FROM OUT OF A
DARK CORNER

FROM OUT OF A DARK CORNER

Evelyn Roth

iUniverse, Inc.
New YorkBloomington

FROM OUT OF A DARK CORNER

iUniverse books may be ordered through booksellers or by contacting:

iUniverse
1663 Liberty Drive
Bloomington, IN 47403
www.iuniverse.com
1-800-Authors (1-800-288-4677)

Because of the dynamic nature of the Internet, any Web addresses or links contained in this book may have changed since publication and may no longer be valid.

ISBN: 978-0-595-48708-0 (sc)
ISBN: 978-0-595-60805-8 (ebk)

Printed in the United States of America

iUniverse rev. date: 4/26/2010

THIS BOOK IS DEDICATED TO MY MOTHER

WHO SUFFERED FROM THE LAST OF THE GREAT

STIGMAS - - MENTAL ILLNESS

Contents

PREFACE

I want to recommend an unusual book that tells a true story that is both unique and uplifting without being soggy. From Out of a Dark Corner, by Evelyn Roth, is the story of a woman who grew up in a traditional Jewish family in the Bronx, but whose childhood and youth were marked by a mother who was mentally ill, confined to Rockland State Hospital on a number of occasions, and eventually ended her own life. Evelyn married and moved to Miami, going to college and graduating when she was in her late forties. With grown children and a largely absentee husband, she felt an impulse to volunteer at a halfway house for mental patients. She was fearful that such work might have a negative effect on her, and her therapist advised against it, yet the need to help people who suffered in a way that her mother did, overcame all other considerations. She became a favorite of the people she helped at the Halfway House, bringing out their musical talents and leading them in sing-alongs and amateur musicals. She was especially impressed with one of the patients who had a remarkably beautiful voice, and she not only befriended him but fell in love with him. Through her love for this man she overcame many obstacles (including his domineering mother who treated him as a child) and helped him shed the obsessive-compulsive habits that had kept him partially institutionalized.

"Marty" became well enough to sing professionally, leave the Halfway House and marry Evelyn. They have been happily married now for over 15 years. Friends and fellow workers do not know that he was once semi-institutionalized for mental illness. Doctors are amazed that he was able to overcome his obsessive-compulsive pattern without the aid of medication. It is truly a story of love conquering all – told in an earthy, honest manner, that is never cloying and never shrinks from the difficulties and frustrations that were dealt with and eventually overcome.

I know both the author and her husband, and I know this story to be as true as it is inspiring.

DAN WAKEFIELD.

Chapter 1
Friendship Haven
1977

The old gray warehouse on South Dixie Highway looked like any other facility for storing merchandise and equipment. The cracks in the concrete gave a hint of what lay past the door. The hours of operation were explained on the partition:

Mon. through Fri. - 8:30 A.M. - 3:30 P.M., Sat., - 6:00 P.M. - 9:00 P.M. The canopy with the words: "Friendship Haven, Everyone Has Something to Offer" was in tatters and barely hung on its frame.

I wondered what I had to offer as I looked around and saw white-faced young people slowly walking to four vans parked in the lot. Their hair was disheveled, their clothes shabby and their shoes well worn. The men needed a shave as well as a haircut and the women matched the grayness of the building.

I knew the place was a psychosocial rehabilitation center for severe mental illness, and yet, I felt so uneasy standing in the parking lot, that I almost left. What kept me there was the promise I made to myself a long time ago to try to help at least one person with mental illness. Perhaps that was because I didn't understand or help my mother when she was sick.

As a child of 5, I saw my mother crying out with pain and then laughing as the grip of insanity took hold of her. She wasn't my mother anymore but some strange being who looked wild as she lay on a small bed in Yonkers, New York, spilling salt in her long, black disheveled hair. Her eyes rolled in their sockets as I knelt by the bed. She kept staring at nothing, as I pleaded,

"Mother, mother, please, don't you know me? I'm Evelyn. Why are you spilling salt in your hair?"

I was answered by almost silent sobs and then high-pitched laughter.

She then disappeared for over a year to rot in the snake pit, Rockland State Hospital. That was over 70 years ago but the nightmares of seeing the image of that creature have not completely left me. Now and then I still hear her pounding on my Miami bedroom door.

"Let me in, she cries, let me in!"

Drenched with sweat, I awaken and run to lock the door. With a sigh of relief, I realize that she isn't there.

I learned over the years that she suffered from manic-depressive psychosis and, in the 1930's, 1940's and even 1950's, there was little psychiatrists could do to help her. My brother, Murray, who was almost two years older than me, took charge of her when she sang in Yiddish, a sign that she was getting sick. He searched for her when she wandered the streets of the Bronx, where we lived after moving from Yonkers, and when he found her, sat with her and made sure she had something to eat. He'd say,

"Mother, you'll get better, you'll get better!"

My father ran away when she got sick; he was too frightened of her. One time, she ran after him with a knife, yelling, "*Kalif, selfish, I'll kill you!*" while my brother tried to wrench the knife out of her hand. My grandmother, whom I fondly called Baba, had a neighbor call the police and my mother was dragged away again to Rockland State Hospital.

I was always curious about the shock treatments my mother got when she was in the hospital. She told me about these when she came home, but didn't describe them in detail. She just said they bothered her memory and were horrible.

"What did they do to you, I asked?"

She answered, "God forbid you should ever know about such a thing."

When she was released from the hospital, she gave me an orange to eat which she carried all the way back from the hospital. She was very thin and I hardly recognized her with her rouged cheeks. Always with me was the fear that I would get sick some day. I knew it was just a question of time. After all, insanity was inherited and I couldn't avoid it happening. I feared that I, too, would have to get shock treatments some day in a mental hospital.

****

I walked into Friendship Haven and entered a small room with a desk and then a larger one with some old stuffed chairs, small tables, a television set and a piano. A pimply-faced young woman sat at the desk and asked if she could help me. I told her that I wanted to look around and just see the place. Maybe, I added, I could do some volunteer work. The woman, whose name was Nancy, searched for a pencil and a piece of paper to write my name down. She couldn't find this so I took a pen and pad from my pocketbook and scribbled my name, Evelyn Roth, and handed them to her. There didn't seem to be anything too wrong with Nancy except that she was very pale and her dress was old-fashioned. She seemed glad that I came and asked if she could show me around.

"Sure, I said, I'd like to see everything!"

We went to a playroom that had a pool and ping pong table. Two men were in the midst of a heavy game of ping-pong.

"Hey, this is all-right," I said to Nancy. "Maybe I'll get a chance to play with them!"

Nancy didn't say much. She took me to an outside patio area where small containers of newly planted seedlings stood.

"This is our nursery," she said with pride. I looked at the pathetic, browning leaves of the plants and said,

"That's great, you plant things. Did you plant anything?"

She lowered her head as she answered,

"No, I'm not too good with that. Do you want to see the work place?"

"Sure, why not. Do you work there?"

"No, I'm not good at typing," she replied.

She took me to another large room with used typewriters and desks that were evidently donated by someone. An older woman sat by a typewriter and methodically pressed one key after the other. Another lady sat alongside her, probably a volunteer.

Nancy seemed very tired if not drugged. Her expression never changed as she showed me around and began walking back to her desk.

"Isn't there anything else here, Nancy? I mean it's a large building. Does anyone live here?"

"Yeah, but I don't feel like going up the stairs. You can go see it," she offered.

I walked up some worn steps to a hallway. Alongside it were different rooms for men and women. Each room had two and three beds and a dresser. The doors to the rooms were open but no one was in them except for one heavy-set man who lay on a bed. It didn't faze him that I looked into his room; he seemed to be in a stupor. The room was clean and the bed was made up with a neat blanket and pillow. A separate bathroom for men and women served their needs. There were some offices with names on the doors that apparently were for the staff. I wanted to say hello to some of the staff persons but there was no one around. Actually, the whole place was practically deserted except for the one person I had seen.

I went downstairs to the social hall area and knocked on a door that read Helena Gold, Social Director. An impatient voice answered through the door,

"Who is it?"

"Can I come in?" I asked. "I'd like to volunteer here."

"No, not now, the voice said. "Call me."

"Oh, can I just ask you where everyone is?"

"Didn't I tell you I'm very busy?" the voice answered again from inside the office.

After that dismissal, I didn't think I'd come back. Yet, I was curious about the dismal place and asked Nancy on the way out why the center was so empty.

Yawning and rubbing her eyes, she told me they went on a trip to the Redlands Fruit and Spice Park.

"Our social director takes care of that," she added. "I have to get back to work now," she said as she feverishly fiddled with some papers.

I phoned Helena the next day and was told she was at a meeting. I tried a few hours later and was again told she was at a meeting. By 5:00 P.M., someone said she was gone for the day. I left my name and phone number with whomever answered the phone. There was a terrible racket in the background as I tried to leave this message and I could barely hear what the person at the other end of the phone, who had slurred speech, was mumbling.

No one called me back the next day. My better sense again told me to forget the whole thing but this was not possible. A magnet more powerful than myself was pulling me to this somber place. So far, I hadn't been able to find anyone with any semblance of normalcy. I was beginning to think that the people who worked at Friendship Haven were as disturbed as the residents, or perhaps they became that way after constant exposure to the depressing atmosphere. This wasn't a mental hospital, or was it?

I finally reached Helena by phone towards the end of the week. As if nothing had happened, she asked me what she could do for me.

"I understand you need volunteers," I said.

"We sure do," she said in an eager voice. "We're having a meeting next week, on Thursday. Can you come to it?"

"Sure, I'll be glad to. Where's the meeting going to be and what time is it?"

"It's in the social hall where the piano is and it'll be at 2:00 P.M."

Thanking her, I felt relieved that I had finally made some progress.

On Thursday, I parked at an Army and Navy discount store that was next door to Friendship Haven. A Colonel Sanders chicken restaurant stood alongside the store. Some men in shabby clothes were sitting at the booths. They didn't speak to each other or change the frozen expression on their faces. I figured the people sitting there were from Friendship Haven.

Something very morbid surrounded the area of the abandoned warehouse, a deadness that couldn't be penetrated and perhaps was contagious. Would I, also, join the entourage of zombie-like people if I hung around them?

The meeting began promptly at 2:00 P.M. Seven ladies were assembled and sat raptly at attention as Helena spoke.

"Welcome everyone. I'll go into some explanation of what we do here, find out what talents you have and what you can contribute to our social and other programs. This is a psychosocial rehabilitation center. It's for major mental illness. The people here have all been hospitalized at one time or another. After they recover, they come here and we help them to make the transition back into society. This isn't a place for the neuroses; do you know what I mean?"

"I do", I said. "I just earned a degree in psychology and was particularly interested in one of my courses - abnormal psychology. You have real sick people here - those suffering from schizophrenia and manic depression, right? I guess most of them have to take drugs, right?"

Helena, a woman of about 30, with half glasses resting on the tip of her nose and devoid of makeup, peered my way.

"Well, I see we have an expert here. What is your name?"

"Evelyn Roth," I answered.

"Well, Ms. Roth, considering you know so much; you can run, all by yourself, the next meeting of volunteers."

The ladies laughed at her comment, but I didn't find it so funny. This Helena was real sarcastic, so it looked like I'd have a problem working with her.

"Can I continue Ms. Roth?" she asked.

Everyone was quiet and ready to listen intently at what was being said.

"The residents here take medicine. A van with a psychiatrist comes around once a week and each person gets a chance to see the doctor and find out if medication has to be adjusted. You'll notice that we have a lot of young adults here. We take older people, also, of course, but younger people have a good chance at rehabilitation.

"We offer work programs here in computers, photography, video and cooking skills. We're in touch with outside agencies and restaurants such as Wendy's, the University of Miami and Burger King. Many of our members begin in dishwashing programs and bussing jobs and go on to other things. We have a staff of trained social workers. If residents are interested in attending classes, we put them in touch with the Office of Vocational Rehabilitation that helps them to go to school to learn different trades. We have an active social program here on Mondays and Thursdays. That's when everyone has a good time and mingles with others. I'd like to find out what your particular talents are and fit you to the needs of these people. You know, our aim is to get them back into society as functioning members."

"Have you been successful with that?" I asked.

"I think we have. Oh, and there's something else. These people don't like to be touched. So, I would avoid doing things like embracing them to tell them not to worry, that everything's going to be all right or touching them in general. You'll want to do that, I'm sure, especially with some of them who are pathetic. But don't do it!"

"What about shaking hands?"

Helena threw me a look that shut me up immediately.

"I'd like you to all introduce yourselves to one another. Here's a sheet of paper. Write down your names and addresses and what particular talent you have. It really doesn't have to be a talent. We need all kinds of help."

I wrote down that I played the piano and sang.

After telling everyone to leave the sheet of paper on the desk in her office, Helena got up quickly and left the room. I turned to a heavy-set woman next to me by the name of Sandra.

"When are we supposed to come here?" I asked her.

"Well, their social program is Mondays and Thursdays. I'll come on Monday if my husband lets me. I don't know what I got myself in for. I mean, those people are pretty sick!"

"Yes, they are, but maybe we can help them."

I went back and told a young staff person named Olivia to give Helena a message that I'd be back on Monday to try to set up a music program.

"You can't do that without Helena's permission," Olivia said.

"Well, I hope she'll let me. That's what I'm pretty good at."

Monday arrived and I drove on Bird Road to Friendship Haven. On the way there, I passed Allen's drug store and parked in their lot. I had forgotten my comb and also noticed I didn't have any rouge in my makeup bag. I purchased the two items and combed my hair while glancing in a small mirror I carried with me. I patted rouge on the upper corners of my cheeks and pursed my lips, applying red lipstick. I couldn't look as wan as the people I had seen at Friendship Haven. I wanted to cheer them up without getting pulled down myself.

I parked in the lot that was becoming more familiar and walked into the social hall. I saw Helena talking to two men who were smoking and sitting on lounge chairs. A guitar was slung over Helena's shoulder as she sat on a folding chair near the men. I walked over to her.

"Hi, Helena, well, I'm here!"

She stared at me for a moment as if to remember whom I was.

"I'm busy right now," she said. "I'll be with you soon."

I walked over to the piano and sat down on the bench. I didn't want to play anything as I knew that would disturb Helena. Instead, I busied myself looking for music in the bench. I found a worn "Stephen Foster" songbook and a green covered edition of "Piano Pieces for Children." I turned to "Serenade" by Schubert and as I silently fingered the notes, an image of a large framed woman came to me.

Interrupting her cooking, she walked over to the piano to listen to me play. I was eleven years old and had just learned the piece. It turned out to be my mother's favorite song and she asked me to play it over and over. The odor of onions wafted into the parlor and irritated my eyes as I played.

Helena interrupted my reverie of so many years ago.

"Well, we're glad you're here. We need help with arts and crafts. One of our volunteers just moved. Olivia has already set up a table in the next room and will help you to get started."

"Helena, I'm not good with arts and crafts. In fact, I haven't done any of it. I like music. Maybe I can do a sing-a-long. The holidays will soon be here and I can type up some Christmas and Chanukah songs. Maybe, we can have a talent show."

"I do sing-a-longs," Helena said. "In fact, I just did one. Maybe next week you can join us as we sing. Right now, I need help with crafts."

I hated arts and crafts. I couldn't stand working with glue that always stuck to my fingers. I hated the assorted junk such as sticks, ribbons, wire, cans, wood and paint that was needed to create more junk. It looked like I didn't have a choice. Maybe I could start with crafts and work my way into music. For someone who wasn't getting paid or anything, it was hard to believe I was going to take orders. No wonder there were few volunteers.

"Helena, I don't understand the instructions you gave us at the meeting the other day. What's wrong with giving these people a pat on the back to make them feel good?"

"No. That's not a good idea. What did you say your name was?"

"Evelyn. Evelyn Roth."

"Well, Ms. Roth, you're going to have to follow the rules here, even if you want to do otherwise. We have experience, plenty of it too."

"How long have you been here?"

"About three years."

"I meant to ask you, Helena. Does anyone ever get violent here?"

"We have very few incidents. These people are screened before they leave the hospital. If they have a history of violence, we don't accept them. Their behavior has to be under complete control."

"What you do must be hard work. There must be a lot of stress."

"You have to care and want to help these people, and I do."

Helena's last statement surprised me. I didn't think of her as a caring person. Her businesslike attitude hid any shred of warmth she might have.

"I want to help too. All right, I'll try with the crafts. How bad can it be?"

A rectangular table with my six "students" awaited me as I entered the large room off the outside of the patio area.

Olivia was seated at the table and spoke to me as I sat down.

"Hello", she said, "I'm Olivia." She waved to me as she introduced herself.

"I know you're Olivia. Someone pointed you out to me the other day when I was here. I'm Evelyn and I'm pleased to meet you."

Olivia, a pretty young woman with long black hair, spoke to the ladies at the table.

I'd like you to meet Evelyn. She's going to help you with your arts and crafts."

Everyone said "Hi Evelyn."

I looked at the assorted ice cream sticks, paste and gold spray paint I saw on the table and didn't have the slightest idea what to do with them.

Olivia interrupted my thoughts.

"We're going to make jewelry boxes. Isn't that great?"

A young woman spoke, "I won't have anything to put in it. I don't have any jewelry!"

"Peggy", Olivia said, "you can use it for other things. How about planting something in it or saving money in it?"

Everyone snickered. "We don't have any money."

"I have!" yelled a young woman seated at the end of the table. I save dimes, pennies and nickels. I'm going to shine them up and put them in my box when it's finished. That way, everything'll look pretty!"

Looking at my pupils, I said,

"I'd like to know all your names. I hope I remember them, though. I'm not too good with names so maybe you'll have to repeat who you are."

Olivia got up to leave. She turned towards me.

"Well, I see you're going to have a lot of help. I'm outta here. Got lots of work to do!"

One of the women waved to Olivia as she left. "Hasta la vista!"

"What about your name? I asked, pointing to a petite blond-haired girl."

"I'm Lisa, she said.

The young woman who complained of not having any jewelry called out,

"I'm Peggy."

'I'm pleased to meet you, Peggy."

As I spoke to her, I tried not to stare at her pretty, but badly pock marked face, that glistened under the neon lights of the room.

"What about your name" I asked, pointing to a dark haired girl with long, unkempt hair.

"I'm Rose", she said, looking away with a slightly bowed head.   .

I turned towards a girl of about 18, sitting quietly.

"And you. What's your name?"

I was answered by silence.

"She's Mary," offered Peggy, "and she doesn't like to talk."

I looked at Mary's sad face and then at her hair that she wore in a tight bun at the nape of her neck. I wondered how she could stand pulling back her hair with such force. Not a strand was out of place. With her straggly hemmed skirt and oversized blouse, she had the austere look of a "40-year old-maid school-marm" of years ago.

As Peggy and Lisa, in particular, were eager to assist me in arts and crafts, I asked them to show me how to glue sticks together to make a box. They carefully picked up some ice cream sticks, applied a small amount of glue to each one, and then placed them alongside one another to create the bottom of the box. They then took two more sticks, criss-crossed them and glued them to the bottom. One by one, they built up the box until it had a depth of three inches. They were so intent and serious with their task that I couldn't help but get caught up in the job at hand.

I thought about bringing Peggy some liquid makeup to apply to her face. Maybe if she used that and a dash of powder, the marks on her face wouldn't be so noticeable. She had big blue eyes and even features but they were almost hidden by her unsightly complexion.

The concern I felt for these young girls was beginning to overwhelm me. I had a home, a husband, and a young son in high school. How I would detach myself from Friendship Haven after the day was over, and pay attention to my own home life, was going to be a problem. My son would soon be leaving for college and I knew that my new busy work was a way of filling the "empty nest" that I would face when he left. A friend I had spoken to about this concern said she would be spending more time with her husband after her children left home. My husband, a C.P.A., who worked day and night, was not someone I could look forward to doing this with. Even when he was home, he had little time or patience to listen to me. College, which I had attended for seven years while raising my son and daughter, was over for now. Whether or not I would pursue a master's degree in psychology was still an unanswered question.

It was almost 3:30 P.M. and the members of Friendship Haven began walking towards the vans parked in the lot that took them to satellite apartments or homes they shared with their parents. I gathered together the sticks, glue and paint, put them in a large brown grocery bag, and placed it and Peggy's box in the closet. I walked over to Helena's office and knocked on her door, hoping she would be a little nicer to me, for a change. There was no answer and I knocked again. Helena opened the door with an annoyed expression on her face, as usual.

"I'm very busy. Can't you see that?"

"I just wanted to say good-bye and that I liked very much working with the people here."

"Good. When my door is locked, except for emergencies, I don't want to be disturbed."

Her words felt like ice water had been thrown in my face.

I walked towards my car and again worried that I wouldn't be able to tolerate Helena's coldness. Whenever I had any contact with her, I felt as if I was a small child who was being bawled out by her mother after doing something bad. I felt good about myself after I had graduated from college. I was worried that Helena would undo that feeling and even cause me emotional problems. I didn't want to become so distraught that I would run the risk of becoming a member of Friendship Haven instead of just a volunteer. I fought the fear of following in my mother's footsteps my whole life, and still continued the battle.

I drove home and wondered what I needed all the aggravation for. As I thought about this, I felt a strange hollowness. I seemed to be a "mother figure" to Peggy and the girls. They were glad when I came over to the craft table, which was with the small amount of joy they could feel. I knew they took medicine because as we were working, Peggy said she had to leave the table for a minute to take her pills. She looked bloated and I wondered if it was from the medicine. I was curious as to why Mary didn't talk and thought I might be able to draw her out. An image of Peggy's pitifully scarred face arose before me as I considered my dilemma but it was mostly Lisa's eagerness at making a simple, little wood box that touched me the most. These were lost souls cursed with the last of the great stigmas, mental illness. My promise to help at least one person with mental problems nagged at me. I was so distracted that I didn't realize I had driven home until I was in my driveway.

I went into my house, prepared a cup of coffee, and browsed through the yellow pages of my telephone book to find a craft store called "Diamond Lil's". I then went to my garage and removed the caps from soda bottles that I had prepared for deposit refunds. After this, I looked through a bathroom drawer for liquid makeup and face powder. I put the bottle caps and makeup in a plastic bag, marked it Friendship Haven, and placed it on a chair next to my pocketbook. It was time to prepare supper for my family so I would have to go to "Diamond Lil's" the next day. I planned on also going to a music store, which was in the vicinity, to purchase a new music book. I hadn't practiced the piano for years but knew it would be just a matter of time until I organized a musical sing-a-long at the Friendship Haven piano. I would try not to rub Helena the wrong way and go along with what she said.

I was surprised how busy I suddenly was. I took out a pad from my kitchen drawer and started to make notes. Tuesday - go to "Diamond Lil's" to buy colored chips - mostly blue, red and yellow - extra yellow that Peggy asked for, paste and paint. Go to music store to get book. Thursday - ask Olivia if she has some petty cash she can give me for expenses.

I added Friday on my note pad. "Go to Rubindale's butcher to buy two kosher chickens. Get some marrow bones." I tried not to forget that I still had a family and a dog to feed.

Chapter 2
Marty

The forgotten human beings of Friendship Haven lived in their own world, cut off from other people. I had a great deal of compassion for them because they were so appreciative of any little thing done for them. Actually, except for Helena, the members of the center were doing more for me than I was doing for them.

I certainly didn't have much clout in my own home. My husband was the self-made boss in our family. He controlled the finances that resulted in my son and daughter looking up to him and down at me. My 20-year old daughter was at college and I hardly heard from her. In her attempt to be more or less on her own, she broke away from me in a very harsh way. I had been very close to her until shortly before she left for college.

I felt like I didn't have a family, certainly not one who acted like they cared about me. I thought my children should be proud of me for graduating college with honors at age 48 and raising them at the same time. I never neglected them and considered myself to be a very devoted mother.

As time went on, Friendship Haven became almost a second home to me. Not only did I go there Mondays and Thursdays, but also sometimes on Wednesdays. While I got along fine with the members of the Center, I continued not getting along with Helena. One of the volunteers said that she was changing, becoming more and more impatient. The volunteer had known her years ago and said she was a different person then, calm and more caring. Helena often said that she cared for the members of Friendship Haven, so her behavior was an enigma.

I didn't believe in Helena's rules about not touching anyone and tried to do this when she wasn't around. Some of the members of Friendship Haven had no one who gave a "damn" about them. Whenever I patted someone on the back or gave them an affectionate hug, it was like putting a balm on their wounds. A young man, named Philip, showed me a deep scar across his back from his father who cut him with a knife when he was about six years old. In spite of this, Philip grew up to be a very caring young man and I was always happy to see him.

Maybe, I thought, Helena was a stickler for rules because she had gotten into trouble at one time or another by not following them to a "T". Not all the members of Friendship Haven were docile. A few of them became violent at the least provocation. While there were strict rules prohibiting anyone with a history of violence to attend the halfway house, it wasn't always possible to weed everyone out. Side effects from the anti-psychotic medicine most of them took caused extreme agitation in some of them. Manic-depressive psychosis and schizophrenia were two of the main illnesses that the young adults suffered from. That is, if they were diagnosed correctly. The psychiatrist, who came in a van each week to see them, spent perhaps ten minutes with them. He mostly doled out medicine in place of psychotherapy, and the members were seldom followed up as to how the drugs affected them.

I felt that the halfway house was certainly better than a mental hospital. The problem was, though, that there were too many sick people and not enough outside facilities to care for them. Getting enough funds for Friendship Haven was a difficult task. Peggy and the others needed to be with people on the outside. Because of her disheveled appearance and that of the others, outsiders didn't want to mingle with them. In fact, some of them had no family support whatsoever.

The stigma of mental illness was almost as strong and distasteful as the 1930's, when my mother was sick. Little progress had been made over the years for the care of the mentally ill. People still called them crazy and treated them almost like lepers.

Volunteers began dropping out of the programs at Friendship Haven. Sandra stopped coming because the violent behavior of a few of the members scared her. I saw a husky man pick up a chair with the threat of hitting a member over the head with it. All the while, he yelled, "fuckin bastard, I'll kill you!" Two male counselors stopped the assault while everyone else stood fixated with fear. We heard of attempted suicides and completed ones among the population of the halfway house. Depressed and distraught adults carried them out in satellite apartments they lived in or other places. Mary, the girl who sat at my crafts table, and never spoke, cut her wrists and was barely alive when she was rushed to Jackson Psychiatric Hospital.

The young adults went back and forth to Jackson Hospital and the psychiatric division of Cedars of Lebanon. If they were lucky, they stayed in the county psychiatric wards for a month or so. If their stay went on for too long a time, they were shipped to South Florida State Hospital for a very long time. So went their life.

I was now going to Friendship House three or four times a week. Even though my craft table was in a room a few doors away from the social hall, I strained to listen to the sound of piano playing from one of the members. If Ben, a young black man wasn't playing, Harriet, a middle aged woman with red hair, would sit down with an old Nostalgia song book and carefully try to read a piece of music. She'd shake her head from side to side in frustration, saying over and over to herself or whoever was around that she couldn't make out the notes anymore. As she struggled with the music, her hand patted her wispy red bangs that refused to lie flat on her forehead. She spoke in a slow Brooklyn drawl and before she finished a sentence, you had to remind her of what she was trying to say. I felt compassion for her because at least she tried to play the piano, instead of just sitting and staring at the walls. She was older than most of the other people in Friendship Haven so I wondered if she was getting any help at all.

My mind wandered from my beading project as I heard someone playing an Elvis Presley tape, "Are You Lonesome Tonight" on a cassette player in the social hall. There was no music for about an hour. Then I heard a voice that was so haunting and beautiful, I almost cried. I recognized the music from a play of the 1920's, "No No Nannette." I asked Olivia, who was standing near the craft table, who was singing. She shrugged and said, "Oh, that's only Marty. He lives here."

I couldn't understand Olivia's lack of enthusiasm. It seemed that a blanket of depression engulfed the staff as well as the members of Friendship Haven. I constantly worried that it would take hold of me, a very scary thought.

I had to see for myself who the owner of such a magnificent tenor voice was. I asked a volunteer, named Pearl, to take over the bead stringing and went over to the piano. Harriet was now playing "Too Many Rings Around Rosie" and a tall, middle-aged man, with an oversized white apron tied around his thin waist, was singing it. I waited for him to finish his song before I spoke to him.

"Is that you singing?" I said to him. "I've never heard anything like it."

I was answered by a frightened look on the man's face. As I took a few steps closer to him, he jumped back as if he had been burnt. His gaunt unshaven face was a greenish pallor and his black, uncut hair made his face appear even thinner. His outdated slanty eyeglasses made his eyes look like two slits. He wore tan, threadbare shoes and an old cloth belt around his pants to hold them up. I attempted to introduce myself and shake his hand, but again he jumped back as if I was about to strike him. I tried again.

"What's your name?" I asked.

"It-It's Marty," the man stuttered.

"You have some voice," I said. "Would you sing something else?"

When I asked this, the man brightened a bit.

"W-W-W What do you want to hear?"

"Anything!"

The man asked Harriet what else she knew how to play. She looked through some pages in her book and, instead of playing, abruptly got up from the piano and walked away. I couldn't figure out what upset her so much.

"I know how to play," I said to Marty, forgetting for a moment that Helene didn't want me to play the piano. "What would you like to sing?"

"D-D-D Do you know any B Broadway?"

"I'm sorry but I don't play by ear. I haven't got any of that music with me."

"I- I- I have some. I can bring it next time."

"Where did you get the music from?"

"F-From the library."

"You go to the library? That's great! I have to get back to arts and crafts but I come here on Thursdays also. We can continue, O.K?"

Marty managed to say O.K. without stuttering. In two seconds he disappeared.

When I went back to my craft table, I was happy to see Pearl still working with the girls. I just hoped she would take over my spot. In fact, I considered asking Helena again if I could finally do the music. As I did before, I'd remind her that the Chanukah and Christmas holidays were approaching and that I thought it would be a good time to get together a sing-a-long or even a full program. I could work with Marty, Harriet and Ben on that. I could even try to get Ritchie, the self-proclaimed handyman of Friendship Haven, to play. He had a Masters Degree in engineering. He was also a pretty decent violinist when his violent temper calmed down enough to allow him to play.

I came to Friendship Haven a little earlier than usual on Thursday and knocked on Helena's door. There was no answer. I knocked again. As always, an impatient voice answered,

"Who is it?"

"It's Evelyn. Can I please talk to you a minute?"

"Alright," Helena said in a tired voice. "Come In!"

Helena didn't ask me to sit down in her tiny office. She flipped through some papers and, peering through her half glasses, said

"What is it? I'm very busy!"

"Well, now that you have such a talented volunteer as Pearl, who really knows crafts, I was wondering if I could get together a music group. I feel it would be a plus for Friendship Haven and I think I can do a good job of it!"

I couldn't believe I was almost begging to do this. Helena made every little thing she did seem like it was the greatest favor in the world.

"Well, we'll see," she said as usual. That wasn't good enough.

"Helena, I'm really not doing any justice to arts and crafts. Nobody is making anything too good, thanks to me. Why won't you let me try the music? If you don't like it, I can stop."

"Let's see," she said. Some of the board members are coming here to take a look around. I guess it wouldn't hurt them to hear some music. But it has to be decent."

"It will be. Thanks, Helena."

It was hard for me to believe Helena had a human side to her. I was wondering what the catch was. I was really excited. This would give me a chance to get back to the piano after I had been away from it for years. I always liked to sing but hadn't done that for a long time either. I eagerly waited for Monday.

I drove to Allegro Music Store after I left Friendship Haven. I felt happy as I looked through the music books. I found a terrific book, "The Best of Broadway" and bought it. I didn't care what it cost and didn't expect to be reimbursed for it. As I thought about the musical program I would organize at Friendship Haven, I stopped thinking about my home situation and the loneliness it brought me.

Perhaps I could make a difference in the lives of the members of Friendship Haven. They were already making a difference in mine.

On Monday I put my music book, "The Best of Broadway", two maracas and ten song sheets from the play, "Fiddler on the Roof", in a brown burlap shopping bag. I placed it next to me as I drove to Friendship Haven. As I entered the stale smelling social hall, I looked around for Marty, Ben and Harriet. No one was at the piano. I went into the craft room and saw Pearl setting up small glass jars and colored crepe paper. I said a quick hello to her, relieved that she was at the table instead of me.

As I walked back to the social hall, I saw Ben playing the piano. I stood by him as he played and sang, "You Are the Sunshine of My Life", by Stevie Wonder.

As I sang, I saw Marty whiz by the room wearing the same checkered pants and white apron as a few days before. He seemed in an awful hurry and did not hear me as I called his name and asked where he was going. It was about 30 minutes before I caught a glimpse of him again. This time I followed him as he went to the kitchen. I watched him pick up a large pot in the kitchen sink and drop it. Without noticing me, he ran out of the kitchen and disappeared again. A half hour passed before I saw him coming out of the bathroom.

"Heh, Marty" I said. "It's hard to keep up with you."

I extended my hand as I said this. He again jumped back as if I had smacked him and clenched his fists to try to hide his hands. When he unclenched them, I noticed they were wet and very red.

"Marty, I have the book, 'The Best of Broadway'. Do you want to sing something from it?"

"I'll be right back."

I didn't see him for another twenty minutes and felt very annoyed. I sat down at the piano and tried to play "Stranger in Paradise" from Kismet. I had never done the piece before and was rusty at it. Within a few minutes, I heard Marty singing from someplace, "Take My Hand, I'm A Stranger in Paradise....." My irritation left me and a sweet sadness took its place. I felt as if a heavy weight was on my chest from holding my emotions in check. I didn't know what it was about Marty's singing that had such an effect on me. The haunting quality of his voice seemed to come from his very soul. It was as if with his music he could express himself in a way he was unable to do with mere words.

Marty continued singing as he walked closer to the piano. He kept his hands closed. When he finally opened them, I noticed they were not only wet, but blistered. He made no attempt to dry his hands on his apron so I took out a few tissues I had in my purse and handed them to him, saying,

"Marty, here, dry your hands. What's the matter with them anyway? Why are they wet and in such awful condition? Is it from washing dishes? Why don't you tell Helena or someone that you can't wash dishes for awhile?"

"I- It's my turn to do the dishes," Marty answered.

"What do you mean by that? Are they going to force you to do them? Aren't you in pain? Do you have any gloves to put on?"

Marty looked embarrassed as I spoke and his unshaven face took on an even deeper purplish-green color. His appearance was such a stark contrast to the beauty of his voice that it was as if the melody came from someone else.

"Marty," I nagged. "Why don't you take off your apron? You're not going to wash any more dishes today, are you?"

He only shrugged as if to say he didn't know.

I realized I sounded bossy, something I hated in Helena. I tried to calm myself down.

"Marty, Helena said I can get together a sing along. Maybe we can do a program for the holidays. Do you know any Chanukah or Christmas songs?"

"Y-Y-Yes. I used to sing Chanukah songs when I went to Hebrew School."

"That's great. Do you remember any of them?"

"I- I know 'Chanukah O Chanukah'."

"I don't," I said. "I've never sung it. Maybe you can teach it to me. I'll try to pick up a Chanukah songbook. I like Christmas songs too, like 'White Christmas' and 'Jingle Bells'."

I saw Harriet enter the social hall as I was speaking to Marty.

"Hi, Harriet" I called out. She answered "Hello" and said nothing else. No sooner did I greet Harriet that Marty disappeared again without a word. I thought that he should at least excuse himself and planned on saying that to him the next time I saw him. I asked Harriet if she wanted to play something.

"Awright," she said as she sat down on the piano bench. She had her worn "Nostalgia" book in her hand and turned to "It's a Small Hotel".

I sang, "There's A Small Hotel, With a Wishing Well".......... No sooner did I begin singing, that Marty appeared again from I don't know where. I had to say what was on my mind.

"Marty, why do you disappear every ten minutes or so?"

He answered, "I've got to wash my hands from those dirty dishes."

"But you already washed them," I said.

"They're still dirty."

"No, they're not. They're too clean. You rubbed the skin off. Do you have some cream to put on them?"

"No."

"Maybe Helena has some. Why don't you ask her?"

Marty had a very troubled expression on his face. I knew I had better stop discussing his hands and talk about the music.

"You know so many songs, Marty. Where did you learn them?"

"I read a book in the library called 'The Musical Theater' and studied the libretto and composers of different music. My father used to listen to the radio a lot and I learned music from that too, especially opera."

"You know, I feel kind of stupid compared to what you know. Marty, you seem to be very smart. Have you had any college?"

Marty looked almost pleased as he answered me. "Almost two years!"

"Wow. Which college?"

"City College of New York."

"Oh, so you're from New York."

Harriet interrupted as I spoke.

"Ya gonna sing or not."

"I'm sorry, Harriet. Yes, we're going to sing."

I leafed through some pages and found, "On the Sunny Side of the Street."

I showed it to Harriet. "Do you think you can play this?"

"I dunno. Maybe if I do it slow."

"It is a slow song. You don't have to rush."

Harriet carefully played the notes with her right fingers. Here and there she struck a bass chord with her left hand.

"That's good," I said to her. "You read well. Did you ever have any lessons?"

"I had for about six months. No, I don't play good."

"I can help you. Look through your book and if you have trouble with a song, let me know."

"Ya mean it?" she said.

There was emotion in her usually flat voice. I couldn't help thinking that some of the people in Friendship Haven were not so depressed that they couldn't come out of it. If they didn't take so many drugs, I was sure they'd be less zombie-like. Marty and Ben still had a lot of life left in them, especially when it came to music. I would try to encourage them to develop their talents. Maybe, some day, they would be able to live outside of the halfway house, in the world that so far had shut them out.

The next few days went by in a blur. The people in Friendship Haven needed me in a way that my family never did. It seemed that lately my big role as a wife and mother was to prepare food, clean the house and little else. I felt anyone could do that.

Before I went to Friendship House on Thursday, I went to Allegro Music Store. I found two terrific books there -- "Christmas Song Book" and "Hebrew Festival Melodies." I even bought two bells that would sound festive with some of the Christmas songs. I sang "Jingle Bells" as I went to my parked car. Even though it was a hot day in Miami, I felt invigorated.

Jingle Bells transported me to Yonkers at Christmas-time when I was a child.

My Pop pulled my brother and me along the glistening snow in a wooden sleigh. The snow thrilled us as we glided along the paths of Trevor Park. The roofs of the small houses were blanketed with snow and the narrow, hilly streets frozen with ice. Chimneys were alive with smoke from fires as families sat around them to warm themselves. Christmas trees with red, blue, green and white lights graced windows, heavy with frost. I envied the families with the fragrant pine trees but knew we couldn't have any because we were Jewish. I'd have to content myself with my Baba's Chanukah Menorah, but it was a poor substitute.

As I entered Friendship Haven, I was eager to get my budding group together to do the songs in my books, particularly "White Christmas" and "Chanukah O Chanukah." Marty and Harriet came over to the piano. I asked Harriet if she would sit down and play "I Had A Little Dreidle" from the Hebrew festival book that I brought. She said she didn't know how to play it but would try something else from her book.

Soon Marty was singing, "Did You Ever See a Dream Walking." He still had his apron on and wore the same worn pants. His shirt was different from the week before; it was a faded pink instead of a yellowed white. His collarbone stuck out from his hairy chest. I noticed some buttons missing on his shirt. He rested his hands on his upper thighs, as if to hide his palms.

When Harriet finished her song, I asked her again if she would like to play some easy music from my new books. She repeated that she didn't know Christmas or Chanukah songs and told me to play them. I turned to "White Christmas" and asked Marty if he would sing it. He said he liked that song and would have to rehearse it. I told him this was as good a time as any.

Marty never stuttered when he sang. As "White Christmas" filled the dim rooms of Friendship Haven, the place took on a new brightness. You didn't smell the stale cigarette smoke as much or notice the grayness of the former warehouse walls. It had this effect on the people there also because several of them came over to the piano to listen or hum along. Peggy surprised me by singing in a lovely soprano voice that blended with Marty's sweet tenor. I handed Lisa a bell as I played "Jingle Bells". She actually smiled as she shook the bell in perfect rhythm.

Helena walked by as we were doing "Jingle Bells" and threw me a quick look of approval. I couldn't believe that I was doing something I truly loved and helping people at the same time.

After I finished the Christmas songs, I took out my Hebrew festival book and turned to "Chanukah O Chanukah". Much to my surprise, Marty sang it in Yiddish.

I asked Marty where he learned Yiddish. He said his grandmother spoke Yiddish. When he visited her as a child when she lived on the lower East side in Manhattan, he picked it up. I told him that my grandmother spoke to my mother also in Yiddish and that I still understood it. It seemed we came from the same Orthodox Jewish background and had both lived in the Bronx. I couldn't help thinking, "there but for the grace of God go I", as I listened to Marty.

Marty never really smiled, even when I complimented him. The most he did was curve his lips a little when something pleased him. Even when he did this, the expression in his eyes was worrisome or forlorn. He reminded me of Jean Val Jean in "Les Miserable's", so pathetic was his appearance.

I was dying of curiosity to know more about him. He was very intelligent but his quick disappearances irritated me. So did his stuttering although I knew he couldn't help it. The first thing he said to me when he saw me each time was, "Y-You've been busy?"

With this question, I would try to think about what I did when I wasn't going to Friendship Haven. As I didn't do much, I didn't have anything to report.

Marty was eager to know what went on with people who lived in the outside world. He questioned other volunteers, asking them, "y-you've been busy over the weekend, y-you've been busy?" Pearl told him about her family and an outing they had on their boat. Marty listened carefully to everything she said, as if he was trying to live his life through her.

It was almost 3:30 P.M., which was the end of the social program for the day. I still wanted to go over some more songs, but there wasn't time. Those who were taking the van went out the door before 3:30 P.M. Marty was among them. I saw him take off his apron and noticed the same cloth belt that gathered the waist of his oversized pants. I had the urge to buy him a shirt or something, but knew this wasn't my place.

I closed the piano and put my music books in a shopping bag. I thought about which songs I would type for the holidays. I would use one sheet of paper for Chanukah and one for Christmas. I'd bring a Chanukah Menorah to Friendship Haven, help Harriet light the candles, and sing the holiday blessings. At least I knew that prayer from childhood. I was sure Ben could play "Jingle Bells" and would go over it with him the next time I saw him. I wanted as many people as possible to be part of the program. I hoped Harriet could learn the simple "I Have a Little Dreidel". I had so many songs in mind for Marty that I had to be careful not to make him the only "star" of the show, so to speak.

I saw Ritchie as I was leaving and placed my hand on his shoulder for a moment to get his attention. He shrugged but let my hand rest there. Remembering Friendship House rules, I removed it as I said,

"Ritchie, could you please bring your violin next time? We sure could use you. If you played along with me, we could have a terrific program. I know you can do it."

He cracked his knuckles a few times and said, "Alright, I'll bring it next time."

He was always running someplace, as if the place was on fire.

I had a picture in my mind of Marty singing White Christmas as snowflakes fell and frost decorated windows and the sliding glass doors of the halfway house. Although I didn't think it would ever happen, I hoped it would snow at Christmas when I planned my program at Friendship Haven. I also imagined the awe from the members, many who had never seen snow.

I wasn't too concerned about the Chanukah program. Marty or someone else could tell the story of Judah Maccabee and his Syrian oppressors. Maybe I'd even dress some of the members up to depict some of the heroes of the time.

On Monday, I entered the familiar entrance of Friendship Haven. I opened the piano and placed my newly purchased sheet of "White Christmas" on the wood music rest that barely hung on its frame. I was playing and singing the nostalgic song when Harriet came over to me. Her speech was more slurred than usual. Probably her medication had been increased.

"Helllo," she said to me in a slow drawl. "Howarrre you?"

"I'm O.K., Harriet. As you can see, I'm preparing for our Christmas and Chanukah programs.

"I gotta go now, Harriet said. I smell something good coming from the kitchen. See ya! See ya later, alligator!"

Harriet's sense of humor surprised me. I looked around for Marty. I'd have to control myself when he sang White Christmas. I didn't want to cry in front of my group. On the other hand, maybe it would show that I was as human as they were. Actually, I didn't feel that different from the people in Friendship Haven, and it worried me.

Marty came over to the piano as I was flipping through my Hebrew songbook. He badly needed a shave. His skin was more sallow than the week before. Even though the other people in Friendship Haven looked depressed and unhappy, Marty's misery was different. I wanted to place a comforting hand on Marty's thin shoulder, but decided not to. Besides, he probably wouldn't tolerate my doing this; every time I wanted to shake hands with him, he jumped a few feet back. He was very appreciative of my bringing in music for him to sing to, but, on the other hand, he was very irritating. He repeated sentences over and over.

"D-Did you have a busy weekend? Were you busy?"

When I was about to answer him, he disappeared. He came back in a few minutes or so and asked me, "Y-You've been busy?"

He loved songs from the 1920's but I preferred Ben's music that was from the 1970's. I felt young as I sang those songs with him but with Marty, I felt old and dated.

I had put on weight towards the end of my senior year at Florida International University from eating too many cookies with my coffee. I was 48 but looked older because of the weight. It bothered me that I couldn't fit into the dresses I liked. There didn't seem to be too much reason to look my best as no one else did in Friendship Haven. Helena wore plain cotton dresses or slacks. It was always hot in the social hall because of the lack of proper air conditioning and the incessant smoke from cigarettes. Some of the members had yellowed fingers from their chain-smoking.

What surprised me was that I felt pretty comfortable with most of the people in Friendship Haven, especially those who didn't seem heavily medicated. Side effects from Halcyon and Thorazine that were common anti-psychotic drugs, caused dizziness, disorientation, sleepiness and depression. Most of the members were on S.S.I., a welfare program, and could not afford private psychiatrists. I wondered what medication Marty was on whenever I looked at his thin, wasted body.

Marty came back from, I don't know where, and watched me run over White Christmas again. He was very quiet. I asked him to pull up a chair next to me so that we could rehearse the song together. It took him about 20 minutes to do this. Everything Marty did was slow. When he finally sat down, I looked at his raw, blistered hands. This time, I decided not to say anything.

"Do you have Mel Torme's song, that has the words, "Chestnuts Glowing on an Open Fire?" he asked me.

"Please sing it, Marty. I don't know the name of it."

As Marty sang, I thought I'd melt into the piano bench.

"That's beautiful," I said. "I think the name of that is 'Merry Christmas to You', but I'm not sure. I don't think I have that in my

Christmas songbook, but I'll get it. I heard that song years ago when I was taking a course at City College."

"You went to City College?" Marty asked.

"I wish I really did. It was just a non-credit chorus course that I went to at night. Why do you ask?"

"Did I tell you I went to City College?"

"Yes you did. That was a very hard school to go to. I think you said you went for two years or so. Maybe you'll go back to college some day."

Marty looked sadder than usual when I asked him this.

"I- I- I don't think so. I had trouble."

"Well, the fact that you went is something. You know, I can tell that you're very smart. Somehow you're different than the other people here. You still have an interest in life. You go to the library and take out music. I know you don't drive so it's some trouble doing this, isn't it?"

"No, it's no trouble."

When Marty didn't stutter, he sounded fine. His speaking voice was not much different from his singing voice. It had a lovely tone to it.

Marty sat down and I noticed one of his knees shaking up and down. I didn't want to say anything about that. As usual, a large white apron covered his oversized pants.

"Why don't you take off that apron, Marty? You're not washing dishes now."

He reluctantly took it off.

Marty sat at the piano with me for at least fifteen minutes. He seemed very restless, as if there was something important he had to do.

"Marty" I said, "You seem a little nervous. You know, singing always helps me when I'm upset. Does it help you?"

"My father had a collection of opera records and I used to sing along to them. That made me feel better. We had a holiday program here last year and I liked it. Helena played her guitar."

"Did you do any solos or Chanukah songs?"

"N-No."

"That's a shame. People should hear you. I'll be honest with you. I've never heard anybody sing like you. You could have made it on Broadway. Did you ever have any voice lessons?"

"I didn't have any lessons," Marty said. "I like Broadway music. Did you ever see a Broadway show?"

"I saw 'Voice of the Turtle' years ago. When I lived in the Bronx, I didn't get into Manhattan much except when I worked at Yeshiva University on Madison Avenue. Would you believe that I never even saw the Statue of Liberty?"

"I went to the Statue of Liberty," Marty proudly said.

"You did! How did you get there?"

"I took the subway from the Bronx."

"Where did you live in the Bronx?"

"On the Grand Concourse."

"I don't believe it! Wow, it's a small world. My piano teacher lived on the Grand Concourse. We used to go there for recitals. It was a beautiful place, but I understand it doesn't look so great now."

Marty wanted to talk some more but I thought it was a good idea to get back to the music. As I turned towards my song sheet to play it again, I realized I had been having a nice conversation with him. In fact, we had a lot in common, both being Jewish and coming from the Bronx. I couldn't tell how old Marty was. His appearance was so unkempt that, maybe, if he had a shave and decent clothes, he would look younger. He might even be in his late 30's, which was at least ten years younger than I was. He wasn't at all bad looking but his cheeks were too hollow and he was too skinny. He had nice black hair with a widow's peak.

Even though it was hot in the social room and most of the members there sweated and had an unpleasant body odor, Marty smelled nice. His checkered pants and faded shirt were freshly washed. So much so, that when he stood near me at the piano, I could still smell the soap he used. Sometimes, the nice odor of his clothes was camouflaged with tobacco smoke that the room was thick with.

I pulled myself back to the task at hand.

"O.K., now, Marty. Let's get back to work! I want you to sing 'White Christmas' as a solo. Use the full power of your voice and let yourself go. You wouldn't even need a microphone if you did that.

Can you open your mouth when you take a breath and when you sing the high notes?"

I must have said the wrong thing. Marty looked forlorn as he said,

"I'll try, but it's hard to do that."

"Why?"

Marty began walking away from the piano as he stammered,

"I-I-I'll be right back, Evelyn."

That was the first time he addressed me by my name.

I didn't see Marty for the next twenty minutes but I caught a glimpse of Ritchie flitting about with his hammer and some other tools. I went over to him.

"Ritchie, we have to rehearse for our Christmas and Chanukah programs. When are you available?"

Ritchie was sweating. Before he answered me, he pushed his eyeglasses that were resting on his nostrils higher on his nose. He peered at me with impatience as he said,

"I dunno. Who's gonna do the work around here?"

"Ritchie, you can take a half hour off, can't you? I mean the music is good for you. I don't think anyone would mind that. Do you want me to speak to Helena about it?"

"I don't care," Ritchie said.

"But I care, Ritchie. Besides other songs, I was hoping to do 'Fiddler on the Roof' for our Chanukah program. You'd make a great fiddler. I can even get you a cap to wear."

"I dunno," Ritchie said again. "We'll see." and he took off.

I wanted to help these people but it sure was taking a chunk out of me. As I mulled over the problem, Marty returned.

"Where were you so long, Marty?"

"I had to go someplace," he said. "I can sing now."

I played the introduction to "White Christmas" again. I waved to Marty to come in.

He did, right on cue.

His singing was too much for me. I knew that in the future I had better carry some tissues with me. My eyes began to burn from tears I could not control. It probably was also because of the irritating smoke in the room. I kept my eyes glued to the piece of music, as I didn't want Marty to see me cry.

When I regained some composure, I looked at the man who had so moved me. He was a man, even though the plastic apron he wore and his unmasculine appearance challenged the onlooker to think of him as one. Again, I thought of the book I had read awhile back, "Les Miserable's". Marty looked like he had spent time in prison or a place resembling that. What a waste of a human being, I thought. And with such a voice! People on the outside should hear him sing. He needed decent clothes, a haircut, new eyeglasses, more weight, but most of all, he needed someone to care about him.

I looked at Marty's skinny chest after he finished his song. A few black hairs stuck out from his shirt. Marty caught me looking at him and a very scared expression crept into his face. I quickly looked away.

"Your singing is so lovely Marty," I said.

Marty didn't hide his hands for a moment and I noticed that they were wet, always wet. With great effort he tried to smile as I complimented him on his singing, but he didn't quite make it.

"Y-You really think my singing is good?" he said to me. "It's good?"

"Good! You must be kidding. Don't you know the talent you have? My God, hasn't anyone ever told you?"

"N-Not really." Marty said. "My father used to tell me that I sang well and he wanted me to have singing lessons."

"So why didn't you?"

Marty didn't answer as his fleeting smile changed to a far away expression.

"Where is your father?" I asked him.

"He died about a year ago."

"Do you have any other family?" I asked him.

"I have a mother who lives on Miami Beach. My sister and brother live in New York."

Marty liked to talk and I thought that was good for him. It was good for me, too. It made me forget my loneliness at home.

"Marty, you never told me why you can't open your mouth more. Is it a secret, or something?"

Marty looked embarrassed. "I have T.M.J."

"What's that?"

"Tempomandibular joint disease. I also have fizzing in my ears."

"What's that from?"

"I guess it's from what's wrong with me," Marty said.

"What's wrong with you?" I asked. "I don't see anything so wrong with you. You've very intelligent."

"You know everyone in this place has something wrong with them. They're sick."

"You're not sick, I mean, not in the way the others are. In fact, I'm going to say something now. My instincts are telling me to say it. Marty, you're going to make it in the outside world. You're going to get out of here. You're different than the others. Really, Marty, there's hope for you."

"Hope? But you don't understand. You don't know what's wrong with me!"

"Well, I know something. You wash your hands a lot and don't dry them. That's awful. I don't know why you do that to the point where they're almost bleeding! Why do you do that?"

"I don't know," Marty said. "They're dirty, I guess."

"Why do you think they're dirty? What do you wash them with to make them so sore?"

"I use Ajax cleaner!"

"What!!!! What for? No wonder they're so blistered. I want you to stop doing that. Just stop it. Will you?"

"I- I- I'll try. What should I use, then?"

"Soap; use Ivory soap!"

"That won't get them clean!"

"Yes, very clean. Please, Marty. Stop hurting yourself, because that's what you're doing! Also, why don't you dry them afterwards?"

"There's nothing to dry them on. There's an old towel in the bathroom but everyone uses it. It's not clean."

"So dry them with the toilet paper?"

"Toilet paper's not clean."

"Why is that? It's clean before someone uses it. I don't understand you!"

"Well, you know. People go and then they take a piece of toilet paper." Marty blushed a bit when he said this, but with his sallow complexion, it was hard to notice any change.

"I'll tell you what. I'll bring you a box of tissues, just for you to use. Does your mother have any cold cream that you can smear on your hands, or Vaseline?"

"Maybe. I can ask her when I see her. I'll see her this weekend when I take a bus to Miami Beach to visit her. It takes me more than an hour to go there because all the buses are local. I- I- I'm sorry. I have to go now and help out in the kitchen with supper."

"Ask them for gloves, Marty. Your hands can't take any more abuse."

"Th-That's very nice of you. Th-Thank you. I'll see you."

"Yes, Marty. I'll see you on Thursday, we should live."

I left the halfway house and as I walked out the door, I kept thinking about Marty. How pathetic he was! I remembered a social work course I had taken at Florida International University. In it we were asked to write a paper about ourselves and what our goals were. I wrote that I wanted to help at least one mentally ill person.

Outside of washing his hands too much and not wanting to be touched, I certainly didn't think Marty was crazy; nor for that matter, Ritchie, Ben or Harriet. I couldn't give too much time or energy to all the people in Friendship Haven because I'd accomplish little. I knew it would be Marty whom I would give most of my attention to. It was strange but I eagerly looked forward to this difficult task. Meanwhile, it would not be too unpleasant because I would hear Marty sing as I tried to help him. That was reward enough.

Chapter 3
Sing-A-Long

I was busy during the week typing and practicing songs on my piano. The time flew by and I hardly noticed my husband who sat and worked at the kitchen table without saying two words to me. My son wasn't around either. He had a bunch of friends he played football with. Sometimes he'd bring one of them home and they played scrabble while drinking cokes. If I disappeared, perhaps my family would notice me when they got hungry, but I wasn't sure. Thinking about Thursday, which was the next social program day at the halfway house, made me feel almost good. I'd even have something to write to my daughter instead of pathetically asking why I never heard from her.

I arranged two columns of songs on my sheet of paper -- one for Christmas and the other for Chanukah. I did some research on the meaning of Chanukah from Herman Wouk's book, "This is My God" and typed that up. I never knew the details of Judah Maccabee's victory over his Syrian oppressors, and the meaning of the eight lights of the Menorah, so this was an education for me also. I asked Peggy if she would say something about Christmas and she agreed, after breathlessly asking me what she should say. I told her that I was Jewish and didn't know that much about the holiday. She said she'd ask her mother who went to church every Sunday and to Christmas mass. I thought it was great that Peggy was interested in doing this.

Olivia told me that patients from Jackson Psychiatric Hospital were being invited to Friendship Haven for the holiday. She added that the Director, Marvin Schiff, planned on dressing up as Santa Claus and giving everyone presents. She said they needed volunteers to go to merchants for donated gifts and asked if I would help with this. I hated to ask people for items but agreed to do it anyway. Getting something new would mean a great deal to the people in Friendship Haven who generally wore hand-me-downs.

As it was only two weeks until the holidays, a flurry of activity took place. Ritchie hung green and red crepe paper streamers along the walls and even attached some balloons to them. Joan, in arts and crafts, and her students, prepared mistletoe and hung the colorful wreaths over the entrance of Friendship Haven. Cans of cranberry sauce, pumpkin for pies, frozen pie shells, stuffing, cabbage, mayonnaise and turkeys were donated from supermarkets and stored in the huge refrigerator in the kitchen. I thought the Christmas dinner would be catered and was surprised to hear from Olivia that the members would cook it. I asked her if I could help to prepare *latkes,* pancakes, for Chanukah that would fall practically the same time as Christmas. She said she'd ask Helena about it.

I found Marty in the huge kitchen. He was standing before the stainless steel sink and staring at a pile of dishes. He didn't have any gloves on. I meant to bring him a pair but had forgotten this with everything else I had to do. I asked him to come over to the piano. He didn't move.

"I-I have to wash these dishes. They told me to do it," Marty stammered.

"Marty, let someone else do it, someone who can't sing like you do. Besides, you don't have any gloves on. Did you ask your mother for some cold cream to put on your hands?"

"N-No, she didn't have any."

"What do you mean, she didn't have any? So why didn't you go out and buy some at the supermarket or drugstore?" I nagged.

Marty just shrugged in answer to my question.

"I don't understand you, Marty. It's a simple thing to go out and buy some Vaseline or cold cream. I mean, what's the problem?"

"I asked my mother for some money to buy it."

"You asked your mother? Can't you buy it without asking her? Don't you have any money on you?"

Marty walked away in answer to my last question. I guess that meant he didn't have any money to use on his own. A grown man and not even a few dollars in his pocket! It was hard to believe. I was only embarrassing him. I'd bring some Jergen's lotion from my house. It was easier than hassling with Marty. I went to look for him in the direction of the bathroom. I knew where he spent most of his time now, in either the kitchen or the bathroom. I found him in the kitchen again.

"Marty, please, will you get out of the kitchen so that we can rehearse? I typed up some Christmas and Chanukah songs. You said you know Hebrew and Yiddish. It would be wonderful if you sang 'Rock of Ages' in those two languages, followed by English. In fact, you could lead everyone and help them sing the songs I prepared. I saw Ritchie working on a speaker and microphone. I mean, wouldn't that be something? You leading the whole place and singing on a microphone!"

"I- I don't, I don't know if I'm good enough to do that. I've never done that before."

"Believe me, you're too good. When we're through rehearsing, you'll be perfect. I can see you don't have a bit of confidence in yourself. I want to help you with that. I think I can, but you have to help also."

"You really think I can do that? Stand in front of the whole room and sing?"

"All of us will sing along with you and help. You'll have the words to the songs in front of you but it would be great if you could memorize some of the songs."

"I sang Rock of Ages in *Heder*, Hebrew school, and some other Chanukah songs too. I remember a few of them but I haven't sung them in years."

"I never went to Hebrew School. I didn't like it. Besides, it wasn't important years ago for a girl to go. I didn't have a Bas Mitzvah or anything. Did you have a Bar Mitzvah?"

"Sure. I went to school for almost four years, three times a week. I used to be able to *daven*, pray, from a prayer book."

"No kidding? That's something. My father reads Hebrew very well. I used to love to hear him daven in the synagogue during the High

Holidays when I lived in the Bronx. He looked so handsome in his yarmulke and *tallith,* prayer shawl. When my son was bar mitzvahed, my mother and father came to Miami for the service. My mother wore a silver sequined dress and my father a dark blue suit. They were called up to the bema and my father and my son read from the Torah. I was so proud of them. Marty. Do you have a picture of your bar mitzvah, or any pictures?"

"Maybe. I'll have to look for them. I have a high school picture, when I graduated De Witt Clinton."

"I'd like to see that. Well, its great talking but we have to get to work."

As I said this, Marty removed his apron and walked with me to the piano. I handed him the sheet of songs I had typed. I looked for Harriet and found her sitting in a chair on the outside patio, smoking. I brought her over to the piano and along the way, grabbed Ben who was starting to play ping- pong. I asked Ritchie to come over with his violin after he hung the crepe paper. He reluctantly agreed. I finally had a group and couldn't believe it. I was hoping for more people to be part of our chorus once we began singing, especially Peggy.

This time, when Marty rehearsed White Christmas, my budding group hummed along with him. As they sang, you could picture snow falling and treetops glistening with it. I thought Perry Como paled in comparison to Marty's singing but, of course, I wasn't objective. These people were so special to me, like trusting children who only wanted to be appreciated and noticed. I couldn't help but feel needed and important around them.

The staff at Friendship Haven decided to celebrate Christmas and Chanukah the evening of December 23rd to give some of the members of the rehabilitation center a chance to spend the evening of the holiday with their families. Chanukah was falling the same week as Christmas so, with Helena's permission, I decided to do a joint program. I ran thirty copies of the holiday songs on a Xerox machine in my neighborhood, not trusting the machine at Friendship Haven that seldom worked. I placed the song sheets, music books, Chanukah Menorah, candles, Jergen's lotion and some colorfully wrapped gifts in a large shopping bag the evening before the celebration in order to be ready to leave the next day. I even brought a scissors along because Lisa had complained that her hair was a mess. I planned on giving her a quick haircut before the fesitivities took place. It was only because I promised this that she agreed to join our group. I would have never attempted to do this except for my experience cutting my own children's hair when they were little. I wanted to cut Marty's hair also but was afraid it might embarrass him. He was touchy enough about the awful condition of his hands and probably wore an apron all the time to hide his tattered clothes. I was hoping that the chance to lead the halfway house in singing the Christmas and Chanukah songs would make him feel like a human being instead of a sick, beaten nobody.

As I entered the social hall, the delicious aroma of food greeted me instead of the stale smell of cigarettes. I sniffed the aromatic air, placed my shopping bag in a safe corner by the piano and entered the kitchen. Sure enough, I found Marty, dressed in his apron, watching Harriet. She was bending down over a large blue enameled oval-shaped pot, basting a turkey. Every now and then, she wiped her sweaty brow on a dishtowel. I reluctantly asked Harriet if she could use some help but was glad that she turned down my offer. I had so much to do that I didn't know where to start. There was a huge flurry of activity in the kitchen as members prepared stuffing, candied sweet potatoes, cranberries and pies. Harriet even rolled dough on a wood board in addition to preparing the turkeys.

"What are you making?" I asked her.

"Apple pies," she answered.

"No kidding? From scratch? Gee, I don't know how to do that. I'd like to watch you but I don't know if I have the time today; maybe another time. I walked over to Marty who was now watching Harriet prepare the dough for pie.

"Marty, could you take your apron off and come over to the piano. We have to rehearse. You're the main star tonight, you know!"

Marty looked solemn as he said,

"I-I don't, I don't know if I can do what you ask me. I'm not that sure of the songs. It's been years since I sang in Hebrew. And you want me to do a solo also?"

"Marty, I don't know what makes you so unsure of yourself. I also don't know why you're here. I'll be honest with you. I see you wash your hands too much but that's no crime. You seem a little sluggish but you're probably taking medicine. Do you mind telling me what you take?"

"The psychiatrist gave me a tranquilizer, Aventil. It does make me kind of sleepy. That's why I don't know if I'll be O.K. tonight."

"Listen. It's still early so we have some time. I'm going to cut Lisa's hair because I promised her I'd do this. Afterwards, maybe we'll have time to go next door to Colonel Sanders and get some chicken to eat for lunch. We can even look around at the Army and Navy store for a few minutes. Would you like that?"

Marty looked down at his faded, blue cloth shoes before he answered me.

"I could use a pair of new shoes. Maybe they have them there."

"Do you have any money on you?"

I could tell by the expression on Marty's face that he didn't.

"If I see something, maybe I can buy them another time." Marty said.

Wondering again how his mother let him walk around like a beggar, I said,

"Sure, Marty, we'll take a look. By the way, I brought some lotion for your hands, and a box of tissues. I'm sure that'll make you feel better."

"I want to thank you. I can't express myself!"

"That's all right. I'm glad to do it. But you can do something for me. After you wash your hands, dry them on the tissues and apply some cream. Don't leave them wet. Will you do this?"

"Y-Yes. I can carry the tissues in the plastic bag I carry my jacket in."

"That's a good idea. I thought of something else. I'll put some of the Jergen's lotion in a small container and you can carry that with you too. O.K?"

"Y-Yes. That's very nice of you. To bother like that."

"Well, I have to get to work. Have you seen Lisa?"

"No, I'm sorry!"

"What are you sorry for? It's O.K. I'll find her."

Marty and I went back into the social hall and found Lisa sitting in an easy chair reading Cosmopolitan. I asked her to come out to the patio so that I could cut her hair. She acted surprised that I hadn't forgotten this and said,

"Ya mean you're really gonna cut my hair?"

"Sure, I promised, didn't I? The only thing is that I don't have something to put around you for the falling hairs. I'll have to think of something. There's a towel in the bathroom. Maybe we can use that."

"I don't want it. It's dirty."

"O.K. I'll tuck some tissues around your neck."

I asked Marty for a few of his tissues. He reluctantly took out one but I told him I needed more. He slowly removed a few more. I stuck one in my pocketbook in case the smoke got so bad later that it would bother my allergies, or if I became choked up with emotion as I did the week before and had to wipe tears I couldn't hold back.

As I prepared Lisa for her haircut, I asked her what style she wanted, knowing full well I was good with bangs and not much more.

"Would you like bangs, Lisa? I think you'd look good in them."

"I used to wear bangs. I like long hair. Can you keep it long?" Lisa asked with excitement.

"Yes. I agree with you. Long hair looks good on you. Also, it's a lovely blond color."

"Ya think so! Ya really think so?" she said with a high-pitched voice. "My mother has blond hair."

"I don't tell stories, Lisa. You'll find that out about me."

When I was done with the haircut, I told Lisa to look in the bathroom mirror. I went with her. The bathroom mirror was cloudy. Chipped tiles on the walls, surrounded by old fixtures and a few damp, yellow towels, hanging on a loose rack, completed the depressing picture. No wonder Marty didn't want to use any towels. Lisa quickly glanced in the mirror and said,

"Wow. I like that. Thanks, thanks a lot."

"Great. Now you can join us tonight in our holiday sing-a-long. You have a nice voice. I heard you humming along with us the other day. How about it?"

"O.K. Now that I'm not a mess. Is my dress alright?"

"It looks fine, Lisa."

After finishing Lisa's haircut, it was too late to go with Marty to Colonel. Sanders or the Army and Navy store. It would have to wait until the following week.

Dinner was set for 6:30 P.M. Platters of turkey, gravy, stuffing, candied sweet potatoes, cranberries, latkes, apple sauce and small rolls sat on patio tables decorated with green and red table clothes. Red and green plastic plates, plastic forks, knives, spoons and cups were set up near the food. A large, glass bowl with chilled orange punch and slices of oranges sat near the cups. A ladle to serve the punch with rested on the side of the bowl. Cone shaped side lights were fastened to the patio walls to give a cheerful glow to the area. Olivia stood by the table to make sure everyone received a fair share of food and possibly seconds. I thanked her for remembering the latkes and applesauce for Chanukah. She told me that Harriet had prepared them.

There were about sixty people seated at the tables, forty from Friendship Haven and the rest guests from Jackson Psychiatric Hospital. Men were freshly shaven and neatly combed. Women wore clean dresses or slacks with colored blouses. I noticed that no one was smiling but people quietly talked to one another as they oooooed and ahhhed the delicious food. I sat at a table with Harriet and Marty. He wore a tan shirt and tan slacks to match. For once, the waist of his pants wasn't gathered together with an old belt. His hair was combed and I thought he looked nicer than I had ever seen him. He had worn shorts earlier in the day so he must have carried his pants and shirt in his plastic bag to change into.

I couldn't wait to begin our Christmas and Chanukah programs that would take place after the dinner. I ate quickly and got up to check my song sheets. I marked the songs in my books with paper clips and small pieces of paper so that I could easily find them. I also wanted to make sure the microphone and speaker were alongside the piano.

"See you soon!" I said to Marty and Harriet as I got up from the table. I looked around for Ben and Ritchie. I planned on having Ritchie play his violin as I played the piano. I hoped Harriet would play "Silent Night" if she were in the mood. Ben was on the program to play "Jingle Bells" which he had practiced during the week. I planned on giving song sheets to the rest of the people as they sang along with

Marty, Lisa, Peggy and I. Marty would hold the microphone as the main singer.

I didn't remember when I was more excited or when I felt more needed as I anticipated our holiday program. I couldn't wait to hear Marty sing "White Christmas." I opened my purse to check the tissues I had put in it. This time I was prepared.

About halfway through the Christmas and Chanukah dinner, Helena walked to the front of the patio, picked up the microphone, and announced that after dinner we were going to have music for the holiday season. She smiled slightly as she said this, something I had never seen in the six months I had volunteered at Friendship Haven. She wore a stylish light- blue dress with medium heeled dark blue pumps. I felt grateful for the opportunity she finally gave me to put on the program - something I never thought would happen.

After Helena's announcement, I went over to Marty and Harriet who were packing some leftover turkey in aluminum foil. Marty told me he wanted to bring some home to his mother and Harriet said she just wanted a bite for later in the evening if she got hungry. I found Peggy and Ben at another table and told them we were about to begin our program. Ben ate with such zest that I knew having turkey or stuffing was a rarity. He asked me if I thought it was all right for him to take a second helping of apple pie. I said that was fine; he was so engrossed eating that he hadn't heard Olivia say there were seconds. Lisa looked very nice with her new haircut and a pale yellow dress. Peggy also looked very nice, as I had managed to pat her face with some liquid makeup before the program began, hiding some of her pitted complexion.

People quietly lingered over their plates even when there wasn't a scrap of food left on them. I often made turkey or chicken with stuffing for my family and didn't think it was a big deal. Yet everyone here found the food so special that it was very difficult for them to accept the end of the meal.

Ritchie came out of someplace and went over to the makeshift stage. He tested the microphone and speaker saying, "one, two, three, one two three, testing, testing." The sound was a little loud so he lowered the volume. I went over to him and said I didn't have enough light by the piano. He told me that he had hooked up lights on the sidewalls of the patio and would soon turn them on. I felt nervous and rummaged in my pocketbook for a valium. I swallowed it with some punch and felt better in ten minutes or so. If the program I organized was good, maybe I'd be hired as a member of the staff.

Everyone finally finished eating so my musical group went over to the piano. I picked up the microphone.

"Hi everyone" I said. "I'm Evelyn. We're about to begin our holiday sing-a-long. Please give a big welcome to Marty who will lead us along with Ben, Ritchie, Lisa, Harriet and Peggy. We're giving out song sheets. If there aren't enough for everyone, please share them with the person sitting next to you."

In a light blue and white pants suit that I had just bought in Jackson Byron's, white earrings and black pumps, I knew that I looked younger than my 48 years as I made announcements. I had recently lost 15 pounds with Weight Watchers, which helped.

Marty stood a distance from me as I said to the audience that he would be the master of ceremonies. I had written out a sheet of paper for him with our program on it, but as soon as I mentioned his name he walked away towards the social room. I caught up to him.

"Where are you going?" I asked.

"I'll-I'll be right back," he said.

"Marty, I know your 'right back'. We have a program to put on. You can't disappear now! In fact, what you're doing is very rude."

"I-I'll be right back," he said again.

I went back to the patio and told my audience that we were having trouble with our sound equipment. Ritchie looked at me confused so I took him aside and told him that Marty had to leave for a minute. I asked Ritchie to play something on his violin meanwhile to fill in the time. I left the area again but could not find Marty. He usually went to the bathroom so that's where I headed. I knocked on the door.

"Marty, Marty, are you in there? Please, if you are, please come out!"

"I-I'll be right out!" he said.

I waited another five minutes and knocked again.

"Come out, or I'm going to find a way to get in there!"

That did it. Marty came out with an expression on his face of utter defeat. I did notice, though, that his hands were dry. He must have used the tissues to dry his hands.

I walked over with him to the piano and handed him the microphone. He poked through the pocket of his shirt and found the program I had prepared for him.

Shoulders hunched over the microphone that was on a stand, he said very haltingly,

"H-Hello. I'm Marty and you all know me. We're going to sing the songs on the sheets. Evelyn, Harriet and Ben are going to play the piano. We'll also hear from Ritchie, Lisa and Peggy. Here's our first song. Join in."

Marty picked up the microphone with his right hand, which shook. I played an introduction and nodded for him to come in. He led the people in "Rudolph the Red Nosed Reindeer" and within a few minutes, his hand stopped shaking. I was surprised how at ease he suddenly seemed with close to 60 people in the area. As I watched him, I hit a few wrong notes but Ritchie drowned them out with his violin. I was especially proud of him. I thought about when I first saw him at the halfway house, standing in a corner of the social room and cursing while he tried to play the "Star Spangled Banner" over and over. Now, with his chin cupped under his violin, and a fresh light blue shirt and dark blue pants, he looked and acted very "together". It was obvious he was enjoying playing as he swayed slightly to the music with his foot bobbing up and down to keep time. After he finished playing, there was a lot of applause and even a few whistles. This encouraged Marty to go on.

"Now Harriet's going to play 'Silent Night' Marty announced. Please sing along with her, Lisa and Peggy."

Everyone's voice, including Helena's, blended together to produce a lovely melodic sound.

A cool breeze, probably from the ocean, blew in to remind us that it was December. One or two stars glistened in the almost black sky and it was almost as if they were blinking to the rhythm of Harriet's playing. In a mysterious way, the night was not only beautiful but romantic as well.

Ben was next on the program. He played "Jingle Bells" with fervor as his dark, handsome head bobbed back and forth to the music.

It was nearing the end of our program and time for Marty to sing "White Christmas." He announced his song and took the microphone with a now steady hand. It is difficult to describe on paper the lyrical and lovely quality of Marty's voice that filled the patio of the old abandoned warehouse. It was so quiet while he sang that anyone hearing him would think there was no one in the large area, instead of the over fifty people that were there. The people in the room tried to control themselves but some were unable to stifle sniffles or tears that the singing brought on. Others sat quietly with their private hopes and dreams. I had trouble accompanying Marty because I felt like crying. I held myself back because I didn't want to fall apart in front of everyone.

It is over 20 years since that Christmas program and, even now as I write about it, I get choked up with the memory of it.

After Marty finished singing "White Christmas" Santa Claus appeared from somewhere. "Ho, Ho, Ho!" the jolly bearded person in red and white with an enormous large belly yelled. "Ho, Ho, Ho! Merry Christmas to everybody. Happy Chanukah!" Santa added. There were squeals of delight from everyone as Santa gave out presents. Santa went over to Marty to try to shake his hand. "You did a good job, Marty, a good job!" Marty jumped a foot back as Santa extended his hand.

"Shake his hand," I whispered in his ear. Marty slowly extended his hand and Santa grasped it. Santa wasn't the least bit surprised at Marty's behavior so I knew he must be someone who is familiar with Friendship Haven. After Marty did this, he disappeared. I was sure he went to the bathroom to wash. In his mind, he had good reason to do this. Touching someone was something I had never seen him do and I knew he'd feel dirty afterwards. Some day I'd find out why.

I went over to my group and told them what a great job they did. They were busy opening their gifts, careful to save the wrapping paper. Peggy was delighted with her talcum powder and, after opening the pretty box, dabbed her face with the soft puff.

"Ooooooo that smells good!" she said. She asked me what I got and I told her that it was a bottle of cologne. I offered it to her but she told me to keep it as I had worked hard. Ben, Ritchie, Lisa and Harriet decided to open their gifts later, as did Marty. He told me he wanted his mother to have his gift but I explained to him it was for a man. I gave him my bottle of cologne for his mother.

Ritchie gathered together the sound equipment and put it away. I managed to stop him for a moment to tell him he played great, especially his rendition of "Fiddler on the Roof". Others went over to him and told him that also. Ritchie only nodded his head and said "good" in answer to everyone's compliment. Ben and Lisa came over to me to ask how they had done. I said they were both terrific and sincerely meant it.

"Ya wanna hear 'Bridge Over Troubled Water?' Ben asked me.

"I will, another time, Ben. I'm tired. It's been a long day! By the way, how are you getting home?"

Ben looked sullen which meant he had a problem.

"Do you need some moola?" I asked him.

"I could use a little," he answered.

I gave Ben two dollars to make sure he had carfare. I told him again how great he had played. He walked away with a quick step instead of the shuffling pace I had always seen him use.

I couldn't find Marty to say good-bye to him. Earlier he told me he was taking the van downtown and then would take a bus to the beach. I figured he was in the bathroom but I didn't feel like going there again and knocking on the door. Maybe he needed the time to be by himself. I knew I wasn't going to put up with his incessant hand washing and other peculiar behavior. I'd treat him normally so that some day he'd go out into the so- called normal world. This was quite a task but my faith in Marty kept me going.

As I was getting ready to leave Friendship Haven, feeling very good that the holiday program I had planned was successful, Helena stopped me on my way out and said to me, "well done". That was the first time she ever really complimented me. I was hoping her mood would last, but didn't count on it.

A feeling of elation rode along with me as I drove home. As I neared my house, it subsided and I felt a let down. My psychiatrist,

Dr. Harris, whom I had been seeing for at least ten years, didn't think it was a good idea for me to be involved with the mentally sick people of Friendship Haven from the very beginning. He added that it would only awaken memories of my own sick mother. He was right, but I had to continue my work to feel a sense of importance. I certainly felt that after the successful holiday program.

I was seeing a psychiatrist because of bouts of depression that began soon after I got married. I asked the doctor to encourage me to get divorced but he said this was not something he could do. He was concerned that I would be even more insecure without my husband, who seemed to represent the mother and father I never had as a child

When I first saw the good doctor and told him what happened to me when I was five, - the sight of my mentally sick mother lying in the narrow bed in Yonkers, - he said that was the most terrible thing he had heard a small child witness. My father was never around at the time to shield my brother and me from seeing such a horrible sight or offering us any solace. In fact, just the opposite. I recall him almost passing out at the time and my brother catching him so that he wouldn't fall. Maybe I was testing myself by going to Friendship Haven, trying to prove that I could stand being around sick people without going crazy myself. I had both the inheritance and the environment that was considered necessary for someone to go insane.

For New Year's Eve, Friendship Haven planned a special Friday evening coffee house. The center had this every Friday night but this New Year's there was going to be sandwiches in addition to assorted pies, cakes, coffee and tea. Members could dance to tapes and records on the stereo player. I was curious about these coffee gatherings and planned on going. I didn't have anything special to do New Year's Eve. One of the volunteers told me she had gone to one of these parties a few weeks earlier and had seen Marty dancing. She said he was a good dancer and added that she was surprised because he was always so solemn. I hadn't danced in years and thought I'd try Marty out or anyone else who wanted to dance.

I left supper for my husband and son and told them I had a commitment at Friendship Haven. I added that I'd be back early in case they wanted to go see the Christmas decorations at Merrick Park in Coral Gables. My husband said he had work to do and my son said he was invited to a party.

I parked my car around 7:00 P.M. in front of the Army and Navy store and sat in it awhile, thinking. The attraction that excessive hand washing had for Marty continued to baffle me. He must feel dirty, I thought, but why? At least he now wiped his hands on the tissues I gave him so that was an improvement. Maybe some day he'd be at ease shaking hands with someone when he was introduced. I knew this would take a long time as I was pretty sure that his problems didn't happen overnight. I'd be patient and little by little he'd make progress. He had already accomplished a great deal by being the master of ceremonies and singing for the holiday program but this was only the beginning.

I didn't realize I was sitting in my car in front of the Army and Navy store for such a long time because, before I knew it, my dashboard clock read 8:00 P.M. I got out of my car and entered the social room of the halfway house. Ritchie put on a tape on the cassette player and soon Paul McCartney sang, "I Wanna Hold Your Hand" as the Beatles accompanied him. I loved their music that made the 60's so unforgettable. I was in college then and hearing this song helped me to relive this special time in my life. An Elvis Presley number, "You're Nothin' But a Hound Dog", followed the Beatle's tape. A couple did a rock step to it. The young man and girl followed the rhythm of the music, swinging their arms and stamping their feet. The only difference between them and other people I had seen dancing to rock songs was that the expression on their faces didn't change much as they danced. The drugs they took drained them of life and spirit -- a necessary evil in their treatment.

I asked Ritchie if he had seen Marty but he said he hadn't. Marty had mentioned that he'd try to go to the coffee house party New Year's Eve. This was the main reason I went and not seeing him disappointed me and made me feel strangely empty. I watched the dancers for about half an hour and got up to leave. As I walked out the door, I practically bumped into Marty coming in. He wore the same tan pants and shirt that he did during the holiday program.

"Hey" I said to him. "You made it. That's great! You know I was going to leave but I guess I'll go back for a little while. It's only 9:00

P.M. Marty. Are you going to sleep in Friendship Haven tonight? I know you visit your mother often but I don't know if it will be safe to take a bus on New Year's Eve to go to the beach."

"It's all right. The van takes me downtown and there are a lot of people at the bus stop."

I waited for him to bring up the holiday sing-a-long the week before but he said nothing. Maybe he was afraid to mention it because he thought he didn't do well. I had to say something.

"Marty, by the way, you sang great last week, really great!"

"Y-You mean it?" Marty stammered.

"Of course I mean it. Didn't you hear the applause? I'll tell you something Marty. I enjoyed listening to you sing 'White Christmas' more than I enjoyed Bing Crosby doing it."

"Bing Crosby is very good. I don't sing like that." Marty said as he shook his head.

"No, not like that but more powerful. Like I told you, you have a Broadway type voice. You know. Like John Rait."

"John Rait! He's a great singer. He's in 'Pajama Game'. I guess you're trying to make me feel good," Marty said with a shrug.

"Marty! You should feel good about yourself, but I guess you don't. How can you? You walk around with hardly a dime in your pocket. That doesn't make you feel like a man. Also, a man has to dress nice, not with an apron around him most of the time."

I was surprised at all I said and waited for Marty to say something. He didn't so I continued. No one could hear me over the loudness of the music.

"Marty, I'm sorry I didn't go to the Army and Navy store last week with you to look at shoes. I don't know what happened."

"Th-That's alright," Marty assured me. "I can look at shoes next week. Will you go with me? I don't know how to pick out shoes."

"You don't? Then who picks out clothes for you?"

"My mother. She's a *maven*, expert, at it."

"That's good. So why don't you go with her to Penney's and let her help you buy a new pair of pants and a shirt. I'm sorry, Marty. I know I'm butting in too much but I can't help it."

"Th-That's alright," Marty said again, looking uncomfortable.

Maybe Marty got used clothes from Friendship Haven, the same as most of the other people there. That would be a shame because he wasn't at all bad looking. I thought about how he'd look in a suit or a light blue jacket and dark pants. Maybe I could go with him to help him pick out an outfit. I knew I was getting in too deep but I didn't have much control over it. With Marty's voice and brains, he could have gone far. Maybe it wasn't too late. He didn't seem as sick as the other people in Friendship Haven. Even though he took a major tranquilizer, he was still pretty alert. He never hallucinated or anything and was always in touch with reality; at least when I saw him. In fact, I didn't see any signs of psychotic behavior in him. So he washed his hands a lot, so what? I wasn't sure what the name of this condition was. I'd look through my abnormal psychology book from Florida International University or ask my psychiatrist about it.

Someone had donated old records with songs of the 40's that were very romantic. Ritchie put them on the record player and a few couples danced to "It's Been a Long, Long Time", "I'll Get By" and "Beguine the Beguine". When this rumba started playing, Marty went over to a tall woman and asked her to dance. I watched the woman move her hips to the music and Marty keeping pace with her. His body swayed to and fro but the expression on his face betrayed his enthusiasm. He had a far away look. I was disappointed that he didn't ask me to dance and I think I was a little jealous as well. I started to walk out the door when Marty caught up to me.

"Why are you leaving so early?" he asked.

"Well, it's getting late and I should be with my family on New Year's," I fibbed.

"I- I want to thank you for coming." Marty said.

"What are you thanking me for? I didn't do anything."

I couldn't ask Marty why he didn't ask me to dance. Maybe he wanted me to make the first move. Looking at him, I felt confused and ill at ease for the first time since I met him. After all, this was Friendship Haven, a Psychosocial Rehabilitation Center, not Roseland Ballroom. It could be that my psychiatrist was right; that it wasn't a good idea to get involved with the members of Friendship Haven. It didn't seem as if I knew my place anymore. I'd have to give it some real thought.

I left the center feeling lousy. Marty went back inside to dance with I don't know who. Maybe I wasn't so important to him after all. I got into my Chevy and headed for home. The emptiness and loneliness I felt stayed with me throughout the evening and the days that followed. I was scheduled to go to Friendship Haven on Monday but this time I didn't really feel like going.

I called Helena and told her I was going to New York for two weeks. I wasn't planning on really going but used it as an excuse to not volunteer at Friendship Haven for a while. I was mad at myself for feeling that Marty practically ignored me during the Friday evening coffee house party. I thought about discussing this with Dr. Harris, but decided not to. I felt it was time for me to figure things out for myself so that eventually I wouldn't have to continue with therapy.

Although my doctor wasn't concerned about it, I felt I was becoming too dependent on him.

I missed the people at Friendship Haven, so I only stayed away from the center for less than two weeks.

It was now close to eight months that I had been volunteering at Friendship Haven. I had developed a nice group of people who sang around the piano. I felt it was time to ask Helena for a paid position. I knew there was an opening for a social worker. The pay was only $8,500 a year, the going rate during the late 1970's.

I knocked on the door of Helena's cubicle but she didn't answer. The door was open a crack and as I stood by, I heard Helena talking to someone. I waited ten minutes and left. I went over to the piano and found six people waiting for me to begin the music. Marty was eager for the Broadway section of music, particularly "Oklahoma". I gave out song sheets with "golden oldies" and Broadway numbers. I also brought along cowboy hats for the men and women to wear, at my expense. I didn't want to go through the red tape and frustration of trying to get reimbursed for them. Marty was very reluctant to wear a hat, saying his head was small and that a hat wouldn't fit. I had a small size black straw hat that I thought he could wear. I took a few steps towards him to help him try it on but he jumped back.

"Marty, why don't you put the hat on? It might fit. After we rehearse "Oklahoma" and some other Western songs, maybe we can put on a play, sort of a take off on 'How the West Was Won'. What do you think of that?"

"T-That's a good idea. I like the way Alfred Drake sang in Oklahoma."

"I know you won't believe me when I tell you that with training you could sing as well as him. Maybe you can take some voice lessons some day."

"I'm a little sorry I didn't take them when my father was alive."

"What a shame, but you know, it's never too late."

Marty finally put the hat on, but with his slanted, old fashioned eye glasses and apron which he was still wearing, he looked silly. No one commented about this because the people in Friendship Haven were used to odd appearances. I told Marty to take off his apron and eyeglasses. He looked a lot better afterwards, sort of a hollow cheeked Gary Cooper. Ben, who was slated to play "Deep in the Heart of Texas," was dapper in a black, felt hat. Ritchie didn't want to put on a hat but I was happy to settle for his playing his violin. By now, he was playing quite well and keeping excellent time to music. In fact, as he played along with me, he helped me with my rhythm, a weak point.

I gave Harriet a tambourine and Lisa a maraca. Robert, a tall handsome young man, with an excellent voice who usually played ping-pong, joined us. He gladly put on a large beige hat while he held a pair of shiny castanets in his hand. He told me awhile back that he was in Friendship Haven because he had fooled around with L.S.D. He was now on lithium that controlled to a degree his manic-depression. To look at Robert, especially with his cowboy hat on, you couldn't tell there was much wrong with him. He had a nice personality and loved to sing "Sunrise, Sunset" in his deep baritone. I played ping-pong with him when I had the chance. He was an excellent player.

I was having a ball with my group around the piano and wasn't in the mood to approach Helena about a job just yet. When I finally decided to speak to her about it, she wasn't around. I asked Olivia where she was and she told me that she was on a leave of absence. Olivia was taking her place meanwhile.

One Monday Helena unexpectedly showed up with the Director. They walked by the piano and heard the rehearsal of the Western program. Helena nodded her head to acknowledge me and then abruptly walked into her office. I asked Ritchie to lead my group while I followed her. I knocked and this time she opened her door.

"Yes," she said impatiently.

"Helena, I heard there was an opening for a social worker. I'd like to apply for that position. I've been here a long time and get along very well with the people."

Helena didn't answer and stared at me for what seemed an eternity.

"Evelyn, she said with a patronizing tone of voice. "I'm very busy now. This will have to wait."

"For how long?"

"Look, I said I'm busy!" she said louder. That dismissed me.

The following Thursday, a young woman who I hadn't seen before, came over to the piano. She introduced herself as Barbra. She had a very sweet face with large, dark eyes and long, black hair. I could tell immediately by the way she was dressed and acted that she was not one of the members. She asked everyone's name and said she was the new social worker. I couldn't understand this. There must be two positions open for social workers I thought.

Barbra listened to the music and told me it was absolutely super.

"Barbra," I asked, "when were you hired?"

"Actually today."

"You know, I applied for a job here over a week ago. I haven't heard anything as yet."

"I don't know anything about that but I do know that what you're doing is the best thing in the place."

"Thank you. That's very nice of you. I still don't understand about that position. I'll have to ask Helena about it."

"I'm sorry." Barbra said. She hummed to some of the songs and waved so long to everyone. As she left she repeated,

"Evelyn, you sure do great work! I hope things get straightened out for you!"

I felt so good because of Barbra's encouragement that I knew I finally had an ally on the staff.

I managed to catch up with Helena around 5:00 P.M. as she was walking out the door.

"Helena, what about that job I asked you about? I met Barbra who was just hired. Do you need two social workers?"

"No. We don't have the budget for that. Did you really think I'd hire you? I need someone who'll do what I tell them to do. You do things without anyone's permission. We have rules and regulations here that have to be followed. I explained this when you first came."

"But why didn't you say something to me?"

"I tried to on several occasions but you insisted on doing things your way. I need a professional. You act like you're my boss instead of the other way around."

"What about how well my group is doing?"

"Well, I will admit that's not bad. But as a member of staff, we just wouldn't get along. I have to go now."

I stood dumbfounded. I worked so hard for my degree while raising small children and attending Florida International University, graduating with honors. True, I didn't follow orders all the time. I embraced Lisa or Harriet to comfort them when they didn't feel well. I placed a hand on Ritchie's shoulder, telling him what a good job he was doing. He said afterwards, "It feels so good just to be touched. Do you know what's its like not to even feel a human touch?"

I knew I'd have to leave Friendship Haven and look for paid employment elsewhere. The halfway house was just a business run by someone who followed stupid rules and regulations at the expense of sick people. Helena and the rest of the staff never even questioned the rules. Little did anyone know on the outside that the dollars they donated were going mostly for a staff that did hardly anything for the people they were supposed to help.

As I walked out the door, I saw Marty waiting for the van to take him downtown. He came over to me when he saw me.

"H-How did I do today?"

"You were wonderful."

Marty managed a very slight smile as he said,

"You try to make me feel good."

He caught himself and quickly clenched his teeth and became tight lipped.

"Marty, why are you so afraid to smile?"

"I think I told you that I have T.M.J. I can't open my jaw too wide and my teeth are very crooked."

"Oh yes. I remember you telling me about your jaw problem. How about just a little smile? Do you mind if I see your teeth?"

Marty hesitated and then moved his lips slightly apart.

"I can't even see your teeth. The upper part of your lip covers them. Really, Marty, don't be afraid to smile. You look nice when you do."

"Are we going to sing more songs from Oklahoma next week? That was a good play," Marty said with a great deal of excitement.

"I hope so." I said.

I fidgeted in my purse for a pair of sunglasses. I didn't want Marty to see the sadness in my eyes. As I looked at him, I thought that soon I would not be seeing him anymore. He sensed something was wrong because even through his thick eyeglasses I could tell he was worried.

"I- I want to thank you," he said. "I can't express myself!"

"That's alright. You express yourself very well."

I walked to my car while waving goodbye to Marty who was now getting into the van, probably to go to the beach. I got in and slowly drove away from the people I loved and a home that had become more like a first one to me than a second one.

Disappointed at not getting a paid position, my enthusiasm for my work at Friendship Haven began to wane. I hung around my house more, accomplishing little. I missed Marty and my group very much and worried about them. I was concerned that Helena had told her staff that I wasn't suitable for a paid position. There was a lot of talk at the halfway house, and while everything should have been private, it wasn't.

Marty and most of the other members of the center tried to treat volunteers and staff members with respect and appreciation. Some of the staff had a superior attitude, as if they lived in a completely different world than the members, - a so-called normal world. I didn't feel that way at all. I just felt lucky not to be a member of the center myself.

At 23, a psychiatrist in New York gave me a choice of outpatient electro-shock therapy or a stay in a mental hospital. This was because of headaches and depression from the constant strain of my mother's illness and a bad marriage. I chose what I thought was the lesser of the two evils, shock treatments, which made me much worse. They were given to me at Flower Fifth Avenue Hospital. We all stood in line waiting to be shocked. As the machines were in curtained booths, I heard the screams of people before me as they suffered this barbaric treatment. When it was my turn, I was placed on a gurney and someone smeared my temples with something cold and greasy. Then an electric conductor was placed on my forehead and a burly man held me down with all his might. I lost consciousness and the next thing I remembered was seeing my poor mother waiting for me to take me home on the Third Avenue El. It was the early 1950's and few anti-depressants were on the market.

Years later, Dr. Harris said I never needed shock treatments. My memory loss from them was terrible. I was unable to recall barely anything during the two years prior to the treatments. I felt that my brain was damaged and it took the good doctor hours and hours of talking to me to convince me otherwise. This, and my inability to handle electric plugs and sockets, gave me much grief.

Most of the members of Friendship Haven had shock treatments. After they came out of the hospital, they discussed them with other people who also had them. They talked about the treatments as if they were the accepted thing to endure when you were sick.

As my mother suffered through these treatments many times in Rockland State Hospital and Halcyon Rest, a private mental hospital in New York, I was sure I was following in my mother's footsteps when I, too, went through that horror.

Once a person has a record of being in a mental hospital, they are stamped for life. No one left Friendship Haven to live in the outside world. Being labeled crazy led to a self-fulfilling prophecy -- if you're crazy enough to have to go to a hospital, and become a member of Friendship Haven, you're expected to act that way. Any small oddity that was normal in the outside world was looked upon as "nuts" if a member of Friendship Haven displayed it. The kind of segregation they suffered and still do, and the menial jobs they are offered, only adds to their "Catch 22" situation.

Thinking about all this, I decided to volunteer at the halfway house only one day a week and try to finish what I began. I'd have to put my personal feelings aside and remind myself why I went there in the first place -- to help at least one person find his or her way back into the so-called normal world - a world that so far, I was allowed to live in.

With my Best of Broadway book under my arm, I entered the social hall room and walked over to the piano. The cigarette smoke bothered me more than usual. It was probably because I hadn't been exposed to it for a while. I didn't see Marty. I walked into the kitchen and sure enough found him standing over a sink of dishes with his large white apron fastened around his over-sized trousers. He was staring at the dishes but didn't touch them. I tapped him on the shoulder and he turned around. I was surprised to see the expression of relief on his face when he saw me.

"H-Hello. I hope you don't mind my asking, but why don't you come around here more? You haven't been around here much lately."

"I've been busy with my family," I fibbed.

"I meant to ask you. When you were in New York, did you see a Broadway show? Did you see the Statue of Liberty? Did you ride the subway?"

It surprised me that Helena bothered telling my group I had gone to New York.

"I only saw that one show I told you about. I didn't ride the subway much."

I felt lousy as I tried to answer each question. Marty looked the same as he usually did -- unshaven with a greenish complexion. His posture was stooped. I couldn't help recalling how tall he stood at the microphone just a month earlier during the Christmas and Chanukah programs. As I looked at him, I knew I would never knowingly desert him. He showed me he had guts by leading so many people in a lovely musical program and singing beautifully.

Marty and I walked out of the kitchen to the piano. I asked him if anyone had done any music during the two weeks that I had been gone. He said Ben and Harriet played a little but that there wasn't any singing. As we spoke, Marty noticed my Broadway book.

"Do you have 'Kismet' in that book?"

"I don't know, Marty. Let's both look."

Marty turned to the index of plays. He found "Kismet" with one of his favorite songs, "Stranger in Paradise." As Marty fingered the pages, I noticed that the palms of his hands were very raw.

"Do you want to sing 'Stranger in Paradise'? I brought along a tape recorder. We could practice it and then I could record you. Would you like that?"

"B-But we have to rehearse. I can't sing it without rehearsing."

"O.K. Let's give it a try."

As I began playing the piano, Ben came over.

"Heh, man! Where'ya been?"

I was surprised that Ben noticed that I hadn't been around.

"I took a little vacation. I'm just going over some piece with Marty. Afterwards, how about you playing 'Isn't She Lovely.' Like I've said to you, you play it as good as Stevie Wonder."

"Sure nuff. Ya got it!"

Ben left the room and Marty and I went to work. After a half hour or so, I put the tape recorder on and Marty sang "Take My Hand, I'm A Stranger in Paradise". As the haunting refrain filled the social hall, it was as if Marty's very soul entered the dingy room and changed it to a place of beauty and serenity. For a short while, I knew Marty was happy. So was I.

My happiness didn't last long. One Thursday morning, as I was preparing to go to Friendship Haven, I received a call from my brother in New York. He said, "Mother is dead. She passed away last night."

The year was 1977. When my husband told me the news, I screamed and was unable to stop. My mother died suddenly of a heart attack. My father went into the kitchen to take a drink of water and found her lying on the linoleum floor in their Bronx apartment.

The guilt that seized my brother at the time remains very strong to this day. He was in California when my mother passed away and blamed himself for not being near her so that he could help her as, always. He told me before he left that he couldn't take the stress anymore of caring for her when she got sick, something he had done since he was a child. He added that our Pop should have taken some responsibility for her and not have run away all the time.

The year before, my brother had to call the cops to take my mother to the hospital. She got so distraught when she saw them that she cowered in the hallway of her apartment and soiled herself.

I wrote to my brother while he was in California and said, "Mother is getting sick again. She sang 'Popirossen' to me over the phone and spoke only Yiddish." These were signs that soon she would be out of touch with reality.

My brother didn't answer my letter. Within a few days my mother was gone. When I went to her small, crowded apartment on University Avenue the day before her funeral, I found a note in her handwriting that read "take salt every hour." My mother had high blood pressure and the high salt intake would definitely endanger her life. My brother and I think she killed herself rather than go back to a mental hospital.

Now I would never have the chance to tell her that I was sorry for being mean to her in the past and not understanding her illness. I hated her when I was a child for all the things she didn't do as a mother. When she went away to Rockland State Hospital, I thought she died. How could anyone explain to a child what my mother suffered from? I blamed her for the messy house she kept, for having to clean and clean before a boyfriend came over when I was older. I longed for the mothers my friends had, nice mothers who kept neat houses and didn't go crazy every year or two. I prayed to God to give me a mother like this, instead of the one I had. I even wished at times that she would die, may God forgive me.

In between my mother's bouts of sickness, she was sad, but functioned pretty well. With her swollen legs, she carried heavy shopping bags up a steep hill to where we lived on Fulton Avenue. She took me on the Bronx Third Avenue El train all the way to Coney Island where Steeplechase Amusement Park was. I loved the exciting rides. She bought me a cute little turtle, named Dopey, near the Roxy Theatre in Manhattan where we saw Betty Grable in "Down Argentine Way", and afterwoods, took me to Fu Man Choo's Chinese Restaurant.

When my Baba and Aunt Essie visited my mother at the hospital and brought her kosher chicken and soup, they were told to leave it. My mother never got to eat this as someone stole the food. It was good that she was a heavy-set woman as she lost a lot of weight in the state hospital.

My Uncle Sam, who was very fond of my mother, and felt a great deal of pity for her, drove her to the hospital once when she was very sick. I was about 7 at the time. The image of my mother in his car is still vivid in my memory. She lay on the floor of the car, with her feet up in the air, laughing and crying the whole way to the hospital. My father kept trying to pull her dress down over her bloomers pleading,

"Sadie, Sadie, stop it, stop it." He cried and my brother and I who were in the car cried with him. Why we were there to see such a terrible thing, I'll never know. It was cold and my uncle tried to wrap my mother in a coat. This was impossible as she wouldn't stop writhing and screaming. My uncle tried to take my mother to the entrance of the hospital but this was also impossible. He called two guards who put her in a strait jacket and dragged her away.

When we visited her a few weeks later, she hung on to a wire fence in the yard of the hospital, pleading with us to take her home. Again my brother and I were not spared this terrible sight. The somber, gray building of Rockland State Hospital, with its black bars on its windows, looms forever in my memory.

My mother got sick almost every year after that horrible time.

Perhaps it was the guilt I felt, after my mother passed away, that caused me to hurt my back. I bent down in my home in Miami to pick something up and felt excruciating pain. I was laid up for close to two months. I wanted to let Marty know about my injury and that I was sorry we couldn't put on the Western musical. When I was able to, I tried to reach him on the Friendship Haven phone but, as usual, this was impossible. I also tried to leave a message for Helena, but doubt that she got it.

I was worried that without the music, and someone who cared about Marty, in particular, he might regress.

After two months, I was able to get around a little. I hesitated to stop by Friendship Haven because of the rejection I felt by Helena. Also, I was concerned that the people I had worked with had forgotten me. It still bothered me that Marty practically ignored me at the coffee house gathering a few months ago and didn't even ask me to dance. Maybe he thought I was above him in some way or that it wouldn't be proper to mingle socially with a volunteer. Little did he know that I needed the people at Friendship Haven probably more than they needed me.

Because of that need, and curious how my group was doing, I drove to Friendship Haven one Monday with the thought of just spending a short time there. I looked around for Marty and felt tremendous relief to find him by the large, stainless steel kitchen sink.

Marty was so happy to see me that I thought he was on the verge of embracing me. He caught himself.

"W-Where have you been? W-What happened to you?"

"I hurt my back very badly. In fact, the doctors thought I slipped a disc. I tried to get through to you to tell you what happened to me, but, as usual, the phone here wasn't working. I hope you weren't too aggravated. I'm really sorry."

"T-That's alright. Someone said your mother died. Is that true?"

"Yes, it's true. I spoke to Olivia before I hurt my back and told her I'd be out because of the death."

"Y-You were gone so long I thought you forgot about us."

"No, No way," I said as I stared at Marty's shadowed, scared face and sad eyes.

Ben and Harriet came over when they saw me. Ben said, "Heh, great, you're back. Ya been missed."

Harriet patted her bangs as usual and said "Hhellllooooo. It's nice to see you."

"Great to see you also, gang" I said. "I can't do the music today. You know, I'm in mourning for my mother," I fibbed.

As far as I knew, there was nothing in the Jewish religion that said you couldn't sing songs after a short period of time, especially if it was a *Mitzvah*, a blessing. I just didn't feel like singing.

"When I come here again I'll play the piano," I told Marty.

"When are you coming back?" Marty asked.

"I don't know exactly. Soon, I hope. Tell you what. Why don't you keep my Broadway book for awhile? I have it in the car. That way you can still practice some of the songs we worked on. Would you like that?"

"H-How can I sing without the piano and you helping me? It won't be good."

"It'll be alright, you'll see."

Marty took off his apron and walked me to my car. I stood for a few minutes looking at him. He was a head taller than me, even though his posture was stooped. He wore a tattered belt gathered at his waist and oversized checkered pants, the same as when I first met him. His hands were blistered and raw, and even though he tried to hide them, I saw them.

There was no use mentioning his hands. It was obvious he had gotten worse, and now the guilt I felt about my mother was doubled by the sight of Marty.

"Don't worry," I said to him. I'll come around. Take care of yourself. Use that lotion I gave you for your hands and the tissues. So, long, Marty. See you soon."

He stood in the parking lot, watching my car as I drove away. His worried face and thin wasted body rode along with me as I left the driveway. I almost turned around but decided against it. The words of my psychiatrist came back to me,

"Evelyn, I don't think it's a good idea to work in Friendship Haven."

I called Barbra and Marty from time to time. Barbra was running into a great deal of difficulty. She told me that they were threatening to fire her because one day she kicked off her shoes in Ben's presence. The staff accused her of deliberately doing this to excite Ben and exacerbate his foot fetish. She denied this, just saying her feet were tired and that she took off her shoes to rest them.

Barbra added that she could do little to help the people in Friendship Haven. She said the staff gave her tons of paperwork and that she didn't have time to even talk to the members. If she so much as patted someone on the shoulder, she was reprimanded for it.

I called her one day and she told me they had fired her.

"Barbra, I'm not surprised. It seems that the best people can't stay there. I remember how kind and loving you were to the members. I never forgot your kindness to me, either. When you told me how good my work was at the piano, you made me feel great."

"I don't know what I'm going to tell Ben. He and I had become good friends."

"I'm in the same boat. I don't know what to tell Marty and the others."

"By the way, Evelyn. Marty told me he likes you."

"I know he likes me."

"I mean, really likes you."

"Barbra, I'm sorry but I don't like him that way. How can I? I mean I feel sorry for him. He's so pathetic and lost. Actually, it's awful of me to say this but at times he irritated me. He repeats himself so much. He asked me the same thing over and over like, "Were you busy this weekend, were you busy, were you busy?"

"I know, Evelyn, but he's a hell of a sweet guy. He appreciates any little thing you do for him."

"I know Barbra and that's what makes it sad. I'm awfully sorry what happened to you but maybe it's for the best."

"I don't know about that, Evelyn. What's going to happen to these people? Who's going to give a damn about them without the two of us there?"

"I agree but we can't get sick over it. You know, I was really getting upset there. It was like hitting a solid wall trying to get through to Helena and the rest of the staff. All they talk about are their rules and regulations and the hell with the rest. Well, I better go. Do you think anyone heard our conversation?"

"No, there's no one around."

"But they do have a switchboard."

"I wouldn't worry about it. I hate having to look for another job now."

"Me too. But first I'm going to volunteer at Haven School for the Retarded. Maybe I'll like doing that work. So long, Barbra. I'll call you soon. And good luck."

"Same to you, Evelyn."

I went to Haven Center and volunteered for a very nice teacher. The children and young adults in the class were slightly to severely retarded and I taught them skills such as tying their shoelaces. I also taught a boy of ten to play a beginning piece on the piano. Even though I was told he was beyond help, I made headway with him. I asked the staff if my work could lead to paid employment but I didn't receive a clear-cut answer. One day, a husky boy of 18, who slobbered all the time, grabbed the teacher and tried to bang him against the wall. I knew then what I was up against. The teacher very kindly said to me that they needed strong men for the place as some of the retarded students had intense neurological damage that caused them to become violent.

Chapter 4
Poisoning

In addition to my mother dying during the year 1977, I lost two of my best friends to cancer. They were only 39. I didn't know what to do with myself or where to look for a job. It was impossible not to think about my mother or Marty. I worried about him and the other people at Friendship Haven. If only I didn't feel so rotten around Helena, I might be able to postpone looking for paid work and just continue my volunteer work with the people I loved.

It seemed that my degree in psychology was almost useless in the job market. Even if I earned a master's degree, I was told that there were too many people in the field.

Social work and Psychology had become glamorous during the '70's. Young people were eager to pursue these areas of study as they thought they could make a difference in a society that was seeing an increase in child abuse, spousal abuse, drugs and crime. If I were still in contact with the students in my psychology classes, I would tell them that their idealistic endeavors would cause them grief as they tried to grapple with tons of paper work and strict rules and regulations. Their clients would take a back seat in a system not geared to help them. Unfortunately, I found this out after much disappointment and frustration.

I still couldn't bring myself to go back to Friendship Haven so, with time on my hands I decided to fix up my house that was neglected during the years I went to school. My small Cockapoo dog, Fuffy, had been scratching herself furiously for weeks. My legs were bitten badly and scabs were forming on them. When I examined my dog, I found her body loaded with fleas that were jumping on my carpet and even my bed.

I called an exterminating company to fog my house. While waiting for them to call me back, I thought of playing tennis again when the weather got cooler, something happy instead of thinking about my emptiness since I lost my mother and close friends. Marty was always on my mind and I planned on trying to call him now and then and giving him what little support I could. I wasn't in the frame of mind to give much of myself, feeling drained of emotion.

I set up an appointment with the exterminating company and busied myself emptying cupboards and arranging to move my large tropical fish, Oscar, and his tank to the patio. I brought Fuffy to my veterinarian for dipping so that she would not bring the fleas back into the house. On a muggy day in August, two men set up their equipment and fogged the rooms of my house. I left and went to a Jack La Lane health club that had given me a month's free trial period. As I drove to the club, I thought of soaking in the whirlpool and letting my cares float away. Maybe this would help me to get the pathetic image of Marty out of my thoughts. Even my car reminded me of Friendship Haven and the times I parked it in their lot, entering the social hall and looking for him. I didn't fully understand the grip Marty had on me.

As I drove along, I thought about Barbra and what she told me about Marty.

"He likes you," she said.

"So, I like him to!"

"No, I mean he really likes you!"

"Barbra, I don't like him that way. How can I?"

I missed Barbra and wondered what she was doing. At Friendship Haven, we were two allies fighting an impregnable system. We hadn't made so much as a dent in that system, as caring for people took a back seat to the politics that ruled the halfway house. There was no room or desire for change and Helena would continue being a mechanical figure who ruled. I still wondered if she had come to Friendship Haven with good intentions but had gotten burnt out by the system. Every now and then I noticed that she genuinely tried to help someone by bending rules but caught herself in time.

I went into the health club and changed into a bathing suit. The whirlpool was co-ed and as I soaked in it, I noticed two men who were talking and laughing with each other as they lay in the foaming tub. Maybe I can meet someone, I thought, as I eyed them discreetly. Then I wouldn't have such a fear of leaving Leo. I leaned against the edge of the whirlpool and kicked my feet. I wasn't so old yet, only 48. I looked around the tub some more as I exercised. The men seemed to be in their fifties. Their pot bellies jutted out of the water as they patted down the hair on their scalp that had large bald spots. Again I thought about Marty, how bony he was and how thick his unkempt black hair was. He never laughed but sometimes managed a forced smile after I complimented him on his singing. These men acted so sure of themselves; they repulsed me. They never looked my way and I figured that men their ages were married and overfed. Even if they weren't, I was sure they wanted younger women. Suddenly, I felt old.

I got out of the tub, dressed in shorts, and did some cycling exercise on one of the bikes. I checked my watch and noticed that three hours had passed since the exterminating company fogged. It was time to go home and open windows.

I opened my front door and was greeted with a strong noxious odor that burnt my nostrils. I got a kerchief out of the trunk of my car and placed it over my nose as I entered the house again. I caught myself on one of my railings when I slipped on the greasy tile floor of my dining room. Everything was covered with a greasy, slimy gook. My baby grand piano, that my mother had bought me as a house gift, and which I loved, was covered with the fetid slop. My favorite music piece, Clair De Lune, which rested on the piano rack, was soaked. Holding the kerchief tightly over my nose, I opened windows and glass patio doors. I ran out to the patio and slumped into one of the chairs next to Oscar. Luckily my son's room hadn't been fogged because he had another fish tank in his room that was too heavy to move. I went into his room and lay down on his bed. I felt dizzy and my vision was out of focus.

There was a phone in my son's room and I called the exterminating company. EMERGENCY, EMERGENCY I yelled over the phone to an answering machine. THIS IS MRS. ROTH. HELP! SOMETHING IS TERRIBLY WRONG. MY HOUSE IS REEKING FROM CHEMICALS. CALL ME IMMEDIATELY! I said as I left me phone number.

As I lay on the bed, I continued worrying about my piano. I had to wipe it or else it would be ruined. I grabbed a towel from the linen closet and wiped the ivory keys while holding a kerchief over my nose. I also tried to mop the floors. Little did I know that the chemicals were all the while seeping into my body even while I tried to cover my nose. As I wiped, I became more and more woozy.

My husband was out of town so I didn't have to worry about his coming back to the house that night. I quickly wrote a note to my son and scotch taped it to the front door. DON'T COME INTO THE HOUSE. STAY OUTSIDE. THE SMELL HERE IS TERRIBLE FROM BEING FOGGED FOR FLEAS. YOU'LL GET SICK IF YOU COME IN. STAY IN YOUR FRIEND TOMMY'S HOUSE!

I went into my son's room again and called the exterminating company. I lay down on the bed and waited for their return call. It seemed like hours passed. They didn't return my call.

By about 10:00 P.M., I heard a knock on my front door. Thinking it was the company, I eagerly ran to open it. My son, who was 16, stood outside the door and asked what was going on. I looked into his serious dark eyes and felt like wiping the sweat from his forehead. I was always close to him, except lately, because his father influenced him and turned him more and more against me.

"Gerald, don't come in here," I pleaded. "There's something wrong. They sprayed too much and everything smells and is greasy. I don't feel well and I don't think it's safe in here. Can you sleep in your friend Tommy's house?"

"They didn't spray my room", my son said. "Why can't I go in there? I have to feed my fish. Why are you making such a big deal out of this? Shirley just had her house fogged and nothing happened."

Shirley was my neighbor who had recommended the exterminating company.

"I'm not making a big deal out of it. Go ahead. Go in if you want. You can see for yourself. But you better stay in your room, just in case. Do you think I should go to a motel and not sleep in the house?"

"Naaaaaa. It'll be O.K! Just open all the windows and air out the place."

My son went to his room and locked his door as usual. I knocked on his door and asked him if he wanted a whopper at Burger King. He yelled through the door that he already ate.

I took some Meclazine for my dizziness, got into my car, and drove to Burger King. It was a relief to breathe air that wasn't drenched with fumes. I ate a whopper and thought about where I would sleep. I drove to Howard Johnson's on Dixie Highway and asked how much a room was. It was close to 11:00 P.M. by now. After the clerk told me a room was $69.00, I decided against it. I figured with my patio door open and a fan placed on the floor of my bedroom, the room would air out and I'd be better in the morning.

I got up about 6:00 A.M. with a terrible headache. Little did I realize that I had breathed the fumes from my pillow on the bed all night. I called my family doctor who told me to come over to see him. Somehow I made it to his office. He examined me and told me to get out of my house for a few days because I was probably allergic to the fumes. Even though it was expensive, I checked into Howard Johnson's and lay down on the bed. My face, arms and scalp felt as if they were on fire. I filled a bucket with ice cubes, put a few in a washcloth, and applied them to my skin. As I couldn't concentrate on reading even a magazine and because of fuzzy vision, I had nothing to do but think. I asked the clerk at the desk for some paper and a pencil and managed to scribble, "Something is terribly wrong with me. It seems more than allergies. I feel very sick and depressed." I wrote the details of what happened in my house and how I was feeling. I ended by saying that I wish I could go back to Friendship Haven to the people I loved. The date of my entry was August 23, 1977.

I stayed at Howard Johnson's for three days and didn't feel any better. My skin still burnt and I was woozy. I called the Epidemiology Department of the University of Miami and left a message for a Dr. David to call me. When he did, I managed, with difficulty, to get an appointment with him. He thought I was interested in a lawsuit and hesitated to get involved with me because of this. I actually had to plead with him for an appointment, saying I just wanted him to examine me.

Dr. David, a pudgy man of about 65, asked me a lot of questions, examined my pupils and was surprised to find that they were constricted. He took a blood test and told me that my white blood count was below normal. He said he wanted to take another test in a week. He stressed my not going home at least until that time.

When I came back for another blood test, my blood count was normal. Dr. David confirmed that I was poisoned.

I went back to my house and tried to stay inside for a short while. This was impossible as my skin began to burn after a few minutes. My husband and son felt all right in the house so they came to the conclusion that it was "all in my mind."

"But you don't understand!" I pleaded with them. Dr. David said I was poisoned."

"You stayed away more than a week." Leo said. You must be better by now. You just think the house is bothering you."

"I don't think anything. I know how I feel here. I'll have to go back to Howard Johnson's."

"And what are we supposed to do meanwhile?" my husband said. "Also you're spending a lot of money."

"Well what can I do? I don't feel good here! I'm probably allergic to the residue!"

"That's crazy!"

"I don't know why you never believe me. Do you think I'd make up such a thing? Why don't you call Dr. David?"

"I'm very busy in the office. I'll call him when I have a chance," Leo said.

After the bills piled up from Howard Johnson's, Leo reluctantly rented a motor home that he parked in the driveway of our house. I felt a little better in it but after a few months, Leo said it was too expensive. Even though practically everything in my house was cleaned or thrown away, I still could not live in it and had to sleep on my patio.

I flew to my daughter who lived in Austin, Texas while she was earning a masters degree at the University of Texas. With an electric blanket over me, I slept on a cot on the porch of her small rented house. It was now winter but I had no choice as I couldn't tolerate the inside of her house because it had been sprayed in the past with insecticide. I also couldn't eat in restaurants for the same reason. When my daughter said my staying with her was interfering with her studies, I flew back to Miami and continued living on my patio or a tent in my back yard that my son had set up.

On a December day, I prepared twenty Dalmane sleeping pills in a plastic container, put them in my purse, and drove to the beach. My plan was to go into the ocean and swallow them. If I couldn't live in the environment anymore and had to stay in a "bubble" so to speak, I figured I'd be better of dead. When I went to get the pills, they had melted into one glob and it was impossible to swallow them.

I was still seeing my psychiatrist, Dr. Harris, who suggested my being tested by a neurologist, as I complained of lack of concentration and severe headaches. I refused to go. If I had brain damage, I didn't want to know about it as there was nothing anyone could do for me.

I had little to do and a lot of time to think. Fortunately by now, my father had moved to Collins Avenue, Miami Beach, and every so often I visited him when I was able to drive. As I drove on the I95 expressway, I thought I was being punished for leaving Marty and the people at Friendship Haven. This reawakened another old feeling of guilt in me, of my letting my brother have all the responsibility of taking care of my sick mother until the day she died. All those years I hated her because of her strange scary behavior.

Now I was behaving rather strangely. My lack of concentration, headaches and inability to live in my own home gave my family an excuse to pull me down even more, saying that I was following in my mother's footsteps. My daughter was fearful that she, too, would inherit her grandmother's and mother's mental illness. I felt like a leper, an outcast, someone to stay clear of. How I longed to be with Marty and the people of Friendship Haven as they, too, were outcasts.

After consulting with doctors trained in allergy, I learned that I had an actual chemical sensitivity and not a mental illness. There was even a group of people I met, when I stayed with my daughter in Texas, who suffered this syndrome. One of the women put me in touch with a doctor who had to live in an anodized aluminum motor home because of his sensitivity. I called the doctor and he told me to go back to Miami and stay on the beach day and night. He thought that the air might help to break down the chemicals in my system. Committing suicide was something I constantly thought about if I was to permanently become part of the group of the "chemically sensitive" who wore used clothing, never went into a restaurant, or were unable to tolerate gas or electric heat.

After a year of being homeless, I got back into my home and slept in my son's room. One day, as I lay on his bed, a letter arrived from Marty.   The return address said Marty Ross, Friendship Haven. I opened the small note that about fifteen people had signed and read, "we miss you...come back." I stared at Marty's carefully written signature and those of Ben's, Ritchie's, Harriet's, Lisa's, Patty's and the rest of the people I had come to know and love. I felt as if a murky cloud had lifted as I read and reread the note. I knew what I had to do.

The Thursday I went to Friendship Haven, and the greeting I received, stands out in my memory as if it were just the other day. People clapped as I entered the social hall with its small, old spinet piano standing against the wall. Marty walked over to me as if to put his arms around me, but, he caught himself.   I looked at his dark, unshaven face, which seemed even thinner and more drawn than I remembered, his thick eyeglasses, uncut hair, baggy pants and white oversized apron, and felt overwhelmed with pity and happiness. By that small letter which he decided to send, he gave me a will to live. These people cared about me and it didn't matter what Helena or anyone else did or didn't do. They needed me almost as much as I needed them.

I had tremendous difficulty around the piano in the social hall, as the cigarette smoke burnt my face. I kept dabbing it with a tissue soaked in cold water and was determined to do some music no matter how bad I felt. I could only stay a half hour before I felt the searing pain was too much for me to bear. Still it was a beginning and a reason for me to go on.

Besides going to Friendship Haven as much as possible, I visited my father, Popsy, as I called him on Miami Beach, and swam in the clear, salt water. I still was unable to eat in restaurants, even though my Pop offered to treat me to the Famous Restaurant on Collins Avenue, where he loved the kosher style food and seltzer water they served.

While he ate, I waited for him outside the restaurant. He always made me a challah sandwich with whatever he was eating and brought it out to me. I couldn't tolerate his room either because an exterminator sprayed it every month.

My Pop went to hear singers on 9th Street and Ocean Drive every Wednesday night. I went with him and listened to Jewish songs of yesteryear. Mostly elderly people got up on the small stage and sang melodies such as "Popirossen" and "Ofn Pripichik," songs my mother used to sing when we lived in the Bronx. I learned most of these melodies from her and hearing the people sing them brought back the good times we had around our old upright piano. As I hummed along, a man who was standing next to me said I had a nice voice and asked me to sing. I said I wasn't prepared but would do so next time.

The following Monday I brought the book "Fiddler on the Roof" to Friendship Haven and asked Ritchie and Marty to rehearse the songs with me. For the first time that I remember, Ritchie didn't balk as he brought over his violin to the piano. He picked it up and cupped it under his chin while he played clearly and sweetly "Fiddler on the Roof", "Sunrise Sunset" and "To Life". He followed me along perfectly as I played the piano and Marty sang. A young man next to me began smoking and my face started to burn. I ignored it and continued playing. Marty sang with such feeling that, as always, the dingy, smoky, gray room was transformed into a bright, happy place. Some of the members came over to the piano to sing or hum along with us, and the expression on some of their sad faces changed. For a short while they seemed to find peace and tranquility as Marty's lovely voice filled the room. Between Marty, Ritchie and myself, I felt we had a nice trio and I thought that we could do something with it outside of Friendship Haven. I knew that I couldn't continue volunteering in the halfway house, that it was only a matter of a short time that I would see things that upset me too much to stay. Still I was grateful for the time that I spent there and for the feeling it gave me of being somebody instead of the nobody I felt I was during the past year.

Olivia told me that Helena had taken a short leave of absence to have a baby. It was wonderful not having her around to give me orders. Ben played and sang for me Stevie Wonder's "Isn't She Lovely." His white teeth shone as he smiled and sang. I tried to show enthusiasm but I was unable to revive the thrill of working with my musical group during the early days at Friendship Haven.

I thought about getting in touch with Barbra who was now working in a rehabilitation center for delinquent girls. I wanted to approach her with the idea of bringing Ben there to play for them. I was sure they would take to his kind of contemporary music.

I kept visiting my Pop and listening to his tales of woe, of being a diabetic and having to stick himself with a needle every day. He met a very nice lady in his hotel by the name of Becky, who was about 75, and who told him and everyone else that she loved him. Even though his hairline had receded, my father was still a handsome tall man of 73, with blue eyes and even features. I sat with him and Becky on the benches with the singers on Ocean Drive but still couldn't get up the nerve to sing. My Pop usually had a napkin in his hand with something for me to eat. He asked me why I didn't sing and I told him that I wasn't ready. I added that I had met a very good singer and that I wanted to bring him over to the beach to sing for the people. As I said this, the man who heard me hum before, went over to me and asked me to sing again. I left the group, walked across the street, and practiced by myself. When I was sure I knew the words and melody to "Bar Mir Biztu Shein", I went back to the group and told the man in charge that I'd like to sing. After I finished my song, there was a lot of applause and I was asked to sing another song. I sang "Are You Lonesome Tonight." This was so appreciated that I felt like some sort of celebrity.

Ocean breezes cooled us and the air added its own sweetness as I sat with my Pop and Becky on the benches and munched on challah filled with cottage cheese that my father had prepared for me. I listened to more songs of yesteryear such as "Yossel, Yossel", "Shein Vi Di LaVone" and actually felt peaceful. Afterwards, I walked with Beckie and Pop to their hotel. Beckie went to sleep and I sat on the porch talking with my father.

"I miss your sweet mother," he said to me.

"I know Pop but at least she's finally at peace and is in heaven."

"She was such a *gitte nishumah*, a good soul, with a heart of gold."

"But she suffered a lot. And so did Murray."

"I couldn't help myself," he said. I'm a weak man. What could I do when she got sick? I was scared!"

"Pop, it's over with. What's the use talking about it? I feel sorry for Murray. He's guilty that he went to California for a few weeks and wasn't around to take care of her."

"He's a good kid. I couldn't help myself," he said again. "It was a pity on your mother."

"Murray more. I know you couldn't help it but he had such a burden. Pop, let's stop talking about it. It brings back bad memories. I'd like to think about good things. Besides, you have a nice friend now. Becky is very good to you!"

"You compare her to your sweet mother? I can't eat anything she makes. Feh! Her icebox stinks. She never cleans it out."

"So her refrigerator smells, so what? But what about the way she washes your feet when they burn. She's good hearted, too, and she really cares about you. You're lucky you met her."

My father rubbed his arm and complained that the needle he injected himself with that morning still hurt him.

"It's the terrible sugar," he said. "If only I didn't have the sugar."

"Pop, be grateful for what you do have. It's no good to complain. I'll help you buy some decent shoes. You're letting yourself go. When is the last time you bought a pair of pants?"

"I have good pants. What do I need new ones for? Where do I go?"

"That's not the point. You're still a good-looking man. Other women in your hotel keep looking at you. There's about one of you to at least 40 women in Miami Beach, so you're lucky you're a man."

"I don't like seeing all the old people with walkers here."

"Pop, I feel sorry for them. I notice that hardly anyone visits them. At least I come."

I heard sniffles as my father blew his nose in a tissue.

He was probably crying but in the dark I couldn't tell for sure. I recalled how he always had clean, pressed white handkerchiefs when we lived in the Bronx because I washed and ironed them. Even though I told my father not to dwell in the past, it was hard for me not to do so.

I thought about bringing Marty over to 9th Street to sing for the people. He already knew Yiddish as we had gone over some of the songs around the piano at Friendship Haven. I couldn't wait to see the response of the people on the benches to Marty's lovely tenor voice. I didn't know if he would get up again in front of so many people to sing but this was something I could help him do.

I tried to go to Miami Beach every Wednesday to see my father and sing for the Jewish people who gathered on the benches of Ocean Drive and 9th Street. The ocean air and salt water helped me to lose some of my sensitivity to chemicals and I was now able to go into the Famous Restaurant for a kosher style meal with my father. I ate the delicious roasted chicken and matzoth ball soup quickly because I still feared I would have a bad reaction to any insecticide spray they used in the restaurant. I watched my father laboriously chew his food as he didn't have any teeth, so to speak. Because of neglect and the poor conditions in Austria when he was a child, his gums grew over his teeth and were so hard and tough that he was able to chew with them. When he smiled, which was seldom since my mother died, you could only see his shiny gums. Years ago he had a wonderful sense of humor that I hoped wasn't lost forever.

There was no entertainment at the Chesterfield Hotel where my father stayed. I thought it would be a real treat for the people living there to hear Marty sing and Ritchie play his violin. Yiddish was practically becoming obsolete except for the elderly people who still spoke it. The response to the Yiddish songs every Wednesday evening on Ocean Drive was so overwhelming that some people had tears in their eyes as they listened to songs of yesteryear.

I was becoming more fluent in Yiddish as Marty and I rehearsed music from Jewish Songbooks and even spoke to each other in Yiddish. Marty knew the language very well, much better than I did. He had practically a photographic memory and hadn't forgotten the Yiddish he learned from his grandmother when he was a child. He also recalled words to Broadway songs from the early 1900's because of the time he spent with his father, listening to records of opera and Broadway melodies

Marty still walked very slowly with bent posture and sometimes his speech was slurred. While rehearsing, he still disappeared every fifteen minutes or so. I didn't want to embarrass him by knocking on the Friendship Haven bathroom door where I knew he was washing his hands until they were raw.

If I could get Marty out of the psychosocial rehabilitation center, even for a few hours, where he would have a chance to mingle with people on the outside, I thought his condition might improve. I still did not see any evidence of psychoses. He saw reality clearly and never hallucinated as others did in the halfway house. I often referred to my college book, "Abnormal Psychology" to check the symptoms of schizophrenia and manic-depression as any amateur psychiatrist would do. I even asked my own psychiatrist to help me try to figure out what Marty suffered from. I was still seeing my doctor once a week to work out my anger at my family for being so indifferent to my needs. What helped the most was my stumbling on a paperback book in the library titled, "Freedom from Compulsion" by Dr. Leonard Cammer. The chapter on "obsessive compulsive disorder" described Marty's symptoms -- his excessive hand washing and repetitive behavior. I was pretty sure that this was the mental disorder Marty suffered from. It was under the chapter of "neuroses", not "psychoses" much to my relief.

Marty's repetitive behavior and hand washing were very annoying. His sudden disappearances added to the annoyance. One minute, he was singing around the piano and the next he was gone, without saying where he was going. He still didn't allow me or anyone else to touch him in any way, even to shake his hand. He jumped back a foot or so when I attempted to do so, as if he was about to be burnt. One improvement I noticed was that he smiled slightly when I told him he sang a particular song very well. He was still very embarrassed about his protruding teeth that no one could really notice as his upper lip covered them. I didn't know anything about T.M.J. and tried to concentrate on his main problem, his rituals and obsessions. When we took a break from practicing our music, he told me he was very angry at the Nazis and God. He repeated this several times. When I questioned him why he felt that way, he said because they killed so many Jewish members of his family during the Holocaust and that God didn't do anything about it. When he spoke of the Nazis, he looked very angry and gritted his teeth. As his face was very drawn, surrounded by thick, black, unkempt hair, his expression at times made me very uneasy. When he was like this, I thought I might be wrong about him -- that he might have a more serious mental disease. His gentleness and meekness gave way to such intense anger when he spoke of Hitler that he became an entirely different person.

As I was poking into an untrodden area, I had to feel my way and listen to my instincts with Marty and the other members of Friendship Haven. People were supposed to be screened for violent behavior before they were allowed to be in Friendship Haven, but several young people slipped through the system, scaring the other members with threats to harm them. Suicides were a constant dilemma and recently another young girl slit her wrists. The counselors were mostly involved in paper work and had poor training in handling people with major mental illness. The psychiatrist rushed through the members as they lined up to talk to him at his van in the parking lot. He quickly wrote out prescriptions for them for anti-psychotic drugs such as Prolixin, Haldol and Thorazine. Medicaid paid for the doctor and their S.S.I. benefits paid for the fee of belonging to Friendship Haven.

I never saw Marty waiting at the van for medication nor did I ever witness him drifting off into a world of his own making. I was so frightened of my mother's bizarre behavior when she got sick, and her grotesque appearance, that I could never be around Marty if he exhibited any of her symptoms.

As mentioned earlier, my mother lost contact with reality when she broke down, sometimes becoming violent. She came to Miami in 1962 when my son was born, in an attempt to help me, but the stress was too much for her. She had a nervous breakdown and rocked my infant son's crib so hard that he almost rolled out of it. She wandered the streets and didn't know her way back to my apartment. As usual, my brother came to the rescue, flying from New York to Miami to drag her back. This was after she screamed obscenities from the window of the apartment building where I lived and after the manager knocked on my door to tell me "to get her out of there." My brother had a very difficult time getting her on the airplane as she had collected bags and bags of stale bread and assorted rags that she refused to part with. I watched in awe as he kidded around with her and helped her to get dressed for her flight back. She laughed and cried simultaneously as he put on her brassiere, bloomers, dress, stockings and shoes. It was hard to believe that she was the same person who a few weeks earlier cooked, washed floors and worried about my pregnancy going well. In between her bouts of insanity she was a kind soul that made her illness all the more terrible to bear.

I always liked a challenge. When I was a child in Yonkers, I welcomed the difficult task of walking to school on a cold, winter day through Trevor Park. Public School 22 was twenty blocks away from the house where we lived and with the thin coat one of my teachers managed to borrow for me, it was quite a feat trudging through the snow and slush to reach the school I loved. My brother, Murray, was always at my side and some times we balanced ourselves on wood railings that protected the beautiful flower gardens, resplendent with violets, sunflowers, zinnias and roses. I couldn't wait for the snow to melt so that I could look at and smell the fragrant blooms of the flowers. I worried that they would not survive the winter but they did.

My childhood and even my later years were both difficult and challenging as I strove not to become sick like my mother and Aunt Ray. My aunt also spent years in state hospitals and because of this, I hardly knew her. With two close members of my family with major mental illness, and with the knowledge as far back as time itself that insanity was inherited, the fear of my becoming crazy was my constant companion. Mental illness both fascinated and scared me. It was either going to be my destiny or a demon that I would eventually defeat.

One Thursday as I walked into the social hall of Friendship Haven, I looked around for Marty but couldn't find him. I had skipped a few weeks of going there because of a cold. I asked Ritchie where he was and he told me he didn't know.

"Do you think anyone here knows where he is? I'm kind of worried about him, Ritchie."

Ritchie squinted his eyes and cracked his knuckles before answering me.

"I dunno. I gotta get back to work."

"I hope he's not sick."

"I dunno," Ritchie repeated, as he walked away with his hammer and nails.

"Wait a minute!" I said as I caught up to him. "When did you last see Marty?"

"Maybe a few weeks ago, maybe more." Ritchie answered. "I gotta go!"

I figured it wouldn't hurt to ask Helena about Marty, but then again it might. She was back from her leave of absence and, as usual, the door to her office was closed. I softly knocked.

"Who's there?" a tired voice answered from inside.

"It's me, Evelyn. Can I talk to you for a minute?"

While I waited, I felt as lousy as I always did trying to confront her. Finally she opened the door a bit and peeked through.

"Yessss. I'm busy." She didn't ask me in.

"Do you know where Marty is? I'm worried about him. I haven't seen him for a long time."

Helena adjusted her half glasses before she answered me. She looked pale, and her hair which was always meticulously combed, was messy.

"You know we can't possibly give out any information about our members. By the way, you haven't been around much the last few weeks."

"I called Olivia to tell her I had a cold. I hope she gave you my message."

"It's better to contact me directly," Helena said, as if this was a possibility.

"But, is Marty alright?" I stammered like an idiot. He's not in a hospital, is he?"

Helena stared at me with a patronizing, sympathetic look.

"I repeat. I can't give out any information. You know that would be unethical. He has a family and I'm sure they are taking care of everything!"

Taking care of everything. That statement really bothered me.

I didn't feel like doing the music at Friendship Haven without Marty, even though I knew the other members needed it very much. I felt very down and tried to tell myself, as before, that I should be less involved with Marty. I played the piano for about half an hour and left.

I was still sleeping in my son's room, even though it was almost a year since I was poisoned. I also spent a great deal of time at the beach, visiting my father. I listened to the singers on Ocean Drive but didn't sing much myself. In spite of my father's sadness, he noticed mine and asked me what was wrong. I told him that a friend I was very fond of might be sick. My father asked me if I was talking about that man who sang and was in a mental hospital.

"Pop, he's not really in a mental hospital. He's getting better. I feel sorry for him. I told you I work with young people who have been in and out of mental hospitals. Many of them don't have anyone who cares. I was hoping Marty would come to the beach some day and sing for the people. He has a great voice."

My father shook his head as he warned me,

"God forbid you should get so close to someone who's sick. Did you forget what your poor mother went through and what I went through? That's the worse sickness in the world!"

My father said he was tired and was going to sleep. As he turned to leave he said,

"I'm afraid to sleep in my room because of the cockroaches!"

"Pop, they spray so much it's hard to believe a bug can live in your room. I still can't go into it without my skin burning. I'm sorry you're having so much trouble. Maybe, it'll be better tonight."

"I have a lot of *tzures*, trouble. I'm lonely and miss your mother. If only I didn't have the lousy sugar," he said again as he walked towards his room, rubbing his arm. I felt sorry for him even though he always felt sorry for himself.

When I got home, I looked in my phone book for a Marty Ross but couldn't find his name. There were so many Rosses in the book that, if necessary, I knew I'd call everyone of them to try to locate Marty. Surely he'd get in touch with me I reasoned. He was doing better than when I first met him. I didn't think he would suddenly slip backwards but then again, I had no way of knowing.

I hoped Marty would still show up at Friendship Haven for their social program. I thought I had better go there at least one day a week in case he did come.

Almost a month passed and I didn't hear a word from Marty. One day as I took the mail out of my box, I saw a post card. The return address said Marty Ross, New York. There was no street number. Immediately I thought he was in Rockland State Hospital where my mother suffered for so many years but as I read on, his card said in meticulous handwriting,

"I'm here with my mother visiting my aunt and brother. It's nice here. Give my regards to everyone. I'll be back in a week."

The relief I felt is impossible to describe on paper. I took the get-well note that he and the people in Friendship Haven had sent me and added Marty's card to it. Afterwards, I lay down on my son's bed, covered myself with a fluffy down quilt which I loved, and drifted to memories of my childhood in Yonkers.

I'm in my Baba's bedroom in her cold water flat. I'm almost 6. My brother and I take turns sleeping with her because her room is the only heated one. Her long, wavy hair flows freely as she undoes the tight bun she wears it in before going to sleep. Her printed flannel nightgown covers her from head to foot as she creeps into her metal framed bed and pulls a feather quilt, an ibba dibba, over her to keep her warm. Her oversized pillow is also made out of feathers and as I put my head on it, I feel like I am floating. An old, small coal stove stands by her bed and barely heats the room. When it isn't my turn to sleep with her, she fixes up a large padded ironing board and places it on two chairs for me. I am very thin so it makes a pretty decent bed.

My Aunt Essie has her own small room and has to get up early each morning to teach at the local high school. My mother isn't around nor is my father. My mother was taken to Rockland State Hospital six months earlier and I'm worried that she'll never come back.

Why these images came back to me, I'll never know. I reread Marty's card, pulled my quilt over me again and snuggled under it. Soon I fell into a sound sleep, devoid of nightmares.

On Monday, I went into the social hall and found Marty standing by the sink in the kitchen. He took off his apron the moment he saw me.

"H-Hello, y-you've been busy, busy?"

"Marty, is that really you? Never mind asking me if I've been busy. It's you I want to hear from. What did you do in New York? And why did it take you so long to write to me?"

Marty didn't answer for a few minutes. Then with his usual worried look he said,

"I-I'm sorry. I had your address from awhile back on a small piece of paper. I took it along with me but didn't remember where I put it. My mother took so many suitcases on the plane that it was hard to pack. I finally found your address in the pocket of one of my pants. You think I'm losing my memory?"

"No way. You have a great memory. Maybe you had too much to do before you left. Anyway, what matters is that you're O.K. I'm really glad to see you. I was kind of worried. I didn't know what happened to you. Tell me, what did you do in New York?" I asked again.

"I took the subway to Times Square."

"That's exciting. Did you see any shows on Broadway? Did you ever see a Broadway show? I mean you lived in New York so many years. You must have seen one."

Marty just shook his head no.

"You told me that you learned most of the music that you know from your father. He must have been something. Does your mother like music?"

"My mother likes to sing. She still has a good voice."

"How old is she if you don't mind my asking?"

"She's 75. She likes to dance too."

"Really! I'd like to meet her. Maybe I can introduce her to my father. As they both live on Miami Beach, that wouldn't be difficult. Mostly, though, I'd like to work out something to have you sing for the people on Miami Beach. Maybe Ritchie can come also and play his violin. I understand he now drives a car."

"Do you think I should move in with my mother permanently? I still stay here most of the time, but they told me they need room for other sick people. They only let you stay here a short time."

"I don't know. Do you get along with your mother?"

"Sometimes."

"What do you mean sometimes?"

As I said this, I realized I had been talking to Marty for a long time and not doing any music. I walked with him over to the piano and sat down on the familiar bench.

"Let's do some music, Marty, and try to talk later. I really think it would be great if we did a little show at my father's hotel. And maybe you could sing for the people on Ocean Drive. You know a lot of Yiddish music and they'd love that."

Marty looked at me with an expression of disbelief.

"A- A show! In front of a lot of people?"

"Why not? You did great here during Christmas. Why couldn't you do it?"

"D-Do you really think so?"

"Yes. I'm certain of it. But we'll have to rehearse. We can do that around the piano here, maybe after hours if they'll let us."

"If we do a show, how can I get to your father's hotel?" Marty asked.

"With Ritchie, or maybe with me."

"With you? Am I allowed to ride with you in your car?"

"What do you mean, are you allowed? You're not a baby. But listen. Do me a favor. Don't mention this to the staff here, O.K."

"No, I won't say anything."

"As I said before, I'd like Ritchie to be part of our program. He's playing his violin great and it would be good for him. I only live about fifteen minutes away from Friendship Haven, so either way, it's no problem."

Marty still had an expression of disbelief on his face as I turned to "Stranger in Paradise" from "Kismet" in my Broadway book and began playing the piano.

As he sang, "Take My Hand, I'm A Stranger in Paradise" I wanted to take his hand, but knew he wouldn't let me. Also, it wasn't the thing to do in Friendship Haven, especially after Barbra got fired for simply kicking off her shoes and resting her feet.

A few of the members were smoking in the social room and even though the cigarettes still irritated me, I tried not to pay too much attention to the sting on my face. As Marty continued singing ---- "Alone In A Wonderland, A Stranger in Paradise", I got choked up, as always. Every time he sang, the dreary room I was in brightened and I was transported to a strange place I had never been before. Unfamiliar feelings bothered me and the emotion Marty stirred in me was something I couldn't understand. It was more than pity, something much more. I needed to have control over what I was feeling, especially in a place such as Friendship Haven, but I was finding this almost impossible. It was as if the line of reality became unclear as I sat at the piano, something I always feared would happen.

My Pop's words came back to me, "*God forbid you should get so close to someone's who's sick mentally!*"

I abruptly got up from the piano bench and told Marty I just needed some fresh air and would be right back. I went outside to the parking lot and stared at my Chevy with its Florida International University sticker on the bumper. This helped me place where I was. I went back to the social hall and sat down at the piano again.

I played "So in Love" from "Kiss Me Kate' and "Bei Mir Biztu Shein" from my Jewish Songbook before I realized the room was empty except for us. I looked at my watch and was surprised to see that it was 5:00 P.M. I quickly stopped playing and told Marty I'd better leave.

"W-When are we going to rehearse some more songs?" Marty asked with his usual troubled expression on his face. I need more practice."

"Don't worry. We'll go over the music when I come here in a few days."

"D-Do you think I should move in with my mother?" he asked me again. "I don't like it here. They're bringing in people now who are very sick."

"That didn't bother you before, Marty?"

"It did but it's getting worse!"

"Well, it's certainly something to think about."

I was very pleased that Marty realized the difference between members who were sick with depression and those who were seriously disturbed and even violent. They were releasing people from Florida State Hospital and Jackson Psychiatric Hospital who really should remain there. The open door policy begun during the 1960's of releasing mental patients from state hospitals was now in full force and the whole atmosphere of Friendship Haven was becoming more and more like a mental hospital instead of a halfway house, for which it was intended. The poor souls who were no longer in psychiatric hospitals were now in run down boarding homes where no one looked after their medications, or in crowded halfway houses.

Marty was definitely improving because he noticed the changes in the psychosocial rehabilitation center. I thought it would be a good idea for him to leave and try to live with his mother but, of course, that decision was up to him. I recall that he told me he got along with her, sometimes. Perhaps now that he was doing better, she would find it easier to live with him.

I wanted to know more about her. There was so much I wanted to know about Marty that I was very impatient to be in a place where I could talk to him without staff snooping around. Maybe I'd get this chance when we did a program on Miami Beach.

Time passed very quickly as I went through my music books at home and prepared songs for Marty to sing. It didn't bother me that my husband did nothing but work at his desk or that I hardly saw my son. I now had my own life and had no intention of giving it up.

When I went to Friendship Haven on Thursday, I saw Ritchie in the social hall carrying a ladder someplace. I stopped him and asked if he'd join Marty and me some day and do some music for the elderly Jewish people on Miami Beach.

"Ya kidding me?" Ritchie said. "I got no time for that!"

"But it would be good for you," I pleaded. "And the people would love it."

"Who's gonna do the work around here?" Ritchie asked, as usual.

"Well, if it's such a problem now, I'll ask you again when you're not so busy. Marty and I are rehearsing some songs he plans on doing and I thought your violin would really make the program beautiful."

"Maybe, sometimes." Ritchie said as he dragged his ladder into one of the rooms.

When Marty saw me talking to Ritchie, he walked over to me.

"Were you busy this weekend, busy, busy?"

"Marty, I don't mean to hurt your feelings but could you try not repeating yourself so much? Just ask me if I've been busy once, that's enough."

Marty looked hurt but I wasn't sorry I said what I did. If he were ever going to live in the outside world, he'd have to work on his habits which were very annoying and not good for himself or anyone else.

85

"Marty," I said as I looked at his face that was cleanly shaven, "have you thought any more about living with your mother? I think it would be a good idea if you left Friendship Haven for good. You're really doing great and I'd hate to see you slide backwards. This place isn't for you. I don't think it ever was."

"Y-You don't think so?"

"No, I don't. You're not sick like the others. So you wash your hands too much, so what! One of these days I'm going to shake your hand, what do you think of that? But when I do, I don't want the palm of your hand to be covered with blisters and rough skin. Stop washing your hands so much. They're clean -- too clean. The skin peels off them; it's awful."

Marty looked startled and scared that I actually gave him an order to stop washing so much. Or maybe because I told him I wanted to touch him some day. I knew that when he did a program on the beach, people might want to shake his hand afterwards and congratulate him. I didn't want him to jump a few feet back when he was approached.

"D-Do you really want to meet my mother?" Marty asked me.

"Yes, I do. You're going to meet my father some day so why can't I meet your mother? I'm sure she won't bite or anything, will she?"

"No, or course not," Marty assured me.

"The beach is nice," I said to him. "Maybe we can find a piano someplace and rehearse there. Wouldn't that be wonderful, to get out of here?"

"My mother has a neighbor, Elizabeth, who plays the piano. Maybe she'll let us rehearse in her apartment."

"That would be great. Eventually I hope Ritchie will join us. He just doesn't have the time now. By the way, do you need help with your suitcase or anything if you finally decide to leave here? Maybe I can help you."

"You'd do that? I can't express to you how I feel."

"That's very sweet but what's the big deal? I'll be glad to do it."

"Then I think I'll leave," Marty said. When can you help me?"

"This week if you decide or whenever you want. I'm not too busy. Maybe I'll stop off at the Chesterfield Hotel and see my Pop after I take you to your mother's place. I may even go for a swim in the ocean.

The salt water helps me get over the skin irritation I still feel. Do you ever go swimming on the beach?"

"I used to once in awhile when we lived in Long Beach. I don't go anymore since I'm in Miami. My mother has a pool in her building and she tells me to go. But I don't."

"Oh yeah! A pool! I love to swim. Can you have guests?"

"I think so." Marty said to me, looking very upset. Perhaps he was getting too close to someone and he couldn't handle it.

Marty was missing two buttons on his shirt and I glanced at the slightly curly black hairs on his chest as I spoke to him. If only he'd fill out a little, I thought, he wouldn't look bad at all. The usual feeling of pity overtook me as my glance left his chest and rested on his drawn face and unkempt hair. Everything about him spoke of neglect -- his old-fashioned eyeglasses, pants, shirt and shoes. His clothes were clean but almost threadbare. He'd have to get some new ones before he sang for people on the outside. Maybe he could get some money from his mother to buy a decent pair of pants, a shirt and shoes. Maybe I could help with this and explain to her that he was going to sing for people and had to look especially nice. I couldn't understand how his mother let him walk around looking the way he did. Maybe she thought that it didn't matter while he was in Friendship Haven because everybody looked ragged.

One Thursday, Marty told me he was ready to leave. I was happy that he made this decision.

"Do you want to leave today? Are you packed?"

"Yes. I only have a few things. I'm sorry to bother you but can you take me?"

"I offered, didn't I? I'd rather leave before the social program is over. Afterwards I-95 will be too crowded. Is your mother expecting you?"

"I called her and told her I might come today. I was waiting to ask you. You sure it's alright?"

"Of course. Why not?"

I told Marty to go upstairs and get his things. As I waited for him, I glanced at the arts and craft's table where my former students were busying themselves with this and that. I saw Patty pasting some sticks together and recalled doing this with her and the others when I first came to Friendship Haven. We made wood jewelry boxes and other knick-knacks that were probably never used. How sad they are I said to myself as I passed the table. They're doing the same busy work they did six months ago and getting nowhere. At least I made some progress with Marty and for that I was pleased.

I knocked on Helena's door but, as usual, there was no answer. I told Olivia I had to go someplace important and might not be back that day. I didn't tell her that I was taking Marty to the beach. They might object and I didn't need that.

After I finished speaking to Olivia, I found Marty waiting for me in the social hall with a small worn, brown suitcase in his hand.

"Did you say good-bye to the people here? Did you have a chance to tell Helena you were leaving?"

"I told one of the counselors. I'll still be coming here for the social program but I won't sleep upstairs anymore."

"Do you need help carrying your suitcase?"

"No. That's all right. It's very nice of you. I'll be right back. I have to do something."

"I'll wait for you outside. My car's parked in the lot. Don't take too long, O.K.?"

"I won't. I'll meet your outside."

I walked over to my snazzy beige and brown 1977 Chevrolet that was the first car I actually owned. Leo had rented it and then bought it for me. I felt important in that car and as I approached it, I couldn't help noticing the other beat up cars that were parked there. I looked at the old abandoned warehouse that was Friendship Haven and was happy to say good-bye to it, at least for awhile.

I waited for Marty for close to an hour and was about to go into the building again to look for him when he came out.

"That wasn't too quick." I scolded. "You probably were in the bathroom washing over and over. Marty, you have to stop that!"

Marty looked ashamed but I felt what I said to him was necessary.

"Marty" I added, "you waste so much time washing and washing that you have little time for anything else that's worthwhile. I don't know what it does for you."

Marty was quiet as he got into the front seat besides me.

"This is a nice car," he said.

"Thank you. I don't drive expressways so I'm going to take Brickel Avenue to downtown and then go over the MacArthur Causeway. You'll have to give me directions to your mother's place."

"I will. I know directions."

"Yeah?" I said to him as I started my car. "Did you ever drive?"

"Yes, with my father, many years ago."

"Why did you stop?"

"They asked me when I tried to renew my license if I ever was in a mental hospital. I asked my father about it and he told me to tell the truth.

I couldn't get a license after that and stopped driving."

"What a shame! You shouldn't have mentioned a mental hospital. Gee, Marty, you sure have been through a lot. But you know! Things are going to get better."

"Y-You really think so, you think so?"

"Yes. But you have to do it. You're so intelligent and have a great memory. I don't know why a psychiatrist or anyone else didn't help you all these years. You never told me what diagnosis the doctors came up with and I guess this isn't the time to go into it."

As I said, "what diagnosis the doctors came up with," Marty looked very sad.

"Please, Marty, don't be sad. I'm sorry. I guess I'm prying too much."

I finally drove my car out of the parking lot but couldn't seem to stop talking. Not only did my car make me feel important, so did putting myself in the role of Marty's psychiatrist. I thought that I couldn't do him any harm. I was pretty sure he suffered from an obsessive-compulsive disorder from reading the book written by Dr. Cammer. He was so bad off when I met him at Friendship Haven that I felt I could only do him some good. I hoped I was right. I was toying with the emotions of a human being so I knew I had better be careful.

My acting like an amateur psychiatrist wasn't anything new to me. I had browsed through books on mental illness from the time I could read, trying to figure out what was wrong with my mother. I wasn't able to apply anything I had read to her mental illness, but had a chance to do so now with Marty. According to what I read, I was pretty sure his problem was in the category of the neuroses which wasn't as serious as the psychotic disorders most of the Friendship Haven members suffered from. This was encouraging.

I drove carefully along Brickel Avenue. Marty was very quiet as he sat besides me. He smelled nice, like he had just washed himself and his clothes with soap.

"I'll tell you something, Marty. That halfway house is just a glorified baby-sitting place. It doesn't really help anyone to get better. The only jobs it leads to are dish washing or maybe bussing tables. The minute an employer knows you're from Friendship Haven, you can't get a decent job. They'll hire someone with a physical disability, but not anyone with mental problems. You have to mingle with people on the outside and be in a healthier atmosphere to get better. Also, you'll need some decent clothes. I can't wait until people hear the way you sing."

Talking so much wasn't helping my driving so I finally shut up and concentrated on where I was going. When we got off the MacArthur Causeway, Marty gave me the directions to his mother's apartment on West Avenue.

I was surprised to see such a high, nicely kept building as I approached the Southgate Apartments where his mother lived. I parked the car in one of the guest slots and took the elevator with Marty to the second floor.

We walked through an open breezeway to his apartment. He knocked on the door.

"Who's there?" an anxious voice called from inside.

"It's me, Ma!"

A small lady, about 75, with gray hair, stylish blue framed eyeglasses, and a neat pink dress with matching earrings opened the door. She shot me a swift distasteful look when she saw me standing near Marty.

"This is Evelyn." Marty said to his mother. "She drove me here."

Marty's mother stood at the door and didn't ask me in.

"Can she come in?" Marty sheepishly asked his mother.

"Yes" the neatly dressed lady said, but I could tell by the tone of her voice she didn't mean it.

When I went into the immaculate apartment, I extended my hand to Marty's mother. She didn't grasp it.

"What's your name?" I asked.

"Betty. But everyone calls me Grandma."

"I'm pleased to meet you." I said.

After standing a few minutes in the small living room, I decided to sit down on a blue and yellow flowered couch. Marty continued standing, looking very uncomfortable.

"Betty", I said, "you have a nice place here. Don't you think it's a good idea that Marty finally left Friendship Haven? The people there have gotten very sick. He doesn't belong there. I don't think he ever did."

"He says he'll still go there" Marty's mother said. "I tell him it's too much of a *schlep*, long trip, for him to take two busses. It's too far and he gets knocked out."

"I agree with you. He's going to sing for the people on Miami Beach and he'll be busy rehearsing for that. Isn't that nice?"

"Yes, it's nice."

I was ill at ease in the small apartment and got up to leave. I extended my hand again. This time Betty limply took it. I noticed her carefully polished red nails as I said goodbye to her.

"Nice meeting you, Betty. Marty tells me you have a nice voice. I'd like to hear you sing sometime."

With that, Betty hit a very high note that I thought was from some operetta. It startled me.

"You have a strong soprano voice. Marty must have inherited his voice from you."

"My great grandfather was one of the biggest Cantors in Poland," Marty offered. "But my mother sings very well also."

"She sure does. Oh, by the way, can you give me your phone number?"

"Yes, the phone is in the bedroom."

I followed Marty into a small bedroom. He picked up his phone and checked the number. Two neat twin beds, a dresser and small end table with a phone and lamp were all that was in the room. There were no bedspreads on the beds, just blankets. The windows were covered with grayish venetian blinds. There was a short pile gray rug on the floor, the same as the living room. Alongside the bedroom was a small bathroom.

As I waited for Marty to give me his number, his mother entered the bedroom and arranged and rearranged the sheets on the beds.

"You have a cozy apartment," I said to Betty as she busied herself with the beds.

"The furniture is all rented," Marty said.

"It doesn't matter. It looks nice. I like the yellow chair in the living room and the couch. I think you'll be better off here, don't you think so Marty?"

"Y-Yes," Marty said.

Betty left the room but only for a few minutes. She went back into the bedroom to tell Marty that it was time for supper.

Marty said, "Ma, I'd like to walk Evelyn to her car. She was nice enough to take me here."

"It's late," Betty said. "I will put your supper on the table but it will get cold. I want to get through in the kitchen."

"It's alright," I said. 'You don't have to walk me to my car, Marty. Well so long again. I'll be in touch with you. Oh, Marty, you still didn't give me your phone number."

As Betty watched, Marty went to a tall mahogany secretary desk in the living room and got a piece of paper. He jotted down his number for me. Marty looked forlorn.

"Heh!" I said to him. "What's the matter? At least you're out of that place. Nothing could be as bad as that."

Marty's mother abruptly sat down on the yellow club chair. As she did this, Marty immediately placed a footstool in front of her and helped her put her feet on it.

Momele," he said as he did this. "Your feet will feel better with the stool."

I walked quickly through Betty's small kitchen to get out the door to the breezeway. A pot was bubbling on her stove. I couldn't make out what was in it. It smelled like some kind of sour meat. I was relieved to leave.

As I rode down the elevator, I thought; poor guy, he needs a peaceful environment and I already knew living with his mother wasn't going to provide that. I didn't know where else he could go. Maybe I could get friendly with his mother and that would help things. I couldn't stop thinking about how Marty ran to get a footstool for her. She acted like a Queen while Marty looked and acted like a pauper. I wondered what she made him for supper. I hoped that he would gain a few pounds being out of Friendship Haven, where the institutionalized food had become loaded with fat and additives.

It was getting late and I didn't like driving in the dark. It seemed to take me forever to get home but I felt that I had accomplished a lot that day.

When Saturday came, I called Marty to try to make some arrangements with his neighbor, Elizabeth, to practice our music. No one answered the phone. I figured Marty was out shopping with his mother for food as he told me he liked to shop. My house was very quiet except for an occasional bark from my small dog. I busied myself preparing some chicken for supper and then went over to my baby grand piano that my mother had bought for me before she died. It wasn't the worse for wear, even after it was drenched with noxious chemicals only a few months ago. A faded blue copy of "Clair de Lune" by Debussey, sat on the mahogany music rest. I opened it up and began playing. I also turned to "Serenade" by Schubert from my old book.

I was also delighted to find something written by my mother on a yellowing copy of "The Warsaw Concerto". In her beautiful handwriting she wrote, "Important. Call Rabbi Gottlieb. Tremont 2-6889."

After playing "Serenade" I got up from my piano bench and called Marty.

"Hello", he said, with a voice that had a lovely musical quality.

"Heh, How're you doing?"

"Alright. How nice of you to call. You've been busy, busy?"

I was happy that he repeated busy only twice.

"It's you I want to hear about. What've you been doing with yourself Marty?"

"I help my mother with shopping on Washington Avenue. You know, it's hard for her to carry groceries."

"I was thinking that maybe you could call Elizabeth and she'd let us rehearse at her piano. Like I told you, I want to do a show at my

Pop's hotel. I'll call Ritchie and maybe he'll also get together with us. What do you think?"

"I can call her. Even though she's almost 80, she still plays the piano. She's a good friend. I'm sure she'll let us come over."

"Great! Can you call her today? Tomorrow is a good day for me to come over. I've done most of my work and have already prepared supper for a few days."

"I'll call you after I talk to her. You sure your family won't mind your coming here again?"

"Why should they mind?"

I was about to say that no one really cared what I did with my time, but caught myself. I didn't want to add my burdens to Marty's problems. Besides, I was supposed to be helping him, not the other way around. As things were going, though, I had to admit that he was helping me probably more than I was helping him.

The hours went by slowly and, as I didn't hear from Marty, I eagerly awaited Monday, hoping that Elizabeth agreed to let us come over to her place. Marty didn't call on Monday either but on Tuesday morning my phone rang. Marty's voice almost sounded enthusiastic as he said,

"Elizabeth told me it's all right for us to practice on her piano. She said she'd like to hear us sing. Can you come over today?"

"Can I! I'll be there in a few hours. I'll bring my Yiddish and Broadway books."

I was much too excited after talking to Marty. After all, I reasoned, I'm just going to rehearse with Marty, nothing more. Still I felt strangely elated.

After straightening up a few rooms in my house, I got into my Chevy and drove through Brickel Avenue to Miami Beach. I parked in the lot of Marty's apartment building and hurried to the elevator. I slowed down a bit before I knocked on his door.

Marty opened the door without asking who was there.

"Hellooo" he said with a lilt in his voice. He was wearing an old pair of shorts without a shirt. I couldn't help staring at his bony chest.

As I walked into his apartment I said, "Aren't you cold, Marty, without a shirt on?"

"Florida is so hot. Why should I be cold? I'm *hallishing*, fainting!"

"Well, as the saying goes, 'if you can't stand the heat, get out of the kitchen.' I don't like the heat either but what can you do? This is where we live. Marty, to change the subject, you'll have to get some decent clothes. Maybe you can go with your mother to buy some new ones. By the way, where is your mother?"

"She's playing poker with some friends."

"Really?"

"Yes. She likes to play cards. I'll put a shirt on and we can go to Elizabeth. I already called her! I'll get ready. It'll take a few minutes."

Marty walked into his bedroom and then into his bathroom. Between the two rooms, he was gone for almost an hour. I knocked on the bathroom door, thinking something happened to him.

"Heh, Marty, what's going on? Don't you feel well? You've been gone so long, I'm worried."

"I'm all right," he answered from inside the bathroom.

"But what's taking you so long?" I asked, as if I didn't know.

"I'll be right out," he assured me.

After another twenty minutes, he came out.

"Marty" I scolded, "how can we do anything if it takes you so long to get ready? I notice you never wear a watch. Do you know it's an hour since you said you're getting ready?"

"No, it wasn't an hour."

"Yes it was. I checked my watch."

"I- I don't have too much conception of time," Marty stammered.

"And why is that?"

"I- I don't know. I'm ready now!"

"It's embarrassing for you to walk around in such ripped shoes. Don't you have another pair?"

"Elizabeth won't mind."

"But I mind."

Marty went into his bedroom again. I followed him. He searched in a closet that had a lot of his mother's clothes but only a few pairs of men's pants. He bent down, took out a blue pair of canvas shoes, and held them up for me to see.

"Are these better?" he said to me.

"A little."

I sat down on one of the beds to wait for him to put his shoes on.
First, he went to a drawer and searched for something or other. He
came back with a foot pad. He sat on a chair and bent down again to
put on his shoes but suddenly stopped.

"Don't sit on that bed!" he ordered me.

"Why not, Marty? I'm not doing anything."

"My mother doesn't like anyone to sit on the bed!"

I continued sitting on the bed.

"You better not sit on that bed!" he repeated. "It's my mother's."

"Heh, Marty, what gives with you and your mother? You take
forever to get ready and it seems like a crime if someone sits on one of
your beds. Do you think I'm dirty or something? It's very odd."

Marty looked out his window and said in a far away voice.

"You know, I'm afraid of the world. Sometimes I sit on a chair and
look out the window for hours."

I got up from the bed and went over to him. I was about to put my
hand on his shoulder but thought better of it.

"What is it that you fear, Marty?"

"I don't know!" he said. "When I sit in this room in a corner, I feel
safe. There's so much people and traffic out there. It bothers me."

"Marty, after we rehearse at Elizabeth's place, why don't we go to
Ocean Drive and have a bite to eat. Would you like that?"

"I- I don't know. My mother is making supper."

"Why don't you leave her a note and tell her you just went for a
walk or something. Can't she keep your supper warm?"

"She doesn't like to do that. She'll be mad at me."

"She'll be mad at you! Do you mind me asking you how old you
are?"

"I'm 38."

"Really? I thought you were older than that. Actually I'm much
older than you. I mean you look young but I'm kind of surprised that
you're that young. Even so, you're not a baby. Why can't you do what
grown people do? Why do you have to check with your mother for
every little thing?"

"You know, she's old and sick."

"She doesn't seem so sick to me if she can play cards. Come on
Marty. Leave her a note that you went to Elizabeth and that you'll be

back in a few hours. It's a beautiful day. I'd really like to take a walk. Maybe one of the restaurants has bagels, lox and cream cheese. Do you like that?"

"I haven't eaten it for a long time. All right, I'll leave her a note but I don't like traffic or too many people. Can we go someplace that's quiet?"

"I'll see what's on Ocean Drive. A few new restaurants have opened. I notice that with the Art Deco movement, more and more elderly people are moving away from the beach. I even notice a few young people now. Things are really changing. That's why I want to do a show as soon as we can. I certainly don't know any disco music, which is what young people want today, so the opportunity to do shows may soon pass us by. Come. It's getting late."

"Do I need a shave?" Marty said to me as he stuck out his chin for me to examine."

"Yes, you do, but there's no time for that now. Let's go!"

We finally walked out of the apartment and took the elevator to the 4th floor where Elizabeth lived. After introducing myself, I sat down at her piano and ran over some Broadway songs. I liked Elizabeth immediately. Her white hair framed a very kind face and her neat blue dress complimented her trim figure. After I finished my Broadway melodies, she sat down and expertly played "The Hatikvah" and a few Jewish songs from yesteryear. I was amazed at her dexterity. After we finished rehearsing, she offered Marty and me some apple strudel and tea. I declined, saying another time. She was so nice I thought I'd get her some flowers or a gift the next time we came.

Marty and I got into my car and I drove to Ocean Drive. After I parked, we walked on a paved path near the sandy beach. I was surprised at the difference in temperature alongside the ocean and went back to my car to get a light scarf and purple sweatshirt. Marty wore a yellow windbreaker but took it off after a few minutes. As we walked, Marty hummed.

"Heh, that's a good idea." I said to him. "Let's sing some of the songs we plan to do for our show."

"Here? Won't someone hear us?" he said.

"So what! You have such a beautiful voice that anyone who hears it will be treated to something special. Let's sing."

"What should I sing?"

"How about 'Stranger in Paradise'? I love that."

As Marty sang the lovely lyrics, I took off my scarf and let the ocean breezes blow in my hair. The air smelled like it did years ago, when I walked on the Boardwalk in Coney Island. I felt like a teenager on a date. Of course, at 48 I was far from a youngster and Marty wasn't my date. Still, I felt carefree and happy, especially since I was looking forward to finding some restaurant that had bagels and lox. I hadn't had that in years either.

The Cardozo Hotel on 14th Street featured a nice menu with salads. I asked the waiter if they had lox. He said they had a salad plate with Norwegian salmon and raw spinach. I said that was great, that I'll have that with some extra bread.

There was no one on the large porch that was converted into a restaurant. Marty sat across from me at a table with a glass top.

"Why don't you sit next to me Marty?" I asked.

As soon as I said that, he looked scared.

"Don't worry. I won't bite. That way we can talk."

"What do you want to talk about?" he asked as he moved a little closer to me.

"We'll find things to talk about. How about a cup of coffee to begin with?"

"I don't drink regular coffee. My mother has some Sanka and I drink that."

"I think a cup of coffee would do you some good. As I said before, you seem sleepy to me or drugged or something. Is the doctor who gives you medicine a psychiatrist?"

"Y-Yes." Marty stammered.

"So what. It's no shame seeing a psychiatrist. I saw one years ago and still do at times."

"Really?"

"Yes. Let's have a cup of hot coffee. It's really kind of chilly here but I love it. I've been wanting to talk to you but never got the chance in Friendship Haven."

"Alright. If you think it'll be good for me."

The waiter brought two cups of coffee with a small pitcher of milk. Marty sipped his coffee and said,

"It's good, this is good!"

I noticed that after he drank his coffee and ordered a refill, he was more alert. So was I.

Soon the waiter brought us a large plate with Norwegian salmon, spinach, cream cheese, vinaigrette dressing and French bread. I asked him to bring us another plate as we were sharing the salad.

Marty looked at the appetizing plate with amazement. I put some lox, spinach with salad dressing, on his plate, and a large piece of French bread.

"Go ahead, Marty. Put some cream cheese on your bread."

"I like bread," he said.

"Good. I'll order some more when you're finished with your piece."

"Isn't this expensive?" he said as he put a tiny pat of cream cheese on his bread.

"No, it's not. Here, take more cheese" I said as I smeared his bread with it. "You need to put on some weight."

He laboriously chewed part of his sandwich, saying, "Mmmmmm. This is good, this is good!"

He put the rest of his sandwich back on his plate, cut it with his knife into small pieces, and ate it with his fork. As I watched he said,

"I have T. M.J. I have trouble biting into anything hard."

"Oh yes, I remember your telling me that. It's O.K. Take your time."

Marty looked upset as a car passed in front of the hotel.

"Can we move to another table, in the corner?" he asked. "I don't like traffic."

We didn't bother calling the waiter but moved our plates, cups and silverware to a table in the corner.

"Marty, when did you last eat out? You seem very ill at ease."

"My sister took me to a restaurant awhile ago but it was inside. I don't eat out much."

"I guess this is a good time as any to ask you something. It's personal, but you know I want to help you."

"T-That's very nice of you. I can't express myself." Marty said.

"I know you lived in Friendship Haven for at least six months, but where were you before that?"

"In Miami Beach, in another apartment. We moved here after my father died, about a year ago. Before that, we lived in Long Beach."

"What did you do in Long Beach?

Marty looked very uncomfortable as he stared at his plate.

"I didn't do much."

"Were you ever in a hospital?"

I knew I was prying too much but if I was going to help him, which I was determined to do, I had to know more about him.

"Y-Yes. But you won't tell anyone?"

"That's silly. Who will I tell?"

"How long were you in a hospital?"

"In and out of mental hospitals for about 20 years. You won't tell anyone!"

"No I promise. I'd like to know what diagnosis they gave you."

"You promise you won't tell anyone?"

"Didn't I just promise? If you're that uncomfortable, you don't have to tell me."

Marty turned towards me and whispered in my ear,

"Schizophrenia."

"What? That's impossible. You don't have that. How could those doctors be so wrong? I read a terrific book by a Dr. Cammer and he explained obsessive-compulsive disorders, you know a lot of hand washing and all. You seem to have that and it's not terrible. You can be cured."

"You mean I'm not crazy!" Marty whispered again close to my ear, with an incredulous expression on his face.

"Of course not. Do you think I'd be with you so much if you were? I had enough with my mother. We'll talk some more about this another time. I know you'll soon tell me that your mother is worried about you and that we better leave. Also, maybe someone else wants to use the table. The place is getting kind of crowded."

"You mean I didn't have to be in Friendship Haven?" Marty continued.

"I don't think so. You were misdiagnosed. What a pity! I think we better go. As I said, we'll talk some more another time."

I drove Marty back to his apartment and headed for home. I wasn't consciously aware of driving and was surprised when I found myself in my driveway. I couldn't stop thinking about what Marty had just told me. How shocking that all these years he thought he was crazy. I was sure that many other young people in Friendship Haven were also misdiagnosed because doctors didn't take the time to find out what was wrong with them.

As I turned the key to my front door, I was relieved to hear the familiar bark of Fuffy. She followed me as I went to my patio. When I sat down on one of my lounge chairs, she flipped her small body over for a belly rub. This made my laugh, in spite of myself. I played with her long, silky ears and, afterwards, went into my kitchen to give her some food and prepare a cup of coffee for myself. I felt a little better afterwards but still couldn't stop thinking about Marty and what he told me at the Cardozo.

Marty and I rehearsed at Elizabeth's apartment several times. Ritchie joined us whenever he could, and finally we felt we were ready to perform at the Chesterfield Hotel, a small, cozy hotel on Collins Avenue between 8th and 9th Streets. The mostly elderly residents of the hotel spent most of their time sitting in their lobby watching television or sitting on their porch. A breeze from the ocean made sitting outside very pleasant. Sometimes, I would join the people, especially when there was a spare rocking chair to sit in. They often spoke to one another in Yiddish so I knew they would enjoy the Yiddish songs Marty, Ritchie and I had prepared for our show.

We performed on a Saturday night and, I must say, our show was terrific. Marty's voice and Yiddish pronunciation of "Ofn Pripichick" and "Der Greene Koseene" were so good that a few people yelled "bravo" after he sang. He finished his performance with "Give Me Your Tired and Your Poor", words engraved on the Statue of Liberty. As most of the people in the hotel were Jewish immigrants from Europe, the music and words meant a great deal to them. My best friend, Ruthie, joined us to sing some Jewish songs in her pleasant alto voice.

After our show, Ruthie and her husband offered to take Marty home. Ritchie said he didn't want to drive anyone in his car because it wasn't acting right. I said "no thank you" to Ruthie, that I'd drive Marty myself. I smiled as Ruthie took me aside and said that Marty wasn't at all bad looking and wanted to know what our relationship was. I was very surprised she said this as I never thought of Marty as really good-looking. He did look better than usual with a short-sleeved pale pink shirt and tan pants. He was also clean-shaven, a task which must have taken him hours.

As I drove to West End Avenue with my car windows open and Marty sitting besides me, the ocean breezes drove along with us and their softness seemed to caress us. Instead of driving directly to Marty's apartment, I parked in the dark lot of a bank across from his place. Ruthie's words kept whirring in my head. *"He's not bad looking."*

I felt uncomfortable with Marty sitting next to me. I always thought of him as a poor soul, someone I needed to help. His singing was so superb at the hotel and he looked so much better than usual, that I felt differently about him than before. As I sat near him, I looked at his face and sensitive mouth and soon my glance traveled down to his almost bare chest. He had unbuttoned his shirt as the Miami heat always bothered him.

Marty and I spoke about our program for about an hour. He didn't wear a watch and even if he did, he told me in the past that he didn't have a clear perception of time. He felt bad that he was always late to everything. Suddenly, he looked very worried as he asked me,

"What time is it?"

"It's about 11:00 P.M."

"Really?" Marty said with alarm. "I have to go. My mother is going to be very upset."

"Why? You're a grown man. You can't stay out late? Oh, by the way, I almost forgot. The manager of the Chesterfield Hotel liked our show so much that he handed me $20.00. Here's $10.00. I'm going to give Ritchie $10.00 also."

"Y-You mean they paid us? I didn't expect that. That's a lot of money."

"Not a lot but it's a start. Now you're a professional. What do you think of that?" I said, as I continued looking him over.

"I can't express myself," he said to me with a soulful look on his face.

How sweet he is, I said to myself. How sweet and grateful for everything.

"I better go" Marty said again. "My mother is going to be very worried. It's late."

"Didn't you tell her the show would end after 10:00 P.M.?"

"I did but it's much later than that now," he said as he opened the car door to leave. I didn't want him to go.

"I don't see what the big deal is. After all, you performed tonight and made some money. What gives with your mother?"

"She worries all the time about me."

"You told me you were close to 40. You're a grown man. Maybe it would make your mother happy if we take her along the next time we do a show. She can sing and play the tambourine. She can help us."

"She likes to dance also. I really have to go!" Marty said as he finally walked out of my car.

I drove home with the image of Marty still sitting besides me. I thought about how beautifully he sang "Come Back to Sorriento" at the Chesterfield and how the people applauded. I was a little disappointed that he didn't shake hands with the people who came up to him to congratulate him after our show, and that he spent so much time in the bathroom afterwards. I had to remind myself that I wasn't so perfect either and that "there but for the grace of God go I." I still saw my psychiatrist every week and even though I hadn't spent time in a mental hospital like Marty (so far, that is) I still got depressed. I never felt down when I was with Marty though.

Now I was the poor soul, as I had no idea how to handle the new emotions I felt that threw me into a turmoil.

My son was asleep by the time I got home at midnight and, as usual, Leo was working at his desk. He stopped his work for a second when I walked in and asked me where I was.

"You remember, Leo, I told you that I had a gig tonight. It ran a little late."

Leo went back to work right after I said this. I was grateful he did, as I wanted to think my own private thoughts about Marty. The attraction I was feeling for Marty worried me. I was afraid I would blab to Leo these new feelings.

I had trouble falling asleep that night, with all kinds of troubling thoughts running through my head. My Pop's warning about Marty came back to me again and again, "*G-d forbid you should get close to him. Don't you remember the aggravation I had with your mother?"* He was right. I wasn't the type to get deeply emotionally involved with someone while I was married, especially someone who had so many problems. Besides spending so much time in the bathroom and all his other habits, Marty had a peculiar relationship with his mother, who acted as if he was her husband instead of her son.

I still sang for the people, who sat on the benches on Ocean Drive and 9th Street, after visiting my father. One evening a man came over to me and asked if I'd sing for the people in the Miami Beach Home for the Aged on 3rd Street and Collins Avenue. I called Marty and asked if he wanted to sing with me at the nursing home while I played the piano. He said he'd like that as he got along very well with old people. I said I'd pick him up but he wanted to take a bus to go there.

I was now seeing Marty a few times a week, something I looked forward to very much. For the first time in my life a man needed me, really needed me. It gave meaning to my life, and without it I knew my life would be as empty as it was before.

One day after we sang, we went on Ocean Drive for a walk. Marty stopped for a moment and said to me,

"I can't express myself," and kissed me lightly on my cheek. I felt a surge, as if some kind of electricity had passed through me. I hadn't felt anything like it since I was seventeen, when I thought I was in love with my first boyfriend, Harry. This feeling was even stronger than years ago when Harry kissed me on the lips for the first time.

I didn't know whether I should tell Marty how I felt after his kiss. I decided not to say anything. I thought it might upset him, as much as it upset, yet thrilled, me. As I drove Marty back to his apartment, I opened my car windows to let the delicious saltwater air in. I knew I could no more control breathing in this air than I could control what I was feeling for Marty.

This time, I quickly said goodbye to him as I parked in his lot, still feeling elated as I drove home.

I wasn't concentrating on my driving along the 1-95 expressway because drivers in back of me honked their horns. The minimum speed limit was 40 miles per hour and I was going 30. I kept thinking about the show we did at the Chesterfield Hotel a few nights ago, and the kiss Marty surprised me with just an hour or so ago.

The elderly people at the Chesterfield Hotel were so happy with our show that after every song we did, they applauded, many with hands and fingers swollen and stiff from arthritis. They loved the Jewish songs in particular and hummed along to them. I called up one of the tenants named Sarah to the microphone to sing "Bar Mir Bitzu Shein". She sang it beautifully, in her deep alto voice. She wore a pretty black and white flowered dress and her gray hair was done up in an attractive style. Even though she was past 80, she pranced around to the beat of the music like a young girl. Ritchie, with his violin cupped under his chin, stopped in front of everyone as he played. It was hard to believe this was the same Ritchie I had met almost two years ago at Friendship Haven, who stood in a corner of a room playing the "Star Spangled Banner" to himself over and over.

I didn't want the sensation of Marty's kiss to leave me so I touched my cheek as I drove. I wondered what it would feel like to be kissed on my lips instead of my cheek. At 49, it was especially wonderful to feel so alive and, I had to admit, "turned on". What I was going to do about it was another matter. I knew I could never "fool around" with anyone while I was married, especially someone like Marty. Also, my religion forbade me having an affair, but thinking about it sure excited me.

I heard cars honking at me again as I thought about going to Dadeland the next day and buying myself a new dress and high-heeled shoes. It had been quite a while since I bought myself a dress. Maybe I could also get some mascara and eye liner to highlight my eyes. Marty was almost six feet tall when he stood straight so high heels would give me some height and make my legs more shapely.

I finally reached my house and parked in my driveway. I didn't know exactly how I had gotten home but somehow I managed it. It was almost 6:00 P.M. and my husband and son weren't home. I quickly prepared supper, undressed, and put on a nightgown. I stared at myself in my bathroom mirror. After a few minutes, I took off my nightgown to get a better look at myself. Not bad, I thought. Nothing hangs too much, even my breasts, which are rather large.

I put my nightgown back on, realizing how ridiculous my behavior was. I was like a teenager and felt a little ashamed of myself. Still I fell asleep thinking what style of dress and shoes I would buy the next day.

Marty, Ritchie and I were now playing and singing Mondays and Thursdays at the Miami Beach Home for the Aged. When Monday came around, I ran to my car and drove quickly to get to the beach. I wore my new low cut dress and high-heeled shoes that I had bought over the weekend. Mascara covered my eyelashes and I knew I looked attractive, even sexy. I had even managed to go to a beauty parlor for a stylish haircut and get a dark rinse to cover some gray hairs. I made sure to bring my bathing suit along because I planned on swimming in the pool of Marty's apartment complex afterwards.

Trying not to let the antiseptic smell bother me from the nursing home, I went over to the black, scratched baby grand piano that stood in a corner of a large room. I introduced Marty, myself, and Ritchie to the residents. Many were in wheelchairs with white sheets covering their laps. I knew this was to hide the catheters that were attached to their bladders. How sad their situation had become; people who had once been needed and active. Yet a few of them stood up as I began our program with "Hatikvah", the national anthem of Israel, followed by the "Star Spangled Banner".

Marty sang both songs beautifully. Ritchie stood next to the piano, looking over my shoulder at the music and playing perfectly. It didn't matter that I was performing in a nursing home. What did matter was that the two guys I had met almost two years ago were finally out in the world, making others happy instead of rotting in a halfway hose.

Another piano player, a 90-year old man by the name of Charlie, was also volunteering in the Home. I asked him to play "Begin the Beguine", which Marty loved to sing and dance to. After Marty sang one refrain, I asked Charlie to continue playing and asked Marty to dance. As I danced a rumba, I shook my hips to the music, swaying to and fro and glancing at Marty now and then. He looked very uncomfortable, and before the song was finished, he abruptly sat down. I was curious why he did this and knew I'd ask him about it later. Meanwhile, I was having fun, singing and dancing and feeling very young.

After our program, I went with Marty to my car parked alongside the curb. I planned on taking Marty home, just six or seven blocks away. When Marty was sitting besides me, I asked him why he sat down so suddenly in the middle of "Begin the Beguine".

In answer to my question he said,

"W Weren't you shaking too much?"

"What do you mean, shaking too much, Marty?"

"Well, you didn't have to move so much, did you?"

I looked at Marty with disbelief. He never questioned me about any of my behavior. It was I who always questioned him.

I guess I was showing off while I danced but I had no clue that Marty noticed it.

"You mean it wasn't nice what I did?" I asked Marty.

"It-It was nice. I-I mean, you certainly danced, didn't you?"

"Why did you sit down in the midst of the song? You never did that before."

Marty looked at me but didn't answer. I thought I noticed a slight blush on his face but wasn't sure. He had such dark skin, especially when he needed a shave, which was now, that his color was always slightly greenish or purplish. He looked so flustered that I thought I'd better let my question drop. I finally drove towards his place, my mind definitely not on my driving. I couldn't help wondering if Marty had ever been with a woman. Ruthie had asked me his age after we did the show at the Chesterfield Hotel, and when I told her he was almost 40, she said he was a lot younger than me. So I'm an older woman, so what, I answered her, feeling a little embarrassed.

Marty interrupted my thoughts.

"It's very late. My mother isn't feeling well. I have to help her," Marty said as I drove along.

"It's only 4:00 P.M. and it's such a nice day. Before you go home, do you want to get something to eat, maybe at Denny's?"

"I- I don't know if I should. Maybe I better call my Mother and see how she his. She's very old and she's alone."

"O.K. then, call her."

We drove to Denny's on 29th Street and sat down at a table in a dark room with a bar. It was a little smoky but I didn't mind. No one was in the room except the two of us. It was very romantic with small candles lit on each table. Marty went to make a call. When he came back he was very upset.

"My mother didn't know what happened to me." he said. "I should have called her."

"But you were only gone a few hours. You're a man, not a kid. What gives with your mother?"

"She's old and sick."

"What about you? Aren't you entitled to any kind of life? It's so nice here, don't you think so?"

"Y-Yes, it's nice. Alright, I'll stay a few minutes."

"How about a hamburger? You sure could use some weight." I said to him as I stared at his thin face and chest.

"Alright," he reluctantly said.

I ordered two hamburgers. "How about a beer?"

"I- I don't drink."

"What's one beer? It'll make you feel relaxed."

I ordered a beer for Marty and a Pina Colada for me. The room was perfect, sort of a hideaway.

I thought Marty glanced for a second at the crease of my breasts in my low cut dress, but I wasn't sure because the room was so dark. Right then and there, I wanted to kiss him, but this time on the lips of his small mouth.

As we ate our hamburgers and sipped our drinks, Marty ripped up his napkin into small pieces and wiped his mouth on each section. He suddenly got up and went someplace. I knew it was the bathroom and it would be a long time before he returned. When he came back I asked,

"Marty, what do you talk about with your psychiatrist?"

Marty rubbed his thumbs and forefingers together about twenty times before he answered.

"Oh, different things."

"Would I be getting too personal if I asked what things?"

"I really have to go!" Marty said, as he got up. I paid the check and walked outside with him to my car. When I parked in his lot, he said good-bye to me and added, "I can't express myself," again kissing me on my cheek. A stronger surge than the one before passed through me, a delicious, warm feeling. I forgot about swimming in his pool as I dwelled on his kiss. I almost told him how I felt but decided against it. Of all people, I thought, to have a crush on. I'd have enough trouble being attracted to someone who was well, but with so many problems like Marty had, my situation was impossible. It didn't even matter that my Pop had warned me about getting involved with someone who was sick like my mother. Short of stopping seeing Marty, there was nothing I could do about my feeling. The chemistry I had for him was incredible. Yet I didn't know how he felt about me. Maybe my feelings were one sided. I didn't know if Marty was capable of feeling anything for a woman except gratitude. I worried that I was in for a big letdown. Still, I couldn't help wondering if he was a virgin. How interesting it would be to find out and how exciting. And me, a married woman, or was I?

My son was soon going off to college and I dreaded being alone with Leo after that. I was grateful for the time I spent with Marty and Ritchie, which filled the loneliness I always felt at home.

I drove home with all kinds of mixed emotions going through my head. Mostly, I worried that Marty felt nothing for me. Also, if he did, I didn't know what I'd do about it. The image of his solemn, sweet face was before me as I drove but luckily this time I kept a decent pace so that cars didn't honk me. I didn't like myself very much at the moment, thinking I was taking advantage of an innocent person with many problems. Still, Marty didn't have a good life before I knew him. Maybe I could make him smile once in awhile; even make him happy. I must have looked cheap as I danced the rumba. Maybe that's why Marty sat down so quickly. He probably couldn't stand seeing the new image of me, a flirtatious, older woman.

I'd have to pull myself together, whatever that meant, and see the reality of my situation. I thought about making an appointment with Dr. Harris. He'd surely discourage me from my involvement with Marty. I planned on calling him the next day.

I called Dr. Harris and made an appointment to see him. I felt good that I hadn't seen him for at least a year. Hanging around with Marty and Ritchie, and doing music in hotels and nursing homes, lifted the depression I felt before I knew them. Still my attraction for

Marty was really bothering me and I hoped Dr. Harris could help me sort things out.

I walked into Dr. Harris' familiar, small office and waited about fifteen minutes for him to see me.

"Hello, Evelyn," he said to me in a warm, friendly voice. "Come in."

"Dr. Harris, I'm in trouble," I said, as I sat down on an overstuffed chair. I've got a big crush on Marty and I'm afraid I'm going to do something real stupid, like put my arms around him and kiss him, or more than that. I'm so turned on by even a small kiss on the cheek from him that it's real hard to be with him now."

"Do you love him?" Dr. Harris unexpectedly asked me.

"Love him? I'm crazy about him."

"Then you do have a problem," Dr. Harris calmly said. "Marty's not the healthiest person in the world," the good doctor added. "But then again you've had a miserable marriage for so long that I can understand what has happened. Do you have any idea if Marty can perform like a man, you know, have sexual relations? You don't want to be brother and sister, do you?"

"No, I don't think so, but how would I know if Marty can do anything?"

"Why don't you find out," Dr. Harris said.

"What? What do you mean, find out?"

"Just what I said. Why get even more deeply involved if you don't know that about him?"

"You know, Dr. Harris, that's strange, because one day last week in Denny's I asked Marty how his psychiatrist was helping him, and I noticed a slight reddish blush to his face when I asked him this. It's hard to tell if he's blushing because Marty usually has a greenish or purplish tint to his skin or dark gray when he needs a shave. Anyway, he stammered that his psychiatrist suggested he find a girlfriend and have a sexual relationship with her. You can imagine how I felt hearing that. For a change, I didn't know what to say. Anyway, it looks like you two guys are in "cahoots". You know, I'm kind of religious and can't commit adultery. Maybe I can just kiss him a little. That won't hurt anything, will it?"

"Well, it could lead to deeper things. How can you stop at that, especially if Marty doesn't stop you?"

"You know, I'm really in a bad spot. I can't handle an affair, especially with someone who's been in and out of mental hospitals. Even my Pop warned me about getting so close to him. It'll make me crazy. Yet, I can't be with him now without being very uncomfortable. Maybe I shouldn't be alone with him anymore. What do you think?"

"Then will you be satisfied?"

"No, I don't think so. My feelings are there already so how can I remove them?"

"You can't and I don't think you want to. Well, it's your decision," Dr. Harris offered. "Another thing. Marty never suffered from the same illness that your mother did. He seems to have an obsessive-compulsive disorder from what you told me. That's not a psychosis."

"Yeah, I know, but I think it would still be impossible to ever really be serious with him; you know, the whole thing, the marriage bit. He doesn't seem to have a dime to his name either."

"You're jumping the gun, don't you think so?"

"Yeah, but anyway, how about telling me to get divorced, please!!! That would help."

"I can't tell you to do that. I'm sorry but our time is up. Do you want to come again to discuss this some more?"

"I think I should. I'll call you. Thank you, Dr. Harris," I said as I shook his hand and left, more mixed up than ever.

I had plans to go to New York in a few weeks and as it turned out, Marty was also going to New York about the same time I was. It wasn't a deliberate plan. It was just working out that way. I was going to attend an affair honoring my cousin, a doctor, for his outstanding work with stress and cancer. I told Marty about this the next time I saw him at the Miami Beach Home for the Aged. Marty was mingling with the residents who were very happy with his singing. He even danced with some of them who weren't in wheel chairs. There was a problem, though. I noticed that every now and then he touched his fly. God, I thought, he's really nuts to be doing that, in public yet. I hadn't seen that before and here I'm considering getting intimate with him. I hoped the social director didn't see what he was doing. I had to do something, quickly.

I took Marty into another room and asked Ritchie to carry on.

"Marty, please, can you sing and sort of wave your hands at the same time to give your song some feeling. Don't keep your hands in your pockets or anywhere else. It will give your song more expression and feeling if you use them to help you with your rhythm. That's also a weak point with me but Richie helps with his terrific violin playing."

I wanted to come right out and tell him to stop touching himself, but felt it was less embarrassing to just tell him to use his hands when he sang.

Marty looked flustered, as usual, as he said, "O-O.K. I'll try to use my hands more for a song."

We walked back to the social hall and I noticed that every time he now started to reach down to his fly, he caught himself. We performed for the elderly people for two hours and were especially pleased that a lady of 98, Celia, got up to sing, "Autumn Leaves". After this, we played it for her every time we saw her. I brought her fresh flowers every week that she put in a vase in her room. She said to me that when she dies, I should bring *bloomings*, flowers, to her grave. I said I would but that she was going to live many more years, especially if she kept singing.

When our program was finished, Marty and I went over to my car that was parked in the nursing home lot. As usual, I asked him if he wanted to go for a bite to eat. I repeated that I was going to New York soon so I won't be seeing him for a few weeks.

"New York!" he said. "Yes, I remember you told me that. When are you leaving? Are your husband and son going with you? I think I told you I'm also going, with my mother."

"That's great! I'm leaving in a few weeks."

"So am I. We always go this time of the year to see my aunt, my mother's sister. As far as having something to eat with you, I don't think I should. It's late."

"You must be hungry. Listen, I'd like to talk to you, just for a little bit. How about it?"

"Well, all right," Marty said as he sat down besides me in my car. I looked at his mouth and almost bent over to kiss it. Wow, I thought, I got it real bad.

We went to the Cardozo Hotel and sat on the balcony at one of the tables. As always, a cool breeze from the ocean seemed to caress us.

"How about a beer?" I asked Marty.

"Now? In the middle of the day?"

"It's almost 4 o'clock. I noticed you like beer. It'll relax you. How about a corned beef sandwich with it? They have good corned beef here. I'm going to order a bagel with lox and cream cheese and a cup of coffee. Their coffee is delicious."

"Al-Alright, I'll have a beer, a draft so it's cheaper."

"What're worried about? I'll gladly pay for it. Order what you want."

"N-No, that's alright. I can't express myself."

"Like I told you, you express yourself very well. You're so appreciative that really, Marty, I never met anyone like you. Sorry to change the subject and I don't want to embarrass you, but was your zipper broken today on your pants? It seemed like it wasn't working?"

"Oh, no!" Marty said surprised. "You mean what you said about my hands?"

I was amazed he caught on to what I was trying to tell him at the Jewish Home.

"You know, I have a hernia," he continued. "I was trying to push it in."

"A hernia? You mean something is sticking out there! Why don't you have it fixed?"

"The doctor says it's not that bad. I figure if I keep pushing it in, it'll stop sticking out."

Poor thing, I said to myself, as I looked at Marty's sweet face. I loved to listen to him speak. The tone of his voice was as musical as his singing voice.

"What kind of doctor do you see?" I asked.

"I go to Clinicare on the beach. My mother goes there too."

"Why do you have to go to a clinic? Can't you go to a private doctor?"

"It cost a lot of money." Marty said, with a very sad expression on his face.

I have to help this guy, I said to myself, and thought that helping him was a kind of destiny for me.

"Marty, something is on my mind," I said to him as we ate our food and Marty sipped on his beer, "you told me I was shaking too much when I danced to 'Begin the Beguine' last week at the Jewish Home, but why did you suddenly sit down?"

Marty didn't answer.

"Please, tell me; don't feel bad about it."

"You won't like what I say," Marty said.

"Please" I pleaded again. I'll like it!"

Marty stopped eating and drinking. "I know it's wrong of me, but you, you......"

"What are you trying to tell me?"

"I got turned on and had to sit down. You know!"

"Really," I stammered. "You got turned on? That's not bad. That's not bad, it's good." I said, not knowing if it was or wasn't.

Well, I thought, he is a man. At least, that's encouraging, except that I didn't have the slightest idea what to do about this discovery. Sure, I thought, it's easy for Dr. Harris to tell me to get involved with him sexually but I knew it would make me crazy leading two lives. I even thought that this was the way I'd finally go nuts like my mother. I couldn't understand why Dr. Harris even advised what he did. I'd have to see him again, soon, to try to clear things up.

I decided not to see Dr. Harris. I felt that in the past I leaned on him too much and was finding it hard to make decisions without him.

I kept thinking about the way Marty got "turned on" when I danced the rumba at the Jewish Home for the Aged. I wanted to talk with him about it, and knowing myself, I knew I would do it the first chance I got.

As my husband was seldom home, one evening I watched by myself a movie on television, one I couldn't forget. It was about an unhappily married woman who went with a group of people to Italy. There she met a man who hardly spoke a word of English. Still, they fell madly in love with each other. Eventually she divorced her husband and moved to Italy.

I thought of Marty as I watched it. I couldn't help putting myself in the place of the woman and imagined Marty, healthy, and nicely dressed, as the man in the movie. I thought it would be a miracle if some day I'd be as happy as that woman; maybe even go to Paris, the city of romance. Thinking about it gave me hope and kept me going. I was grateful that I hadn't gotten sick like my mother, not yet anyway. Perhaps if I was happy, I wouldn't follow in her footsteps and ever lose my mind.

When my husband upset me by not paying any attention to me, which was most of the time, I'd tell him that he was aggravating me enough to make me sick. I added that I feared that some day I'd end up in a state hospital like my mother because of this. He did little to comfort me, even after twenty years of marriage. He was just too busy. Still every time I told Dr. Harris to help me find the courage to get divorced because I was so lonely, he would say that if I do that, I'd even be more alone. He also couldn't give me any guarantee that without my husband, who was some kind of a rudder to me, although a sick one, that I wouldn't indeed break down. I had such an unusually insecure childhood that my husband had become a father figure which I never had, strong but uncaring. So I was in a sort of "Catch 22" situation. I couldn't get divorced and I couldn't live the way I was.

After singing at the Jewish Home for the Aged on a beautiful day in November, I drove Marty towards his home. Instead of parking in his lot, I parked in the lot of a bank that was closed for the evening. It was getting dark and when I stopped the car and looked at Marty, he had a scared expression on his face.

"Why are you stopping here?" he asked me.

"I'd like to talk to you. Do you mind?"

"Well, a little. I have to get home. I told you my mother worries when I don't come in time for supper."

"She worries too much and so do you, Marty. I'm sorry I'm so frank but I can't help it. She treats you like a child and you let her. When I met you almost two years ago you told me you were 38. That would make you 40 now, a grown man. But you don't act grown; do you know that? I'm sorry if I'm insulting you. I don't mean to. I just can't help it. I make most of my own decisions so why can't you?"

Marty listened to me as he squirmed on the car seat. He said he felt warm even though a cool breeze blew from the ocean. I opened the window of my car. He sat very quietly, still looking scared.

"I know I have a big mouth, Marty, but I mean well. I stopped here because I have to ask you something."

"W-What do you want to ask me?" Marty said as he picked on his nails.

"Well I was really surprised at what you said to me about getting 'turned on' when I danced to 'Begin the Beguine' at the nursing home. I never thought I'd hear that from you. You're so shy. Please, tell me, did you ever have a girlfriend?"

I noticed a slight blush creep over Marty's face when I asked him this and his usually wan, greenish face seemed to turn a pale orange. He fidgeted some more as he sat in the car, stared out the window, and said,

"I never had a girlfriend. That's all I need with all my problems. I liked to go to dances when I lived in New York but I never asked anyone out."

"Did you notice any of the girls being attracted to you? I mean you're tall and with some weight and nice clothes, you'd be good looking. Didn't anyone ever tell you that?"

My sister-in-law said I looked a little like Gregory Peck but I didn't believe her. I guess she was trying to make me feel good."

"No. It's true. There is a slight resemblance. You have very dark hair and a widow's peak like he has. But, of course, his face is rounder and his clothes are magnificent. I'll bet you haven't bought yourself a new shirt or a pair of pants in years. Isn't that so?"

"My mother says I have too many pairs of pants already. What did you want to ask me?" he said again. "It's late."

"I'm trying to get to some point, but it's not easy. I might as well come out with it. You know, when you kissed me on the cheek after we sang at the Jewish Home, I got a charge. It really threw me. And you told me you got 'turned on' when I danced the rumba. When I met you at Friendship Haven, I just meant to be friends with you and help you, if I could. Now our relationship is different. I......"

Marty interrupted me. "I better go home. This is all I need. I have enough problems. I don't need any more."

"Why is it a problem that we like each other?"

"Well, for one you're married. You have been very nice to me and I appreciate it. But more than that......"

I knew I had said too much, much too much. Sitting in my car and looking at Marty, I suddenly got scared that he wouldn't want to see me anymore.

"Alright. I'm sorry. I see how uncomfortable you are. Look, we're going to be in New York just about the same time. Where are you going to stay?"

"With my aunt in Long Island."

"I'm also staying with an aunt of mine in Yonkers. There's an express bus that goes to Manhattan a few times a day. Maybe we can meet someplace and go to the Museum of Natural History or the Museum of Modern Art. Would you like that?"

"Isn't your husband going with you?" Marty asked.

"No. He has too much work to do. He'll stay home and mind my son. He's not really interested in going to my cousin's affair. And he hates New York."

"Really? I love New York!"

"Me too. It's very exciting. I love to see the ice skaters in Rockefeller Center. And I love to eat the chestnuts that the venders sell from carts. When I was a kid in Yonkers my Baba used to help me roast them on our old black coal-burning stove. I can never forget that. When I walk along the streets of Manhattan and smell those chestnuts, it does something to me. And those hotdogs with sauerkraut! Those are the best hot-dogs in the world."

"They're kosher too. I eat kosher, do you?" Marty asked.

"Most of the time. I think I told you that I was brought up in an Orthodox home."

"My grandmother was very orthodox also."

"Yes, you told me. Isn't that something? We both lived in the Bronx and came from similar backgrounds. We have a lot in common, don't we?"

"I guess so," Marty stammered.

"You look so ill at ease. Why? I'm not going to do anything drastic. Well, I better take you home."

"Yes. My mother made supper and like I told you, she doesn't like it to get cold."

"I saw what she makes for you. She gives it to you in a small plate, hardly fit for a child. Aren't you hungry afterwards?"

"Well, I eat a lot of bread. I like bread!" Marty said with a pleased look on his face.

"Yeah? I'll bring you a nice challah the next time I see you. By the way, you said your mother wasn't well. I know she's old but what else is wrong with her?"

"She has a goiter. Didn't you notice the big lump in her neck?"

"No I didn't really look. I haven't been to your place much. Maybe two, three times. You sure bend over backwards for her. I never saw anything like it Marty."

"She cooks for me and cleans. I guess you don't like her," Marty said with an annoyed expression.

"No. That's not true. I don't even know her."

Again I knew I talked too much. I worried that one of these days Marty would really get fed up with my nagging. Also, by asking him if he ever had a girlfriend, it might give him an idea to go out with someone. The thought of it actually made me jealous.

"I really have to go!" Marty said very firmly. "I can't express myself."

"Are you annoyed with me?"

"No. Why should I be annoyed?"

"Because I'm prying too much."

Before I drove Marty home, I took one more look at his face, especially his mouth. I wanted to kiss him in the worst way but knew I had better not.

The minute Marty went upstairs, I felt empty. I drove back home, thinking about my next move. It didn't seem like I was going to do anything or get anyplace with Marty in Miami. Maybe New York would be different, although actually getting intimate with him scared me as much as it did him. Still, I looked forward to my trip very much.

My cousin's affair was in late December, and to me, that was the most beautiful time of the year in New York. I hadn't been back for a long time and couldn't wait to see the huge Christmas tree in Rockefeller Center lit up. If Marty and I did manage to meet in New York, I'd ask Marty if he would go to Macy's with me to see Santa Claus. I knew that was childish but, as I said, I felt very young. Maybe I'd even buy a new dress in Macy's and ride the escalator up and down.

I could get tickets to a Broadway show for Marty and me. Chorus Line was playing in New York. I knew he wouldn't have money for tickets but it would be a pleasure for me to treat him.

I should mention something good about Leo here. He wasn't tight and would give me enough money to have a decent time in New York. Perhaps he felt guilty about hardly ever being with me. I didn't understand him and knew I never would. Sometimes I even felt sorry for him, as there was something pathetic about him. All he did was work.

When I went into my bedroom, I looked in my closet and picked out a suitcase. I browsed through my dresses and pants and mentally picked out what I would take. Afterwards, I went over to my baby grand piano and played Clair de Lune, my favorite piece that had carried me through many years. Then I reached for my Broadway book and found some music from the show Chorus Line. I played "What I Did For Love" and sang along to it, feeling a little giddy.

As my cousin's affair in Yonkers was going to be formal, I needed a gown or something very dressy to wear. After browsing through my closet, I found a long, dark blue flowered dress I had worn for my son's Bar Mitzvah party. I tried to wiggle into it but it was just too tight. I'd have to go to May's on Lincoln Road to look for a dress. Somehow, shopping on the beach made me feel more comfortable than going to Dadeland Mall in my own neighborhood. After I found something, I planned on showing it to Marty. I even thought of asking him to go with me but changed my mind. He might feel pressure helping me pick out a dress, something personal you did with your closest friend or your husband. It was getting to the point that I didn't want to do much without him.

Marty planned on going to New York a week before me as he had his niece's wedding to attend. Before he left, I asked him if he had a suit to wear. He said yes, that his sister had bought him something nice when she visited him from New York a few weeks back. I had seen him in a tan linen pair of pants and jacket one Friday night at a dance in his apartment building and figured that was what he was going to wear to his niece's wedding.

A volunteer put on records and tapes every Friday night in the social hall of Marty's apartment building. As Marty loved to dance, he went to them every week. I also began going and mostly watched as he danced with his mother and a few older ladies. One Friday evening I got annoyed with him because I stood around as I watched him dance a rumba and cha-cha with another lady who looked younger than the others. I bawled him out for ignoring me. Not usually a jealous person, I was surprised at my behavior. Marty apologized to me afterwards, at least three or four times. What a bitch I am, I thought to myself, and how possessive I've become. Marty looked better than usual that evening in the tan suit, and even my father who went to the dance with me said so.

After the dance, which ended about 11:00 P.M., Marty usually walked me to my car. Sometimes I'd ask him to sit in the car with me and talk, but he hesitated to do this, worrying that it was late and his mother had to go to sleep. She always locked the front door before going to bed. He didn't want to wake her as he slept in one of the two twin beds in her bedroom. I couldn't wait to meet him in New York, maybe even go to Roseland Ballroom with him. I hadn't been there in years and the thought of it excited me. I even hoped his mother wouldn't have such a hold on him in New York.

Marty left for New York a week before me. Before he left, we exchanged our aunt's telephone numbers. I told him I'd call him the minute I got to Yonkers.

The trip on Eastern Air Lines went very smoothly. I went to the bathroom several times to look in the mirror and put on fresh lipstick. There seemed to be a glow in my eyes as I stared at myself, something I hadn't noticed before. I must have looked attractive as the man sitting next to me on the plane began a conversation with me. Before I knew Marty I felt old and used up. Now I felt young and vibrant, especially when I thought about meeting Marty in Manhattan. I remembered Macy's and other stores on Fifth Avenue all lit up for the Christmas holidays, and the delicious odors of roasted peanuts from venders' carts wafting through the streets.

My brother met me at LaGuardia Airport. He asked how Pop was doing and I said fair. As he drove me to my Aunt May's house in Yonkers, he spoke about our mother. He told me he never forgave himself for being away when she was having another nervous breakdown. He added that he felt responsible for her dying so suddenly. I tried to comfort him and tell him that he shouldn't feel that way, but it didn't help.

As my brother drove the crowded expressways, I looked at his worried face. He was losing his hair and every now and then he'd take his hand off the wheel and rub a bald spot on his head, as if the friction would grow new hair. He had gained weight and looked bloated. I told him it made me very sad to hear about our mother. At least, I said, she was out of her misery but that didn't help him either. It didn't seem like he'd ever forgive himself for being in California when she died.

I thanked him for sparing me the anguish of taking care of our mother when she got sick. Our Pop let him carry all the responsibility of her care, using the excuse that my mother scared him with her violent outbursts. Still, none of it was fair to my brother.

When we got to Aunt May's house, Murray came in for a short while, saying he had to go to work. He was a "runner" for a bookie but, of course, I didn't mention this to our aunt. I felt so sorry for him and the torment he felt, that I put my arms around him and gave him an extra hug when I said good-bye. I told him to take care of himself and added that he had a very kind heart. He wasn't sure when he could see me again so we said we'd call each other and try to meet in Manhattan. After he left, I practically ran up the hill to a supermarket pay phone to call Marty. I didn't want to use my aunt's phone and later answer her questions as to what man I was calling.

I was delighted that Marty answered the phone when I called. We made up to meet at the Metropolitan Museum of Art in Manhattan in a few days. I said I'd call again to arrange the exact day and time.

My cousin's affair was the next day. My aunt loaned me some beautiful light blue shimmering earrings to go with a new pale blue gown I had bought. I had my hair nicely cut and styled in Miami before I left. I dressed in a strapless bra because my gown was low cut, and did a little waltz around the room. I put mascara and blue eyeliner on my eyes and was very pleased at the result. My uncle knocked on my door and when I let him in, he said I looked beautiful like Sadie, my mother. He had always been very fond of her.

The celebration honoring my cousin's contributions as a physician was held in the ballroom of the Jewish Community Center. My cousin had written an outstanding paper on the relationship of stress and cancer and he was also a community leader. It was nice to see some other relatives there but I was surprised that my brother wasn't invited. When I asked my aunt about this, she said that he wouldn't fit in with the crowd.

One of my cousins danced the Lindy Hop with me and told me I looked very sexy. Most of the day, I thought about Marty, and wished I was dancing instead with him.

Even though it was late when my cousin's affair ended, I ran up the steep hill of my aunt's house and used a pay phone to call Marty again. I didn't want to wait a few days to see him and arranged to meet him the next day at the museum. I had bought a stylish, fleece-lined short windbreaker, hat, gloves and slacks for the occasion. New York was having a cold spell, but I loved cold weather.

I took an express bus to Manhattan and arrived at the museum a half hour early. Actually I didn't expect Marty to show up, thinking he'd get cold feet the last minute. I kept looking around for him even though it was early. I noticed a hot dog vender at the bottom of the steps and soothed myself with a hotdog and sauerkraut while I waited.

About 2:15 P.M., I noticed Marty running up the steps. I felt as if I was in some kind of dream state. Could that actually be Marty, all the way here in New York? When he saw me, he ran a little faster to where I was standing.

"Hey, is that you?" I said to him as the two of us embraced as if that was the most natural thing in the world. When we did, I felt Marty's manhood against my jeans, a hardness, that delighted, yet upset and surprised me. It was very sudden and of course, I said nothing. Marty probably wasn't aware of it but I couldn't stop thinking about it.

"Do you want to see the museum now or walk awhile and go later?" I asked him as I looked at his heavy light brown unbuttoned coat and blue sweater.

"I'd like to see it now if that's alright with you," he said. "How was your cousin's party? Imagine; we're both here in New York. Am I dreaming?"

"Are you dreaming? Am I dreaming? It really feels unreal meeting you here. Can I pinch you to make sure you're here?"

"I'm really here!" Marty said very seriously.

"How do you like this cold weather?"

"I love cold weather!" he said.

"No kidding! Boy, we sure have a lot in common," I said as I looked at his sweet face. He didn't look as drawn as usual. His almost black eyes even had a slight sparkle to them, something I never thought I'd see.

We went from floor to floor of the museum and as it turned out, Marty knew the history of the works of many of the artists.

"How come you know so much about art?" I asked him.

"I read about famous artists. I like art and architecture," he said pointing to a painting of a Roman Coliseum. I was very impressed with him. Somehow in New York he didn't seem like the same shy, scared Marty I knew in Miami. He hardly stuttered when he spoke. As we walked along, I wished I could remain in New York forever. It seemed easy for me to forget that I was a married woman with a son still at home. I felt very different, as if I had shed my old self that I dragged around with me in Miami.

After seeing some of the paintings in the museum, we walked along Fifth Avenue with the wind helping us along. I put on my wool hat and Marty wrapped a yellow scarf around his neck. We huddled together as we walked. I took his arm and put it through mine. It felt like we had always walked this way. Still, I was on the lookout for anyone I knew who was visiting from Miami or even living in New York. Even if someone recognized me, I could always say the man with me was my brother and we were huddling together because of the cold. I felt so happy and carefree that even as I walked along, I asked myself if this was me and not somebody else. I still feared I'd awaken to reality and find myself back in Miami in my dreary life.

It got dark very quickly and Marty and I decided that we'd better leave Manhattan. I had to take two busses back to Yonkers and he, a train, to his aunt's home in Long Island. We planned on meeting in Manhattan again the next day, maybe to see a movie. I figured Marty's mother had given him at least a little money to spend in New York. It really didn't matter because I had enough to treat both of us.

Before we parted, we stopped in Burger King for a hamburger and much to my surprise, Marty paid for his. He seemed so much more sure of himself in New York than Miami that I hardly minded it when he got lost in the bathroom at Burger King. So what, I said to myself when he was gone for more than half an hour. That's not so terrible to put up with. There's worse things, I thought, like if he drank too much and took it out on me.

I took his hand when I said goodbye to him. It was wet and still rough with blisters. I was mad at myself for not carrying some soothing hand lotion with me to put on it. All that was ridiculous but I wanted Marty to heal, to stop washing his hands so much and feel secure.

On the way back to my aunt's house in Yonkers, the bus stopped in Getty's Square. I found it hard to believe that Grant's Five and Ten was still there and went into the store to look around. The merchandise was now shabby and thoughts of years ago, when I stole penny items with my brother from the counters, came back to me. I went next door to a Chinese take out restaurant and ordered some Chicken Chow Mein and egg drop soup to take back to my aunt and uncle. I hung around to give Marty time to get back to his aunt's house in Long Island. I planned on calling him to remind him about meeting me in Manhattan again the next day.

I couldn't stop thinking about our embrace on the steps of the Metropolitan Museum of Art. I wondered if I imagined that Marty got turned on. It happened so quickly, that now that hours had passed, I wasn't sure. With several boxes of Chinese food under my arm, I dialed his aunt's number. I felt ill at ease when his aunt answered the phone and asked who was calling. I said just a friend.

It took awhile for Marty to come to the phone. When I heard his voice, I felt very happy.

"Hi there!" I said.

"Well, hello!" he answered without stuttering.

"Do you know you have a musical voice," I said.

"No, no one ever told me that. What do you mean?"

"Well, when you talk it's as if you're singing. Really, it sounds lovely. Did you have a nice time today?"

"Yes. It was nice," he answered.

"Are we definitely meeting tomorrow again in Manhattan?"

"Yes. That would be good!"

"Where should we meet? You know, I may stay at the Pickwick Arms Hotel tomorrow night. It's a very long bus ride getting back to Yonkers."

"I'm sorry," Marty said.

"What are you sorry about? It's not your fault. Where do you want to meet?"

"How about the Museum of Art again? That way we can walk through Central Park, maybe even go to the zoo."

"That's a great idea. What time?"

"How about 2:00 o'clock? That'll give us plenty of time. Is that alright with you?"

"Sure!"

I couldn't get over the way Marty spoke. He had a new confidence about him. I couldn't wait for the next day and thought about what I would wear. I only brought along one pair of jeans but I could at least wear a different blouse than the one I wore earlier that day. I was sorry I hadn't brought more clothes along and thought about going to Macy's to shop. I loved Macy's this time of the year. Maybe Marty would go with me and afterwards we could see Lord and Taylor's and Sack's Fifth Avenue lit up.

That night, I went to sleep very late on my aunt's Castro convertible bed. I sang songs to myself, softly of course, so as not to wake my aunt and uncle. "The Nearness of You" is one of my favorite melodies and I sang it over and over before finally falling asleep around 3:00 A.M.

My aunt asked me where I was running off to the next day and I told her I had to meet a friend. She wanted to know if I was going to be back for supper and I told her I didn't think so. She was disappointed as she planned on making stuffed cabbage. I felt a little guilty, staying with her and my uncle and not being around much. Still, I couldn't help myself and only thought about meeting Marty again.

I got to the museum a half hour early. It was a very cold day, the kind of weather I loved. I had a bulky sweater under my jacket but a pretty pale pink long sleeved blouse under it. I used eyeliner and mascara before I left and dabbed my cheeks with rouge. I was pleased when I looked in the mirror and thought I looked younger than my almost 50 years.

I saw Marty running up the steps at 2:30 P.M. He was out of breath as he said,

"I-I'm sorry I'm late. I'm sorry. I missed the Long Island train. Have you been waiting long?"

"It's alright. Aren't you cold in that lightweight coat?"

"No. I love this weather. There's some lining in my coat. Where do you want to go?"

"Well, we're right in Central Park. How about taking a walk, maybe see the zoo like you mentioned?"

"Sure!"

Again, I put his arm through mine as we walked. I had brought an extra pair of gloves along just in case Marty didn't have any and asked him if he wanted to use them.

"How thoughtful of you."

We walked through the park. Just a few people were sitting on benches because of the weather.

"Let's sing some songs, Marty. I'm kind of in the mood."

"Here? Won't people hear us?"

"There aren't too many people around. And so what if anyone hears us."

Marty sang "Stranger in Paradise" and I joined him. After a few minutes, I stopped singing, as I just wanted to listen to him. There was something very special about that song. I first heard him sing it at Friendship Haven two years earlier. At that time, I tried to take his hand and tell him how beautifully he sang but when I did, he abruptly moved away from me. As he now sang, "Take my hand, I'm a stranger in paradise", I longed to be someplace alone with him so that we could have another chance to embrace. I wanted to put my arms around him so that I was sure it was his manhood I felt the day before and not something I just imagined.

We walked to the zoo but didn't see many animals. They were probably in their dens because of the cold. Afterwards, we climbed a small hill. I sat down on one of the rocks and asked Marty to sit besides me. He said the rock was dirty and refused to sit down. I brushed it off with my glove but he still wouldn't sit down.

"I don't know why you're so hung up on dirt Marty!" I said, but was sorry I did because Marty suddenly looked sad.

To change the subject, I asked Marty if he had ever kissed a girl.

"I remember, after a dance once, I kissed a girl on her cheek."

"Would you like to kiss me? On the lips?"

"Now? Won't somebody see us?"

"Like I said, there's no one around."

I got up from the rock and walked towards Marty. He stood still. I reached up to him as he was a lot taller than me and tried to press my lips to his. He was so clumsy and awkward that at first he couldn't seem to find my mouth. I persisted and our lips finally met. Marty's thin lips were warm in spite of the frigid weather.

What happened to me when he kissed me is as vivid today as the more than twenty years ago when it happened. I felt such a strong surge going through me that I almost lost my balance. If it is possible to have an orgasm from just a kiss, I must have had it. Actually, as I never felt anything like this with anyone, I wasn't sure what it actually was. Marty and I weren't too close together when we kissed because of the bulky clothes we were wearing but it didn't matter.

It took me awhile to speak afterwards. For the first time since I knew Marty, I didn't know what to say. One thing I did know was that I was in big trouble. I was in love with Marty as strange as that was for me to even believe. I was in love with a guy who had severe problems, someone who had spent twenty years in and out of state mental hospitals, who didn't have a dime to his name, and had a strange relationship with his mother. At least with Leo I had some security. I knew I couldn't handle an affair with Marty while still being married, but it was much too late to go backwards. Maybe a solution would be to not see him alone, just to see him at Friendship Haven, with other people around. I really knew that at the present stage of our relationship, it wasn't possible, so I said to myself, "whom am I kidding?"

Finally, when I was able to speak, I looked at Marty's serious face and asked him what he was thinking about. He didn't answer.

"How was that kiss?" I asked.

"I- It was nice!"

"Just nice? I mean did it do anything for you?"

"It was nice!"

I had to ask myself if it was just me who had gotten so excited. At that moment, I wished we didn't have so many sweaters on so that I could feel Marty's body again.

"I better get back to my aunt's place," Marty suddenly said.

"I'll walk you to your train. Do you want to get a bite to eat?"

"No, thank you. My aunt prepared supper!"

I walked Marty to his train and went down the subway steps with him. Before he left, he kissed me on the cheek and said goodbye. Again, I felt a tremendous surge of warmth go through me. I watched him as he walked towards the train platform and missed him the minute he was out of sight.

I stayed at my aunt's house a few more days and even got to eat her stuffed cabbage. It was delicious but then again everything looked and tasted terrific to me after Marty and I kissed each other in Central Park. Still, I worried that I had much stronger feelings for Marty than he had for me because he acted lukewarm afterwards.

I longed to feel again the electrical charge that went through me when we kissed. I needed it, almost the way someone needs a drug. And like a drug, I feared that it would do me in, especially if Marty didn't feel as I did.

While we were in New York, Marty told me he planned on visiting Friendship Haven shortly after he returned home. He said he had some business there to attend to. I knew he was on Supplemental Security Income, a program for people with very low income, and a food stamp program. I figured he had to meet with a counselor in Friendship Haven to discuss his benefits. He hardly went to the rehabilitation center anymore because he told me again that people there were getting sicker and sicker and he didn't want to be around them. I thought it was very hopeful that he was aware of this and knew it was because he was getting healthier.

I called Marty the day I knew he would be back in Miami Beach. He stayed in New York a week longer than I did, a week in which I did boring errands around my neighborhood, feeling out of sorts. I told him over the phone that I'd go to Friendship Haven when he did, do some music, and wait for him while he settled his S.S.I. business with his counselor. I added that afterwards I'd take him back to his Miami Beach apartment. After I spoke to him, I felt better. It seemed that Marty had become someone who made me feel secure, although I didn't completely understand why.

At Friendship Haven, I sat down at the piano and played some Broadway songs. Soon Ben and Harriet came over. Nothing had changed much for them or for anyone else at the center. Ben looked depressed and Harriet more flustered than ever. I asked her if she would like to play the piano but she said she felt too shaky. I figured it was because of some new medicine they were giving her. I was pretty sure that outside of Marty and maybe Ritchie, no one in Friendship Haven would ever have a chance to make it in the outside world.

Marty was with his counselor a long time so I waited in the parking lot for him. It was about 3:00 P.M. when he came out. I walked over to him as he seemed distracted, acting as if he hadn't seen me.

"Hi Marty" I said, "good to see you. Did you accomplish anything in there?"

"W- Well, I guess so," Marty stammered.

"Can I talk to you a minute or is this a bad time?" I asked.

"You can talk to me," he said.

Marty was wearing the same checkered pants I noticed when I first met him. The waist was too big and it was gathered together with a tattered belt. He wore slipper type shoes, frayed at the edges. He had certainly looked better than he did now and I wondered why he looked so unkempt. Saying to myself, I wouldn't nag him about it, I did so anyway.

"Marty, what is it with you? You have better pants than what you're wearing and what's with those old slippers?"

I knew I sounded like a bitch but it was hard for me to realize this was the same guy who looked so nice and manly in New York. I felt disappointed and even angry at him.

"You know I've been in Friendship Haven. How am I supposed to look? Everyone looks like me," Marty explained.

"Are you kidding? What do you mean by that? What about the almost two years that I've bugged you about how you should dress? You don't belong with these people anymore. You know that. I mean I feel sorry for them but you've gotten too healthy for that. You've done shows at the Jewish Home and at the Chesterfield Hotel and you're a real *mensh,* person, now."

"I- I still have to come here. I get benefits."

"I know that, Marty, but so what? Some day even that will end."

"It will end! How do you know that?"

"I just know; that's all. Look, how about me driving you back to the beach. I wouldn't mind doing it and I'd like to talk to you, so how about it?"

"You sure that won't be too much trouble for you? What about your family?"

"Don't worry, Marty. They can manage, O.K.?"

"Oh, alright."

"Maybe you can call your mother and tell her you're having a bite out to eat with me. That would be nice."

"I think she prepared food. She'll be upset."

"You're always afraid to upset her. It's a nice day. We can walk on Ocean Drive afterwards. I'd love to have a bagel with lox at the Cardozo Hotel again and sit on the balcony. I'd also like to talk about New York. Wasn't it great?"

"Yes. It was very nice. I love to travel. I used to go places with my father."

"Really, Marty? I'd like to hear about that. So how about it?"

"I'll call my mother. I'll be right back."

Marty went into Friendship Haven to use the pay phone. He came back in ten minutes, looking flustered.

"My mother isn't home. I don't know what to do."

"Call her from the beach. We'll get there in about forty minutes."

"But I hope she won't worry too much," Marty said.

I looked at Marty every now and then while I drove. My glance rested mostly on his lips. He had thin lips, usually curved in a frown, but I found them very sexy. It took all the restraint in me to not pull over and kiss him.

I parked along Ocean Drive and walked with Marty to the Cardozo Hotel. They were having an early happy hour so I asked Marty if he wanted a beer with the Swedish meatballs and assorted salad they were serving. He said no but I convinced him that it would relax him. I ordered a glass of wine and we sat on some stools at the bar drinking and eating. When we finished, we went to the outside patio and sat at one of the tables and ordered our favorite bagels, cream cheese with lox and coffee. The breeze from the ocean was soft and very soothing as it caressed my face and bare arms. I inhaled it deeply.

Marty went back into the lounge to call his mother. He was very distressed as he told me that she had supper on the table and the liver she had made had gotten cold. She was leaving it for him and going to play poker with her friends.

"Heh, Marty," I said. "Can't you have a good time like other people? Why are you so afraid of your mother?"

"As I told you, she's old and sick! She was at the doctor's office the other day for tests. She's got a big lump on her neck and I'm worried about her."

"And what about you? What kind of life do you have? You walk around without decent clothes and hardly a penny in your pocket. At least your mother had a husband, a very nice one from what you told me. Also, you have a brother and sister so she's lived more than you have. Isn't that so?"

"I-I don't know. I take care of her."

"You take very good care of her. I wish you would take such good care of yourself. It's so nice here. Can't you stop worrying for a minute and just enjoy your bagel? Why do you always have to suffer?"

"I'm not suffering," Marty said, as he cut up his bagel with his knife and ate it with a fork.

"So, Marty," I asked, "how did you like Fifth Avenue all decorated for Christmas. I'm sorry we didn't get to Macy's but we will another time."

"Another time? You plan on going again?"

"Sure. Why not?"

"Doesn't your family mind?"

"I want to share something with you, Marty. I'm not very happy. I guess you know that already."

"But you told me you're married a long time and have two children." Marty said as he slowly chewed pieces of his bagel,

"Yes, a long time. But it hasn't been good. I feel happy and carefree here with you. There, I said it. And, I want to say something else. That kiss in Central Park was wonderful. It turned me on. You know what I mean?"

Marty looked very upset after I said this.

131

"L-Look" he said. "You're a very nice person and very considerate but I have too many problems. I can't take on any more."

"What do you mean too many problems? Am I some kind of problem to you?"

"W-Well you're married. Also I have my mother to take care of. And I wash too much. That's all I need. More problems!"

If a hole in the patio of the Cardozo could have opened up at that moment, I would have crawled into it. A moment ago I felt very good. Now it was as if Ocean Drive with its colorful pale green and yellow Art Deco buildings had become gray, and the shimmering greenish-blue ocean murky. Still, I couldn't give up. If I did, I felt I'd have nothing to live for. I had to convince myself that Marty felt the same about me as I did about him; that his problems were just temporarily standing in the way of any intimate relationship he might have with me.

Like a teenager, I thought about playing hard to get and staying away from Marty for at least a week. Maybe then he'd miss me. I had gone through all this frustrating stuff when I was seventeen and couldn't believe I was going through it again.

I paid the check as Marty thanked me and said, as usual, "I can't express himself." I drove him home, not saying anything to him in the car. I thought about parking awhile across the street from his apartment complex but changed my mind. I had to have some respect for myself. I never really thought that Marty would reject me. Of all people! He spent years in and out of state hospitals and dressed in rags. Yet it seemed I wasn't good enough for him.

I tried to think about the joy I felt with Marty in New York. I had to hang on to that. If only I could get him away from his mother, I thought. I was pretty sure that she was his biggest problem. She certainly resented me. It was hard not to feel it every time I saw her. How I would befriend her, was going to be a big hurdle, if I could do it at all.

I didn't call Marty for over a week and he didn't get in touch with me either. I tried playing the piano but most of the songs I played reminded me of him and his beautiful voice. The sound of the keys seemed flat as I played them and there was no joy in what I did. When ten days went by, I couldn't stand it anymore and called him. His mother answered the phone.

"Hello Mrs. Ross" I said. "Is Marty there? It's his friend, Evelyn, calling him."

"No. He's not home," his mother said very abruptly.

"He didn't go to Friendship Haven, did he?"

"He went to meet a friend," she said.

"A friend? That's good! Could you please tell him I called," Mrs. Ross.

"Allright. I'll tell him if I remember," she said, and hung up the phone.

I didn't get a call that evening and wondered if Marty's mother had given him the message. I was relieved when he called the next morning.

"Hello" he said when I answered the phone. He acted as if nothing was wrong.

"I haven't heard from you for over a week, Marty. I guess you're busy," I said, feeling very dejected.

"I have to help my mother shop and I take her to her doctor."

"I know, Marty; you have a lot to do. I'm going to see my father later in the week. Do you want me to stop off and visit with you awhile?"

"If you want to," is all he said.

"Maybe we can go for a walk, a short one."

"I have to be home on time for supper" he said. "I don't want to aggravate my mother."

"Alright, I don't want you to upset her either. I'll call you before I come over."

I drove to the beach and visited my father at his hotel. Afterwards, we went to the Famous Restaurant on Washington Avenue and had supper. My father loved the sour pickles and seltzer the restaurant placed on each table. I ordered the brisket with horseradish sauce and matzo ball soup. My father ordered mushroom barley soup and stuffed cabbage. The food was delicious. Afterwards, I drove my father back to his hotel. He asked me why I looked sad but I didn't tell him anything.

"See you next week Pop," I said to him as he slowly walked up the steps to his hotel. "Take care of yourself!"

"I have the sugar," he said as he opened the door to the lobby of his hotel. "What can I do?"

"You're a good Pop," I said. "You'll be alright! Give Becky my regards!"

After I said goodbye to my Pop, I drove to Marty's place. It was about 8:00 P.M.

I felt very awkward as I knocked on his door. He opened it and as I walked into his apartment, I looked around and noticed he was alone.

"Where's your mother?" I asked.

"She went to a neighbor."

"So what have you been doing with yourself Marty?"

"I have a lot to do. Have you been busy, busy?"

"Not too much."

Marty was wearing a striped bathrobe.

"How come you're not dressed?" I asked. "Didn't I tell you what time I was coming over?"

"I took a shower. You said you want to go for a walk. I can be ready in a few minutes."

I waited for Marty on his couch and, after close to an hour, he came into the living room.

"I'm ready now," he said.

I said nothing about him taking so long. I couldn't afford to be so critical of him.

We got into my car and drove along Ocean Drive. I parked the car and we walked. I felt chilly even though it was not a cool night.

"Marty" I said after a short while. "Let's go back. Somehow I'm not much in the mood to walk."

"Alright. It's getting late anyway."

"No. It's not late. It's just a little after 9:00 P.M."

I headed towards his apartment complex but instead of going to the parking lot, I parked across the street in front of a bank building that was closed.

"Why are you stopping here?" Marty asked.

"I'd like to talk to you, if you don't mind. Marty, what gives with you? Your mother seems to be your whole life and you act like you're scared of her."

Marty didn't answer so I went on. I figured I didn't have too much to lose.

"You were so different in New York. I'm sorry to say it but I don't think it's good that you're so attached to your mother. It's not normal for someone your age. You should have a life of your own."

"I've been in hospitals," he said. "I told you that!"

"So what! I shouldn't say this but it seems that it makes no difference to you whether you see me or not. I thought you liked me, I mean, really liked me."

"I-I like you but I told you I have a lot of problems."

"Please, tell me, what good is it doing your seeing your psychiatrist? I don't know if he's helping you to stand on your own two feet."

"I don't work. How can I be on my own?"

"There's no reason you can't get a little job. I'm with the school system now and they pay me to help the people at the Jewish Home. You can be my assistant. Maybe I can help you to get certified. You've had almost two years of college and a lot of experience with elderly, sick people. You're awfully good with them also."

"Certified? Me?"

"Yes. You. Why can't you sing and talk to the people just like you've been doing and maybe get paid for it? Wouldn't that be great?"

"Y-Yes. It would be. About what you asked me before. My psychiatrist and I talk about a lot of things! He's helping me."

"Are you still taking a tranquilizer?"

"Just something mild to keep me calm. You're acting like a doctor."

"Not really. Marty, do you think those shrinks all know what they're doing? They give too much medicine. You've seen the people at Friendship Haven. They walk around like zombies."

"I like my doctor. He gives me time and tells me I'll get better. He tells me to have sex! I don't know why I told you that," Marty added, turning a little purple.

"Sex? You did mention that but I kind of didn't believe it."

"N-No? That's what he said! He thinks I wouldn't wash so much if I have that! But sex is dirty."

"No it's not. Heh, he is a good doctor. I have new respect for him," I said, feeling elated. "Well, I'd like to talk to you some more but now it is late. I better get back."

I turned towards Marty and kissed him on the cheek. He moved suddenly away from me as if I had burnt him.

"What's wrong?" I asked. "What did I do? It seems like I scared you!"

"I told you that sex is dirty."

"I wasn't going to have sex with you. I just kissed you. Marty, have you ever been with anyone?"

"I told you that I kissed a girl."

"You kissed me. Doesn't that count?"

"You're a married woman!" Marty said with sudden maturity.

"So what? I told you I'm not happily married, didn't I?"

I was dying to kiss Marty on the lips, embrace him, and feel his manhood again as I thought I did on the steps of the Museum of Art.

"Can I kiss you again Marty, just a little? Don't be scared."

Marty didn't answer so I bent over and somehow found his mouth. If a charge or chemistry or whatever it is could get stronger than before, it happened to me. I felt as if I had a fever.

"Can I just touch you, a little?" I asked as I put my hand on Marty's lap. I kissed him again and moved my hand towards what I noticed was a swelling. I stopped myself before doing anything more. Marty didn't move. It seemed as if he wanted me to do more but I was afraid to. I did turn him on and even though he said he couldn't get involved, he already was. Maybe there was hope for us in spite of almost insurmountable problems.

I said good-bye to him and drove home still feeling flushed, hoping that a miracle would somehow bring us together.

I was now going to the Jewish Home for the Aged twice a week and meeting Marty there. Sometimes Ritchie would join us, strolling through the large social hall with his violin cupped under his chin. He'd even go to the third floor where the bedridden residents were and play Jewish songs for them, which they loved.

I was earning $20.00 an hour through the school system. I'd often give Marty and Ritchie $5.00 when they helped me with my musical program. That still left me with at least $80.00 a week that I put in a bank account under my name. I was just a part-time employee but felt proud that I was making some money.

One Friday, after Marty and I finished our program at the home, I asked him if he'd like to go to Denny's. I was surprised that Marty agreed to go with me and asked him why he wasn't putting up a battle about it. He explained that his mother was going to a dance in her apartment building that night and wasn't cooking.

"So what did she expect you to eat for supper Marty?" I asked him as we walked to my car.

"Maybe she thought I'd eat with you or just take some leftovers in the refrigerator. She wasn't feeling good so she didn't prepare."

"But she's O.K. enough to go dancing?"

"No matter how she feels, she can always dance. She says it makes her sleep better. Maybe you'd like to stop off at the dance later with me?" Marty asked.

"Well, I'll see if it's not too late after we eat. I love Denny's hamburgers and I'm going to treat myself to a Pina Colada. I like anything with pineapple in it."

It was about 5:00 P.M. when we got to Denny's. The bar had just opened. Shadows from the small candles on each table flickered and seemed to dance on the walls. Marty and I sat down in a booth and for the first ten minutes, I just stared at him. I loved his dark eyes with their intense expression.

The waiter brought our menus and we ordered. I convinced Marty to also have a hamburger and a beer. I noticed he dozed for a few minutes in his chair after he drank it.

"Heh Marty," I said touching his arm to gently wake him. "It's so nice outside. After we finish eating, let's park again by the bank building, open my car windows wide, and get some ocean air. Or would you rather just walk?" I asked halfheartedly.

"I danced a lot with the people at the home so I don't feel like walking too much. The only thing is that my mother expects me to go to the dance. I do a waltz with her and sometimes a rumba."

"I noticed she dances with some ladies and, besides, we don't have to sit too long in the car."

"Well, alright, if we don't get back too late!" Marty said.

I drove again to the bank building across from Marty's apartment complex and parked. It was now almost dark. Marty was very quiet as he sat next to me in the front seat. Then he moved as far to the side of the car as he could manage. He looked scared.

"Marty, you don't have to be scared" I said. "I just want to thank you for the wonderful job you did singing at the home."

"T-That's alright!" Marty assured me. You think I help the people?"

"Very much so and me too!" I said, as I wiggled towards him and kissed him on his cheek. He moved even further away from me after I did this.

"Marty, I keep thinking about what your doctor said, about being intimate with a woman. He said you wouldn't wash your hands so much if you did. I don't know the connection because I don't know why you wash so much, but he's the doctor! Like I told you, sex isn't dirty, especially with someone you really care for."

"I-It's dirty. How can you say it isn't?"

"Would your doctor, who's trying to help you, encourage you to do something that wasn't good for you?"

"N-No, I guess not."

"Would you like to kiss me again, the way we did in Central Park? That was real nice, wasn't it?"

"I-Is it going to lead to sex?" Marty asked me.

"Here in the car? No. Don't worry. Let's just kiss a little and see what happens, O.K.?"

As Marty didn't answer, I leaned over and kissed him. Again, I noticed his manhood even though the light by the bank was very dim.

"Marty, I'm going to ask you if I can do something. Please, don't be scared. I want to touch you."

"W-Where?"

"There" I said staring at the swelling in his pants. You're nice, Marty, real nice. Sexy too."

"Me? Sexy?"

"Yes. You!" I said as I very quickly and lightly touched him. He sat completely still. I continued stroking him, getting myself all worked up.

"Is it right what you're doing?" he finally asked me.

"Does it feel good? If it does, it's right! How are you built, Marty? You know what I mean? I can't really tell with your pants on."

"I'm big!" he said without any hesitation and much to my surprise.

"Yeh? Really?"

As I continued stroking him, I was transported to a different time and place.

I was thirty years younger in the Catskill Mountains with an older guy I liked. He kissed me and took my hand and put it on his hardness. He gently pushed my hand back and forth and came in my hand. I felt cheap afterwards and was sorry I got so carried away. I hardly knew the guy but even then I was so desperate to be loved that I was willing to do that at a time when nice girls didn't.

Now, with Marty, I knew I wouldn't feel cheap afterwards because I loved him. Besides, as I kept reminding myself, it was doctor's orders.

"Marty" I said, "can I feel you, I mean, just your bare skin?"

"Y-You want to do that. It's dirty. I have to wash first!"

"No, it's not dirty. Would you like to touch me?"

"Where? Where should I touch you?"

"My bust!" I never could say the word breast.

"We're going to have sex?" he asked again.

"Not really. This isn't having sex."

"But it is sex!" Marty said.

"I guess you can say it's just petting. Could you just unzip yourself a little, O.K.?"

"You sure it's not dirty?" Marty asked again.

"No. I'm sure!"

Marty unzipped himself and I quickly stuck my hand into his pants. The hardness and softness made me feel ecstatic. I felt myself quivering as I bent over again, kissed him on his sweet lips, and guided his hand down my blouse. He clumsily felt me and then removed his hand. I couldn't believe how far we had gotten. Marty zipped up his pants and moved again to the far end of the car.

" I-I have to go!" he said, out of breath.

"That was very nice and it sure didn't hurt anybody, did it?"

"N-No. But I have to go!"

"Alright. I'll drive you over to your building!"

Marty didn't ask me again if I wanted to go to the dance. I parked my car in his lot and walked Marty to the hallway of his building. Instead of heading towards the social hall of the dance, he took the elevator. He didn't say good-bye or anything to me. Afterwards, I sat in my car worrying that I had gone too far. I knew that at the rate I was going it would be a short matter of time until I went all the way with him. That is if he was willing. To be with a man who had never been with a woman really excited me. I had no idea if he could perform like a man. In fact, when I mentioned it the week before to my psychiatrist, he doubted it very much.

Even though I was concerned about my brazen behavior in the car, I felt warm and tingly as I drove back to Miami. I was still turned on even by the time I went to bed. I told myself that I was no longer just a middle aged woman with nothing much to look forward to. My affair with Marty was making me feel young and vibrant. I thought again about buying a nice dress, a little low cut, and a high heeled pair of shoes.

As I lay in bed unable to sleep, I thought more and more about the results of my actions. Could I cause more trouble for Marty than he already had? He had enough trauma in his life without me giving him more. I even wondered if Marty had heard his doctor right. Maybe the psychiatrist didn't really mean going all the way sexually. I didn't know if Marty knew what sexual intercourse was, as silly as that sounded. Maybe I could show him some pictures in a Penthouse magazine to find out what he knew about it.

I got up from my bed and went into my kitchen to get a glass of milk. A new worry hit me. I didn't know if Marty would see me again after I was so aggressive in the car. I didn't like the way he hurried to the elevator after he left me, as if he wanted to get away from me as fast as he could. On the other hand, maybe he was so excited that he ran to his apartment to relieve himself.

I couldn't wait to call him the next day but didn't know what I'd say to him. As I continued mulling over my thoughts, the good feeling I had earlier in the evening wore off. After all, I thought, I'm just another married woman having an affair, an older woman pushing herself on a very troubled man. Another problem was that I was kind of religious. I didn't believe in adultery and remembered from my childhood that it was important to follow the Ten Commandments or be punished. I thought about going to a synagogue near me and ask for God's understanding and forgiveness.

I wasn't sure if I was really married, that is emotionally. Leo was a very hardworking man and was good to the children. We never wanted for anything financially. If only I wasn't so lonely with him.

What I was doing with Marty could lead to a divorce and the insecurity that I dreaded. Eventually, someone could see Marty and me together although I was careful not to kiss him in public places. Everyone knew we worked together so I had that as an out. Still, I knew that if we went further we'd have to sneak around to find places to be intimate.

In a way, I was hoping Marty's fears would stand in the way of his having sexual intercourse with me. And in a way, I hoped he would overcome them because I had never been with a man I really loved.

Even though I didn't know what I would say to him, I called Marty the next day. In spite of the fear that the heavy petting I was doing would lead to sexual intercourse, I could hardly wait to see him.

"Hello!" he said rather breezily to me when he answered the phone.

"Hi! How're you doing?"

I think I heard what passed for a laugh when he answered in a high pitched voice, "Oh, alright."

"Listen, maybe you'd like to go swimming in the ocean. We can go to 89th Street and Ocean Drive where there are showers and bathrooms so that we can change afterwards. It's a nice day. Would you like that?"

"I don't swim much in the ocean and I don't like the sand."

"Oh, be a sport!" I whined. "It'll be fun!"

"W-Well, alright."

"I'll pick you up around noon. We're not singing in the Jewish Home or anything today so it's a good time to go."

"Noon? I have to help my mother with her shopping."

"How about 3:00 P.M? The days are long and hot so I think it'll be alright?"

"O.K. if you want to go."

"Yes. It'll be good for you too. See you at 3:00 P.M."

I packed my bathing suit, cap, and towel and thong shoes in a bag and put on a low cut dress that I had recently bought in Penny's. I threw on some high-heeled shoes and stood before my bedroom mirror. I was lucky there was no one at home because I had to admit to myself that I looked sexy. I knew my sixteen-year old son would be very surprised to see me at that moment.

I drove to Marty's apartment building and parked. I took the elevator to the now familiar second floor and knocked. His mother answered the door. Looking me up and down with a smirk on her face, she called,

"Martele, Martele, there's that lady to see you!"

Marty came to the door and let me in. He wasn't shaved or dressed to go. He just wore some old shorts and worn shoes.

"Marty" I scolded. I told you 3:00 P.M. Why aren't you ready?"

"My mother wasn't feeling well after shopping. I had to take care of her."

"Well, we did make up to go and I came a long way. How about getting ready? You have a bathing suit, don't you?"

"Y-Yes. It's old so I don't know if it'll fit me," he said, with his usual worried look.

"No one will see you and its O.K. with me whatever you have. How about it? I'll wait for you but, please, don't take too long."

"Alright. I'll just be a few minutes."

The few minutes turned into an hour as Marty disappeared into his bathroom. I knocked on the door. I noticed his mother lying on one of the twin beds in the bedroom next to the bathroom.

I quietly closed the bedroom door before I yelled, "Marty, what is with you? Why don't you come out?"

It was hard to believe that he still hung around bathrooms so long. It almost seemed as if he was going backwards.

"Coming!" he yelled back through the door.

After twenty minutes or so, he walked out. He was unshaven and disheveled looking. I didn't think this was the same man who just yesterday turned me on as we petted in my car.

He opened the bedroom door and called out to his mother, "Ma, I'll be back soon!"

"I made you supper," was all that his mother said

"I hope she's alright," he muttered to himself as we went down the elevator to my car.

"She'll be O.K. It's still hot outside so we can go swimming. The exercise will be good for you."

I parked my car and brought out two beach chairs, my bag with my bathing suit and an ice chest. I had packed two sandwiches and some cokes before I left my house.

We walked on the sand, with Marty carefully watching his steps because he saw a dog crouching a few feet away. He asked me if the dog was "making".

"No. Don't worry about it." I said, as if that mattered. "Do you have your bathing suit on?" I asked.

"No. How could I do that with my shorts on?"

"You could have put it on under your shorts. Never mind. I have to put on my suit too. I'll carry the stuff while you go to the men's room. Meanwhile, I'll go to the ladies' room and change."

"Can I help you carry something?" Marty asked.

"No, thanks. I can manage. Meet you outside in 15 minutes, and I mean 15 minutes, O.K?"

Marty looked very unhappy as he said, "Yes, fifteen minutes."

I didn't like how bossy I sounded but if I was going to help Marty get well, I couldn't let him wash his hands in every sink he saw until they almost bled. I didn't want him to use his obsessive-compulsive problem as an excuse for not leading a normal life eventually. Even Dr. Harris told me to attack each of his habits, one at a time. I knew that his mother had a terrible effect on him and also knew that she was the sick one. Marty was just someone unfortunate who was with her almost constantly from the time he was born. At least when his father was alive he told me he traveled with him. It was only a year after his father passed away that I met him in Friendship Haven.

He did come out in fifteen minutes. His bathing suit was old-fashioned and too tight. That didn't bother me at all. My eyes rested for a moment on his chest and then my stare went down him. I didn't think he noticed. He also didn't seem to notice the low cut bathing suit I wore. It was purple with flowers. I had recently gone to Weight Watchers and, with much effort, after five or so months, had lost twenty pounds. I didn't think I looked too bad for 50.

We both went into the soft, lukewarm, aquamarine water. Marty walked into it very slowly, splashing himself a little at a time, reminding me of older women I saw on Brighton Beach in Coney Island when I was a kid. He took some water in his hand and smelled it.

"Is the water clean?" he asked me as he reluctantly trudged along.

"It's salt water, so it kills germs. Why are you always so concerned with dirt?"

"Well, you saw the dog on the beach. That's not allowed. I think I'll report it to the lifeguard."

"Can you do that later? So much time has been wasted already. I'd really like to take a swim before dark."

When he finally got into deeper water, and swam, I splashed him.

"Don't do that!" he said, as he lightly splashed me back.

I swam towards him and put my arms around him. He stood very still.

I cuddled up to him closer and kissed him. He didn't kiss me but just let me press my lips to his.

"Someone will see us!" he said when I finally backed away a little, but not before I felt his manhood again.

"There are hardly any people in the water." I tried to assure him.

I don't know whether there was a sudden surge of warmer water or it was just me, but I felt very flushed. I embraced him again and this time he put his thin arms lightly around me. I felt his hardness again and stroked him on his bathing suit. I wasn't so brazen as to put my hand down his bathing suit, although I thought about it.

At that moment, it didn't matter that his unshaven face was dark and rough or that he looked disheveled only an hour or so before in his apartment. I loved him and that's all that mattered.

"Heh! Marty!" I said as we finally got out of the ocean. "I brought some sandwiches and soda. I'm starved and I'm sure you are too. Let's eat."

"T-That was very thoughtful of you," he said as we walked towards my two beach chairs.

I spread out some towels, sat down, and tried to hand Marty a sandwich.

"I can't eat here. The sandwich will get full of sand."

"No it won't. We'll be careful. Here," I said, again handing him the sandwich.

He reluctantly took it and nibbled on it. It was kosher salami with a sour pickle. He wasn't enjoying it.

"Marty, for Pete's sake. Eat the sandwich. You need to put on weight. If a little sand does get in, it won't kill you, you know."

After I said that, he ate a little faster.

"This is good!" he said between bites.

I loved being on the beach with him. It was very private, with few people around. While Marty ate, I thought about the future. Maybe, with enough time and love, I could help him relieve the tension he always seemed to be under. On the other hand, I could make him even more upset. Still I was thinking of a motel we could go to, some place where no one would see us. Having sex with Marty was the prescription that both my psychiatrist and his recommended. I thought of several motels that were out of the way, where no one would see us.

It was almost six o'clock P.M. when I checked my watch.

"I'm going in for another dip," I said to Marty. "Want to come?"

"No. I had enough!" he answered.

"O.K. See you in a little while."

"Be careful," he said, much to my surprise.

I swam for only twenty minutes or so and then went back to where Marty sat.

"Do you want to get a bagel with lox or something at the Cardozo? We didn't have much to eat."

"No. I have to get home. I told you my mother wasn't feeling well. I have to help her. She said she was making supper."

"Alright. I'll take you back but I don't understand you. It's Saturday night and you act like you're ten years old. You should be independent. Why can't you be with a woman?"

"You're a married woman, or are you?" Marty asked with sudden wisdom.

"I am. Maybe you don't respect me the way I'm acting."

"It's not that. I do respect you. You wouldn't be with me if you were happy."

"No. You're right. I can't get over your maturity now. When I picked you up, you acted like a little boy. It's as if you aged 40 years in a few hours. You're also very smart."

"Smart?"

"Yes. You act like no one ever told you that."

"Well, I was in a gifted class in public school."

"I'm not surprised. What about high school and you told me that you went to City College for a few years. Why didn't you get a degree?"

"I- I couldn't!" Marty stammered.

"Why not?"

"The Korean War was on and I was afraid I'd be drafted. I was nervous in class."

"If you were in college I don't think they would have drafted you, but I could be wrong. I guess it depended on how many men they needed. You weren't in the armed forces at all, were you?"

Marty looked very uncomfortable after I asked that question. I sure know how to pry, I said to myself. Why don't I leave the poor guy alone? And yet, if I do, we'll get no place. How far should I push I asked myself again.

"Marty, I know you've had a lot of problems, so much so that you told me you spent many years in and out of state hospitals. Yet, I don't see much wrong with you except your hating dirt and washing too much. That's nothing to be ashamed of. I also had a lot of trouble. It's sort of 'there but for the grace of God go I" that I didn't have to go to a mental hospital. My mother was so mentally ill while I was growing up and afterwards that I don't know how I survived. My brother, Murray, looked after me and took care of my mother also when she got sick. She had a nervous breakdown practically every year and was completely out of touch with reality. When this happened, she didn't even recognize me. It was really scary and awful. It's a miracle it didn't happen to me. I feared it would, but so far, so good."

"You poor thing!" Marty said softly.

What a tender hearted person he is, I thought. A kind soul and yet he's been through so much. Anyone else would be bitter, but not him. That made me love him even more.

"Well, I've pried enough."

"Th-That's alright," Marty said.

"Marty. I want to be with you," I suddenly found myself saying. "Really be with you. Do you know what I mean?" I asked again.

"Y-Yes. I think I do. But, I don't know if we should."

"Why not? I know I'm very nervy, but do you think you can have sex?"

"I-I think so."

"Do you know how? I mean, you never have but, heh, I don't know how to ask these things. Your psychiatrist said you should have sex, didn't he? I'm sure he meant going all the way."

"I've seen pornography magazines downtown in New York. But isn't sex dirty and what if someone sees us? I- I don't know."

"No, it's not dirty. Actually, between two people who care for each other it's beautiful. I've never been with anyone I really cared for so you can say it's a new experience for me also. I'll find some safe place to go and even wear dark glasses. I never wanted to commit adultery but I'm not even sure I would be, being with you. Did I ever tell you Leo had an affair with some woman?"

"No. You didn't. So emotionally you're not really married."

"I think you can say that. Am I scaring you by talking the way I am, I mean, about wanting to be with you? Do you want to be with me?"

"Y-Yes, I think so but I-I don't know."

"But aren't you curious what sex is like? You're at least over 40 although your mother calls you her baby."

"I-I don't know if you'll like it."

"Don't worry. Even if we just hold one another, it'll be fine. I do have to be careful, though. I think I weigh more than you do so I don't want to break anything on you," I giggled.

Marty didn't find that very funny.

"Can we get together next week? I asked. "There's an out-of-the way motel in Coral Gables. It's not too expensive because I once stayed there."

"How do you sign in?"

"Don't worry about it. I'll give a different name and pay by cash. I'm sorry. I don't know if it's alright the way I'm talking."

"I have to go home. It's very late!" Marty suddenly said.

"O.K., I'll call you. Listen. Don't worry. I'll take care of everything. You have nothing to worry about."

Marty sat very quietly in my car as I drove him to his place. I said good-bye to him and bent over to kiss him. I never got the chance as he quickly got out of the car as soon as I parked

As I drove back from the beach, I searched for motels along U.S. 1. I couldn't consider Howard Johnson because it was too popular and expensive. I slowed my car as I passed a sign that read, Riviera Motel, Reasonable Rooms, Vacancies. I looked over the modest building that had a fresh coat of paint on it. As I continued driving to my house, I thought that it was crazy to sneak into a motel to try to have sex with Marty. Even though I wasn't emotionally involved with Leo, I still had a piece of paper that said I was married.

When Leo went out to play bridge that night, I called Marty. My son was at a friend's house.

"Marty," I said, "I found a motel that I think will be O.K. for us. Could you come in by train to South Miami Thursday? I can pick you up at the station."

"Couldn't someone see us together?" Marty asked.

"Well everyone knows we're friends and sing together so I don't think it's much of a risk. Anyway, I plan on wearing dark glasses and added, with a laugh, maybe even a blond wig I have lying around."

"If we have to hide like that, it means you're still married, doesn't it?"

"You know, I don't really know how to answer that. I am legally, but not emotionally. I told you Leo broke the marriage vows by having an affair. If I could get divorced, I would, but I don't know at this point how that is possible. You still have your mother to take care of, and, I'll be honest, you have no way of making a living. To save taxes, Leo put all our money in his name. I was a schmuck to let him do that, but what can I do now? He's the expert and I thought he was protecting both of us. I don't know what I have. I'm pretty sure if we split I wouldn't have enough for the two of us. Look, Marty, if you're really against our being together, I'll understand."

"No. Th-That's alright."

"So, you'll come to Miami?"

"Yes. What time do you want me to come in?"

"How about 2:00 P.M.? I'll pick you up at the metro train station at University Ave., alright?"

"I don't have much money on me."

It seemed funny that he said that because he never had any money on him.

"Don't worry about that. I have money."

I parked my car and waited at the station for Marty to come in. It was way past 2:00 P.M. when he finally showed up. He wore his best pair of beige cotton pants and blue canvas shoes that I had finally bought for him at the Army and Navy store near Friendship Haven. As he walked towards me, I noticed he was cleanly shaved.

He wore his same old-fashioned eyeglasses and I was annoyed at myself that I hadn't helped him to buy a more modern pair.

"I appreciate that you came," I said to him when he sat down besides me.

He fidgeted in the car seat and looked out the window, saying little. Soon we were at the motel.

I put some dark glasses on before I went in. I brought along a blond wig, just in case, but there was no one around at that hour so I didn't put it on. I registered as Mr. and Mrs. Handel, wrote down a phony address and gave the clerk $35.00 in cash. Marty asked him if he could have two extra towels and soap and the clerk handed it to him without a word.

The motel room was clean but very plain. It had a queen size bed, dresser, end table and lamp. The closet had no door and a few wire hangers were attached to a round, wooden pole screwed into the wall near the top. The air conditioner buzzed loudly but wasn't powerful enough to get rid of a moldy odor. The bathroom was tiny but at least it had a bathtub.

I flipped open the chenille green bedspread on the bed and closed the faded green drapes. Marty took the two extra towels the desk clerk had given him and placed them on the dresser. He then carefully placed the two pieces of soap in one of the drawers.

"Do you want to use the bathroom to wash or take a shower?" I asked him.

"I'll take a shower after. I hope there's hot water," he said as he went into the bathroom and turned on the faucet.

"The water isn't too hot," he said to me through the bathroom door that was open a crack.

This isn't going to work, I said to myself. Marty is more interested in soap, towels and hot water than he is in me.

"Marty!" I yelled to him. "Why don't you undress and just wash up a little?"

"Alright," he called back.

I heard water running for almost an hour and then Marty finally came out, just wearing his under shorts. They were gathered at his waist with a safety pin. He carried his pants and shirt in his arms. He carefully hung up his shirt and pants in the closet. I looked at his bony body and for a moment, thought about changing my mind about having sex with him. I really didn't think he would be able to do anything anyway and suddenly felt very stupid being in a motel with him. If only he didn't have so many annoying habits. I liked his hairy chest and wanted to see the rest of him naked, but also knew I'd be very disappointed if he couldn't or was too afraid to have sexual intercourse. That would end the dream I had of being more to him than just a close friend or sister. Strange as it seemed, I had hoped that some day we could be together. How that would come about? I had no idea.

"Marty, you're so skinny," I said to him after he hung up his clothes. It wasn't a nice thing to say, but I just blurted it out. "I'll have to start cooking for you somehow."

I knew that was not possible because his mother would never let me step into her kitchen. I saw the portions his mother set out for him. They were fit for a two year old. We'd just have to find a way to eat out more often in Denny's.

Marty went to the bathroom again, spent about fifteen minutes there, and came out with two more pieces of soap. He opened the drawers of the dresser, ran his finger over them to make sure they were clean and threw in the two pieces of small soap. He sniffed the pillowcases on the bed and inspected the sheet.

"Do you think the bed is clean? Who knows who slept in it?"

"They change the sheets every day. It looks clean. Aren't you going to get undressed?" I asked.

"I hope it's clean."

He removed his underwear right in front of me, without a bit of embarrassment, and continued inspecting the drawers.

What I saw surprised me. For such a skinny guy he was well built.

"Excuse me a minute, Marty. I'm going to wash up."

I got into the tub and tried to take a bath in lukewarm water. It was uncomfortable. When I came out of the bathroom, Marty was still walking around the room, inspecting the closet.

"I don't have enough hangers." He said.

"Marty, you're not going to buy the place," I said very annoyed. Always a little shy, I got into the hard bed and undressed under the covers. I threw my clothes on a chair. I reluctantly asked Marty to lie down besides me, saying that it would be nice if the two of us could just rest awhile together. I wasn't expecting more at this point.

Marty got into the bed and just quietly lay there. His lips moved as if he was saying something to himself. It looked very strange.

"What are you doing?" I asked him. "Are you praying?"

"I'm not doing anything! Did you wash?"

"Of course," I said. "That's not very nice of you to ask me that."

"Well, you asked me."

"Yes. I did. Heh, you're getting more sure of yourself, aren't you!" I said rubbing my hand on his chest. I was actually afraid of doing anything more, not that I didn't want to.

I lay still for a few minutes and looked at Marty's thin face. He lay under the sheet still moving his lips. Somehow, I turned towards him and took him in my arms. He didn't resist. His skin felt very silky and I pulled him closer to me to kiss him. He lightly ran his hands over my breasts that both pleased and surprised me. Then he began to shake.

"What's wrong?" I asked. "Please, please, don't be scared. We don't have to do anything. I know you've never been with anyone.

Nothing has to happen. Let's just lie here. It's nice, isn't it? I wish we were in a better place but this is the best I could do for now."

I caressed his thin body and was very pleased to notice his manhood. His shaking got worse. How pathetic, I thought to myself. It seems that he wants to be with me but is too scared.

"Marty" I said. "Do you want to skip this for now? We can get together another time."

"I'm sorry," is all he said but he didn't get up. He closed his eyes and moved his lips again.

I looked at his sallow face again, his thick but unkempt hair with its widows peak, and small mouth. I wasn't sure why but at that moment. I was so turned on that I could hardly control myself. I bent over and kissed him, rubbing my hand over him again.

"Don't we need some protection?" he suddenly asked me, again to my surprise.

"No, don't worry about it, I'm alright. I'm too old to get pregnant. Is that why you're so frightened?" I said as I continued stroking him. I knew I shouldn't be doing that, but I couldn't help myself.

"Is it alright what I'm doing?" I asked.

"Y-Yes, it's alright."

"I'll be honest with you, Marty. I don't know what to do. I don't want to upset you. Every time our bodies get close you shake terribly. I'll leave it to you. What do you want to do? I mean do you want to try to do something?"

"You're not expecting too much, are you?"

"No. I told you that. This is our first time! You know what? I think we better stop, just for now and try another time.

Marty looked disappointed but I was afraid of adding more trauma to his life. Even though his psychiatrist and mine encouraged us to have sex, I had no way of knowing how he would react to it.

I gently pushed him off me and lay very still with him besides me. When I did this, he said, "I'm sorry, do you want to try again?"

I looked at his sad face and said, "Do you?"

He didn't answer so I said, "Alright. Let's just put our arms around each other. Maybe you'll relax a little."

"You won't be disappointed" Marty asked again as I helped him get on top of me. He didn't weigh much so it wasn't uncomfortable. He groped around to find me. I helped by softly telling him how brave he was and how much I loved him. In spite of his fear, and shaking, he finally made love to me. Afterwards, he signed deeply and walked with a sprightly step to the bathroom.

It is impossible to describe in mere words how I felt during this time. I never expected him to be able to complete his lovemaking. I feel that he was able to do what he did because he was so eager to please me. Maybe it was also because he finally wanted to think of himself as a man.

I never felt anything like I did that day in that shabby room. I felt completely satisfied, for the first time in my life. If there is such a thing as a peak experience, I felt that also. It was more than the physical act, more than any emotional experience. I felt such love and tenderness for him that I knew that I wanted to be with him for the rest of my life. His nutty habits didn't really matter to me anymore. That he hardly had a penny in his pocket didn't matter either, or his cheap clothes. He showed such love for me that day that even though it's more than twenty years since this happened; I've never forgotten it and am still able to write about it as vividly as the day it happened.

After taking Marty to the University Avenue train station, I drove slowly back to my house. I still felt tingly all over and didn't want to let go of that wonderful feeling. It was as if a completely new life had begun for me in that shabby room in Coral Gables, a life of hope and possible happiness. I thought about all the years I longed for love. I remember even saying to myself that I'd give my right arm for someone to love.

As I went into my house and saw Leo working at the kitchen table, an awful feeling of reality hit me. I knew I couldn't continue to have sex with Marty while still being married. I had a very strong urge to blurt out to Leo what I had just done, but luckily caught myself. Why I felt such a need to do this, I didn't know. Since I had already left Leo some supper in the refrigerator, I just said goodnight to him, explaining that I was tired. He didn't say much in return, busily working on some papers.

I crept into bed and tried to relive the day and the love I shared with Marty. I didn't want the glow I felt to wear off -- a glow that made me feel young and needed. If only I could get divorced and be with Marty!

I knew that wasn't possible so I'd just have to content myself with being with him whenever and wherever we could. I also knew that this was going to be very difficult because sooner or later someone would see us going into some motel together. If that happened, I could always say to anyone who saw us that we were singing in that particular hotel. I could also wear a wig and dark glasses each time we got together. I didn't want to worry about it anymore and fell asleep with my private thoughts and dreams.

In time, Marty and I found a small hotel in Miami Beach to go to. The Shorecrest Hotel became our hiding place. It was on 21st Street and Collins Avenue. I always registered as Mr. and Mrs. Handel and paid cash. Before we signed in at the hotel, we ate in an Italian Restaurant nearby. They always had a special so it didn't cost much. Marty was now more sure of himself and I noticed he was even putting on some weight.

The back of the hotel faced the ocean and I usually went swimming after we made love. Sometimes Marty went swimming with me and we would put our arms around each other in the water and kiss. I'd take another shower after my swim and so would Marty. The trouble was that afterwards he'd wash himself so much in the shower that I'd aggravate myself yelling at him to come out. Since our being together wasn't an every day thing, I felt I could put up with it. He still had habits that I knew would drive me crazy if I lived with him. He still had trouble shaking hands with anyone. He never walked on the grass, fearing it was dirty from some dog. When he sat on a bench, he first wiped it off. He still repeated himself and his favorite question was still, "Y-You've been busy, busy?" Even though he was better than when I first met him, he had a long way to go. I tried not to be self righteous around him but found myself yelling at him much too much. His mother yelled at him most of the time for one thing or another so I had to be very careful not to become like her.

I usually got together with Marty on Mondays and when I came home, I'd find Leo watching Monday night football in front of the television. One particular Monday evening, I almost blurted out that I had made love with Marty. I made an appointment with Dr. Harris the next week because I really needed help with this new problem. Living with Leo and having an affair with Marty was tearing at me.

It wasn't guilt that I felt, just the stress of leading two different lives, exciting as it was.

Dr. Harris told me that I should not under any circumstances tell Leo what I was doing. He thought that Leo might be some kind of father figure to me because my own father was so weak my whole life. Dr. Harris added that until I fell in love with Marty, I didn't really have a strong sense of identity as to who I was. Now I thought of myself as a mature woman, a vibrant one at that.

One day, after Marty and I made love, I became so frazzled at the thought of going home afterwards, that I decided to stay overnight at the Shorecrest. My urge to tell Leo everything was getting out of control, even though I was seeing Dr. Harris. I knew I'd have to do something; I couldn't go on the way I was. For a moment, on the beach that day, I felt as if I lost touch with reality, not knowing where I was and looking at Marty and asking who he was. He calmly said to me, "I'm, Marty, I'm Marty, and I love you." He dragged me back to reality, saying that. I still wasn't completely convinced that some day I wouldn't get sick like my mother. That day on the beach I came very close to it and got very scared. Marty was wonderful in his calmness and love. We were two people who had been scarred because of our childhoods, he with his overbearing mother and me, with my sick mother. We understood each other completely.

Things were far from smooth with Marty's mother. Sometimes, when he went home after 10:00 P.M., she would put the chain on the door and lock him out. That was a hardship because he didn't have any money with him to get a motel room. I began waiting for him after we went out together to make sure his mother would let him in afterwards. When she didn't, I'd go with him to the Shorecrest to spend the night. I'd call Leo and tell him I couldn't get back because of a late gig or a rehearsal at the Greater Miami opera.

Marty and I auditioned for the chorus in the opera. The director listened to Marty sing "Stranger in Paradise" and immediately told him he was accepted. I sang "Are You Lonesome Tonight" and was told that they would let me know because they had a lot of mezzo-sopranos. I was so proud of Marty when I saw him perform in "The Merry Widow". He earned $600.00 for it, the first money he had ever made completely on his own. As I sat at the Dade County Auditorium listening to the chorus sing and watching them waltz with the ladies in the chorus, I thought I would burst with pride. Marty did a perfect waltz with one of the ladies. The makeup people pasted a small mustache and beard on his face, which were actually very becoming. Marty's brother made a trip from New York to see him.

What a milestone! How amazingly far he had come. The director called me one day to tell me they needed a mezzo singer for "Nabucco", so I, too, shared this unforgettable experience with Marty at the Greater Miami Opera

. Marty constantly worried about his mother because she was old and getting frail. She complained about a lump in her thyroid gland. She still resented me and one day when I went to pick up Marty, he looked more upset than usual. When we went downstairs, he told me his mother had run to the roof, threatening to jump off, if he continued running around with me. She was in her nightgown and he had to grab her. He couldn't leave her because he said there was no one to take care of her. He added that his brother and sister had families of their own and couldn't take on the responsibility of taking care of her. So, I was stuck with Leo and Marty was stuck with his mother.

Again and again I had to remind myself that he had no money of his own. He had managed to go to some lawyer with his mother to get himself put in her will, a one-third share of it. Before that, his sister was the soul person to handle his affairs when his mother passed away.

Leo now complained about my not being around much. He said he wasn't a dog, something to be left a plate of food in the refrigerator almost every night. He told me he didn't like my running around and coming home late or not coming home at all. I knew I'd have to do something, and quickly.

When I went to bed at night, I missed Marty terribly. I wanted him to be lying alongside me. I thought about him all the time and was glad my son would soon be leaving for college that would free me more. I had to find out how much money Leo and I had. In the past, he showed me statements with money mostly in his name. When I complained about this, he said it was for tax purposes. He also questioned me why it was suddenly so important for me to know what we had. I was now able to tune him out as my life was no longer with him. It really never was.

One day Leo was very nasty to me. My son was not treating me with respect either because he didn't have a good example from his father. I yelled at Leo that I wanted a divorce but he didn't take me very seriously. I ran into the bedroom and packed a small suitcase and hid it in the closet. When Leo went out to see a client, I grabbed the suitcase and my small dog, Fuffy, and drove to the beach. I went to Marty's apartment and knocked on the door.

"What are you doing here?" Marty breathlessly asked.

He was still very upset at what his mother had done the day before, threatening to jump off the roof. She was sitting in her chair watching television when I went in. Her feet propped up on a small stool, she ordered him to change the channel on the T.V. I looked at Marty and felt terrible pity for him. I knew that he'd have to get away from his mother if he was ever to get well.

"Marty" I said after he found another T.V. channel for his mother, "Let's take a walk. I have to talk to you. It's important."

"Ma" he said. "I'll be right back."

His mother answered him with a dirty look.

As we took the elevator downstairs, I told him I couldn't stay in my house anymore, adding that it was unbearable. I said that Fuffy was in my car and that I was checking into a hotel on the beach. I'd pay for it with loans from my master card. I told him that he had to get away from his mother or else he'd be finished.

"W-What do you mean you left your house?" he asked me with disbelief. How can you do that? W-What are you going to do?"

"Look, Marty. I think we have a chance together. I'm going to see a lawyer to get some kind of legal separation. You know I went to my synagogue the other day and asked God to understand and forgive me for what I was doing with you. I'm still legally married but emotionally I never really was. I have to find out how much money I have. Perhaps, by some miracle, we can make it together. Your mother changed her will and named you in it. If something happened to her, we might be able to have enough to live on."

"Don't say that! I don't want anything to happen to her."

"Marty" I said. "You'll never have a life as long as you're with her. You've been with her your whole life and got sick because of it. You have a chance now. Tell your brother or sister to take care of her. Come with me to a hotel and stay with me for a few days. Let her know that you're not taking any crap from her anymore."

"H-How can I do that. What should I do?"

"I need help, Marty. I had to take my dog along because I didn't think Leo would have the time to feed her or anything. It's not easy to find a hotel that will take a dog. Would you come with me and help?"

"I'll help you. Let me just go back and tell my mother that I'll be back soon and pack a few things in a plastic bag. She worries about me."

"She worries about you? She worries about herself. You have to break away from her and become a man. You know what I mean. You are a man and a wonderful one. But she infantilized you; kept you a baby so that you'd never leave her. I think that's why she had you ten years after your brother was born. Don't you want to have a life with me some day?"

"H-How can we do that? I have no money. I have nothing."

"You told me your mother has a lot of money. I remember you told me she has $400,000. I've been married for over twenty-five years and Leo shows me statements that read that he has close to a million dollars on his name. I think if I got divorced, we'd make it."

"But you say my habits bother you!"

"Yes, but you've improved enough to have made the opera. I know that with time you'll get better and better. I'm not so perfect myself. I'm a terrible sleeper and some times I get mean."

"You're never mean."

"You never have a bad thing to say about me. I do love you Marty. I always will."

"I love you, too" Marty quietly said. "You're the center of my universe!"

"You know, if ever two people were meant to be together, it's us. And you know something else. It's a destiny, for us to be together. God wanted it that way. Excuse the schmaltz!"

"That's all right. I feel the same way."

"You know I never would have met you anyplace. You weren't around, just hiding in Friendship Haven. Wasn't that destiny that made me go there almost two years ago after I graduated from college? I remember going to some open house and Nancy showing me around. I wasn't sure right away that I wanted to do volunteer work there but when I heard you sing the following week, I didn't have any doubt. And look at you now, as the saying goes. You've come so far. You just have a little more of the mountain to climb, that's all. I know you'll make it all the way."

"Y-You really think so? I can't express myself."

"You express yourself very well. Now, let's work out how we can be at some hotel together."

Marty kept saying to me, "Did you really leave Leo?" over and over. He looked very scared as he said this.

"Marty" I answered. "I can't go on this way. I'm under so much stress that I feel I'm really going to flip. I just can't have an affair with you and go home to Leo."

"B-But what am I going to do about my mother?" Marty asked. "She can't get along without me. My brother and sister can't take care of her. I told you they don't live in Florida."

"Marty, it's too late now to think about what we should have done. You know I think I have a solution. I'll just stop having sex with you. We'll go back to being friends. The reason I came here was that earlier today I almost blabbed to Leo about us. Luckily I stopped myself. I grabbed Fuffy and a suitcase and ran out of the house. Why I have such a strong urge to tell Leo, I don't know. You'd feel independent if you stayed with me at a hotel a few nights. That way, your mother wouldn't take you so much for granted and maybe treat you a little better. She treats you like you're her slave. I'm sorry, but that's how I feel."

"Stay away from her? She's sick. How can she manage?"

"She'll survive. Please, help me find a place."

"I'll help you. I'll call my mother and tell her I'm visiting my friend, Herbie. She knows him but I don't like to lie to her."

"It's no big deal. It's just a little small lie. I'm a friend too."

I drove along Ocean Drive with Fuffy sitting between Marty and me in my front seat. Marty kept brushing hairs off himself even though

I told him Fuffy didn't shed. After stopping at some hotels and finding out dogs weren't allowed, I drove up to the Versailles on 34th Street. I decided not to mention that I had a dog when I registered. I gave the clerk cash and said I would be staying for a few nights. I had a lot of money on me because I had made a loan from my master card. I left Fuffy in my car and went to the room the clerk led me to. I was amazed at the ocean view from the huge picture window. Even though it was just one room with a kitchenette and a bath, it was airy and large. Looking out of the window, I felt as if I was on a boat right on the ocean.

The first thing Marty did after hanging up his spare underwear and shirt in the closet, was to investigate the bathroom. That took about an hour. He complained to me that there weren't enough towels or soap in the bathroom. I thought that even if he had 20 cakes of soap and the same amount of towels, it wouldn't be enough. How, I thought to myself, am I ever going to live with him? I felt very down even with the lovely ocean view.

"Evie," Marty called from the bathroom, "do you think I should call my mother now?"

"What did you tell her when you left your place?"

"I told her I'd be back soon. I didn't want to tell her I'd be gone a few days."

"You've only been gone a few hours but if it'll make you feel better, call her and tell her you're spending a night or two with Herbie."

"She'll be angry at me."

"Oh, for Pete's sake, Marty. Won't you ever grow up?"

Marty looked very sad when I said this.

"My mother needed help with the vacuum leader when you rushed me out. She can't help it if she's old and sick."

"And I can't help it if I feel like I'm going to lose my mind. Go call her already! I'll go downstairs, get Fuffy out of the car, and sneak her in when nobody's looking. I better take the stairs. This certainly didn't turn out to be too glamorous or exciting. Wherever we go we take your mother with us. I wonder if you really care about me. Right now, I'm sorry I ever got involved with you. You're not grown up and it's not even your fault. It's mine. I should have known better."

I don't think Marty heard much of what I said because he headed back to the bathroom when he first heard my angry words. It seemed to be some kind of refuge for him. With bent shoulders, he slowly came out after a half hour or so. He didn't say anything as he walked out the door to a phone booth downstairs. I went to my car to get Fuffy.

I wrapped my small dog in the blanket she slept in, and climbed up the stairs with her. I felt so weary that I longed for my bed in my own house. At least I had some security there, even though most of the time I was miserable. After I went into my hotel room, I gave Fuffy some water and dog food that I had taken from my house. Marty still wasn't back.

As it was still early enough to go swimming, I put on my bathing suit and went to my car to get a folding chair. I walked to the beach that was close to the parking lot, sat down near the ocean and tried to figure out what I would do from here on in. I got up and slowly jogged alongside the surf. The water was aquamarine and very appealing. I put on my cap and ran in. After swimming, I felt better. My mother used to tell me that the best thing for the nerves was going into the saltwater ocean. She loved to swim and somehow when I was in the water, I felt like she was with me. That gave me both a good and bad feeling.

After an hour or so, I went back to my apartment room. I looked for Marty again and found him, as usual, in the bathroom.

"What's with you?" I scolded. "I mean, why are you spending most of your life in the bathroom? What attraction does it have for you? You run the water so much that it's like torture listening to it."

"My mother is worried about me."

"Her again? So how does washing your hands help?"

"It makes me feel secure."

"Secure? I can't understand how. Oh, why did I get involved with someone with mental problems after having a mentally sick mother?"

I knew I was undoing all the good work I had done to help Marty up to this point but still, I couldn't seem to control myself.

"Listen, Marty. Let's just be friends from now on, O.K? I mean I can't be intimate with you anymore and still live with Leo."

"Whatever you want is alright with me. I don't want you to be upset."

"You care whether I'm upset or not?"

"Of course I care. I just don't know what to do."

Somehow the anger seemed to leave me after he said this. I knew he couldn't help himself. He was too immature to know what he was doing when he got involved with a married woman. I blamed myself for everything.

I took a shower, washed my hair, and looked out the window at the light blue, yellow, gold and pink sunset. The sky was the closet thing to heaven I thought I'd ever see. It looked like an artist's palette, but more beautiful. Fuffy was sleeping peacefully on her blanket. If only I could feel so peaceful. Maybe if I stayed at the hotel a few nights, I'd feel better.

"Marty, tell you what. Call your mother as much as you want. Maybe if we stayed here a few days things would look a little better."

"Won't that cost a lot of money?" Marty asked.

"Yes, but I need the break. I'm going to make an appointment with Dr. Harris and maybe he can help me. You know Leo and my son don't know where I am and I'm not going to tell them. I'll call and just say I'm spending a few nights on the beach with a friend. Gee, I can't believe how mixed up I am."

"You poor thing."

"Marty, why do you have to be so sweet and yet at times make me crazy?"

"I'm sorry. I have these habits but they'll get better. You said I was getting better."

"Yes, I did. But somehow I don't seem to have the patience to continue helping you. Yet, you've been helping me too. I'm pretty sure I, also, would have spent time in a state hospital like my mother if I hadn't met you."

"You poor thing," Marty said again.

"Listen, you don't have to feel sorry for me. Let's get dressed and go out for something to eat. We'll feel better. With Dr. Harris' help, I'll figure out what to do. You know, I'd really like to get away from Miami. Out of town someplace."

"Where do you want to go?"

"Well, you always said you love to hike. I've never been to the Poconos in Pennsylvania."

"The Poconos! There's the Appalachian Trail there. Did I tell you I was a Boy Scout?"

"No. Really? You? How did you stand the bugs when you hiked? Oh, I'm sorry. You know I have a mean streak in me. My mother used to say to me when I aggravated her, "Evie, you're a rat today.""

"No, you're very caring."

"Not as caring as you. That's why I love you. Yes, I do. What we're going to do about it, God only knows. Come, let's eat."

We went to a small restaurant on 21st Street and Collins Avenue for their early bird special. Marty ooed and ahhed while he ate steaming minestrone soup. Asking me if I knew that he loved bread, he sheepishly asked the waiter for more. He was so hungry that it took him seconds to slurp down the soup. Afterwards, we shared an antipasto salad and eggplant parmesan. Marty looked a lot better after he ate. I ordered a glass of wine and asked Marty if he wanted a beer. He said no. I told him not to worry about money, that it was O.K. for him to order a beer. After finding out that it only cost $1.00, he ordered one on draft. His face relaxed as he sipped his drink.

After he finished eating, Marty looked at me with his dark, soulful eyes and said, "I can't express myself."

"You're always so grateful for any little thing I do. I can't stand it. I want to be with you but we're going to have to control ourselves tonight. Our room has two twin beds. I'll take one and you take the other one. I'm sorry but I don't know what else to do."

"T-That's alright, If you think that will help you. Would it be all right if I asked the waiter for more bread? I love bread."

"Sure. You do understand what I'm trying to do, don't you? I mean going back to just being friends."

"Yes. I understand. I'm sorry I'm so much trouble to you."

"You? Trouble? You saved my life; did you know that? You and Dr. Harris."

"I'll get better, you'll see," Marty tried to assure me.

I rubbed my wet eyes as I looked down at my wine glass. I could hardly speak; I was so choked up at the goodness of this guy. Who was I kidding, I asked myself? Stay away from him? I knew very well what would happen that evening when we went to bed. I'd creep into Marty's bed and put my arms around him. He had put on some weight

163

so I didn't feel anymore that I'd crush him by making love. The velvety feel of his body against mine was so appealing that I'd be irresistibly drawn to it. I'd rub my hand up and down him, stop at his thin but hairy chest, feel his hardness and be gone. Who was I kidding?

The next day, Marty still fretted about his mother and called her every hour. If she didn't answer the phone, he was frantic.

"Do you think something happened to her?" he kept asking me.

"Will you stop it," I scolded. "She's probably playing poker or shopping."

"She's too sick to shop without me. What will she eat?"

"Oh, for God's sake. It's like you're addicted to her. How terrible!

You know, just to change the subject, I'm thinking of getting a legal separation or maybe some kind of open marriage from Leo. What do you think of that? It's too risky our sneaking around together, don't you think?"

"I'm worried about my mother."

"Did you hear what I just said?"

"Y-Yes, but how can we manage? I have these habits and I have no money."

"As I told you, I think we might be able to manage with what I would get from Leo. Your habits are getting better. Do you just want to live the rest of your life taking care of your mother? She's not going to last forever, you know. Maybe you can still have some kind of life."

"Don't say that about my mother. I don't want anything to happen to her."

"Oh, what's the use, Marty? I was hoping we were making some headway but now I'm not so sure. I know practically everything about you and I don't care. You told me that when you were 12, your Great Uncle Itcha offered to have you live with him in Georgia. You said you had a habit then of collecting garbage and stuffing it in your pockets. It was a mistake for your father to suggest your going to a mental hospital when you were so young. He really didn't know any better. If things were caught at that time, and if you had gotten away from your mother, you probably would have been all right. How sad. And now, so many years later, you still can't break away from your mother."

"W- What if you can't be with me?" Marty stammered. "My psychiatrist, Dr. Grossman, said I should never live with anyone because of my habits. What if you can't stand what I do and leave me? What will happen to me then?"

"I won't leave you. I love you and can't leave you. You'll get better and better; you'll see. Let's find out what it's like to be with each other a few days here at the Versailles. The view is magnificent. Of course, this isn't the real thing being in a room on the beach but it's better than nothing. How about going swimming with me?"

"Alright. I just want to call my mother one more time to make sure everything is O.K."

"I guess you have to do that. Afterwards, how about meeting me at the beach? I think Fuffy would like to go with me. I'll just have to carry her down the stairway so nobody sees us."

I sat close to the calm ocean and stared at the sky. There was something very strange about the sky. As I continued staring at it, a white cloud that I was following broke up into pieces. It seemed to form a gigantic head with wings. Its expanse took up an area as far as my eyes could see. In a few minutes, it formed what looked like an angel. I looked at Fuffy who was sitting on the sand next to me, and noticed that she was shaking. She must have felt something strange also, as I did. I had never seen anything like the mystical cloud formation. It felt as if God was revealing Himself to me. I knew that it could have been the stress I was under but still, the sight was so awesome, that maybe I was having some kind of surreal, spiritual experience.

The apparition soon broke up but not before I said a prayer to the odd formation. "God, I asked, please help me. Help me to be with Marty some day."

Soon after, I watched the waves in the water and felt another strange presence. It was as if my mother was swimming in the ocean. She loved the salt water. It was almost Rosh Hashanah, the Jewish New Year, and Yom Kippur, the holiest day of the year. During that time, my mother's image was before me, stronger than ever, as she prayed on the top tier of her synagogue, with religious men with long beards wearing *Talliths*, prayer shawls, on the bottom. I also thought of her with a scarf over her head bending over the Sabbath candles Friday nights. Whenever I prayed to God, I thought about my mother, asking

Him to please make sure her soul was at peace, especially since she had such a terrible life while on earth.

I kept staring at the water, hoping to still feel my mother's spirit, but it was as if she had swum away. I looked for the "angel" in the sky, but all I now saw were grayish clouds with no special form. I felt empty and lonely.

I had to tell Marty what I had seen. Carrying my small dog, I practically ran up the back steps again and went to my room. Marty wasn't around. I went to the lobby and called my best friend, Ruthie, to tell her about my strange experience.

"Ruthie, you're not going to believe this, but I think I saw God."

Ruthie said nothing.

"I think maybe I'm losing my mind. Do I sound crazy to you?"

"No," she finally answered. "You sound alright. What makes you think you saw God?"

I told her about the angel with wings.

"Really, Ruthie, do you think I'm losing my mind?" I asked again.

"No," she assured me. "Who knows?" she added. "People have said they've seen strange things. Maybe you did see something."

"Ruthie, I'm going to make a break from Leo and be with Marty. I just made that decision. What do you think? You know, right this minute, I don't feel lonely anymore."

"That's wonderful. I hope you work things out. When am I going to see the two of you?"

"Soon, I hope. I have to see a lawyer. Maybe I can get some kind of legal separation. You sure I sound O.K. to you?"

"You sound fine. I have to go now. Shalom, you all."

I went back to the room and found Marty wiping one of the dresser drawers. I wasn't too surprised that he still hadn't gone to the beach. I told him what I had seen and also asked him if he thought I was alright."

"Who knows?" he said, his mind far away. "Funny things can happen. Maybe you did see clouds shaped like an angel and felt some presence. No. There's nothing wrong with you."

"Thanks for telling me that. You look so unhappy, Marty. What is it? Did you call your mother?"

"Y-Yes. She answered the phone and said she was watching television. I told her I'd only be gone a few days and that I was with Herbie."

"She'll be fine. Like I told you the other day, what I really want to do is go away to the Poconos in Pennsylvania. You always told me you loved mountains. Your mother could go to New York to stay with her sister or your brother and we can take a real vacation."

"I don't know if they'll take care of her. Is it alright if I take a shower now?"

"Sure. But how about going swimming with me first? It looks like it's going to rain but I think we still have some time. My beach chair is downstairs. I think I'll leave Fuffy here. I'm tired of carrying her up and down. We can run along the surf, get some exercise and swim together afterwards. Do you like that idea?"

"I don't run so well. Is the water clean? Is it alright to go into it?"

"Sure. You'll feel good taking a swim. I love it here. Maybe I can invest in one of the condominiums they're building. You know, I found out they're going to fix up this room and sell it. Wouldn't it be something to live with such a magnificent view? We don't need more than this, do we? It'll be you, me and Fuffy."

"There's just one bathroom and it's just one room."

"I know but maybe they can divide it into two rooms. Anyway, how about putting on your bathing suit? I can't wait to get into that ocean. It looks real clear. You know, as I looked at those strange clouds and the ocean, I felt like my mother or her spirit or something was swimming in the water. Isn't that weird?"

"No. My father is someplace traveling. You know he loved to travel."

"So you believe that the soul lives on, that somehow people don't die."

"My father didn't die."

"That's O.K. if it makes you feel good. Would it take you very long to get ready?"

"No. I'll be out in ten minutes."

Marty went into the bathroom and, as usual, was still in there after an hour. The joy I was feeling suddenly wore off. How can I live with this guy I asked myself without going nuts? Even with all the love I felt for him, I was scared. If I lived with him day after day, I'd have to listen to water in the sink running most of the time, answer all his endless questions what to do about this or that, struggle with far less money than I was used to, go with him to a shoe store while he took two hours to settle on a cheap pair of shoes, and listen to his whining about what the Nazis did to the Jews and how he hated them. Even at this point, he still needed my assurance that sex wasn't dirty. No, I told myself. It's not going to work.

I yelled into the bathroom that I'd meet him on the beach. I sat down on my chair again at the beach and felt a cold wind that blew in from someplace. It was getting darker. I searched the sky for some sign of the eerie cloud formation I had seen earlier, but all I saw was threatening dark gray clouds. As I was about to go into the ocean, I saw Marty walking towards me. His bathing suit was two tight on him but I had to admit he looked sexy. He now wore modern eyeglasses because I had gone with him to a stylish optician to pick out nice frames. I also bought him a watch that he seldom wore because he was afraid to lose it. He treated the watch and eyeglasses as if they were diamonds. How pathetic he is, I thought to myself. Maybe my prayers to God or to whatever I saw earlier in the day will come true. Maybe Marty will get better and better and some day I'll be able to live with him. I did love him very much but wondered if love was enough.

The week before, when I went to see Dr. Harris, he warned me against marrying Marty. I recalled his words.

"Evelyn, he's far from the healthiest person. Why would you want to take on that responsibility? It'll be like living with an alcoholic!"

"Dr. Harris. I'll still feel responsible for him even if I don't marry him. He has no one and I don't feel like I have anyone either. He has gotten a lot better, you know."

"You have to work on each habit, one at a time," the good doctor advised. *He does sound like a very sweet person."*

"The sweetest. He's so caring. I never loved anyone the way I love him!"

"Yes, but being in love doesn't guarantee happiness. Do you want to come in next week?"

"I'm not sure. I don't think I'm going to have to come here much more if I do get a legal separation or something. You know Marty doesn't see his shrink anymore. Do you remember I told you that his doctor recommended

that he have sex? Well, we're sure having that and it's great. I feel satisfied
for the first time in my life!"
  "That's fine. Why don't you call me if you want to come next week?"
  "Alright. Thank you Dr. Harris."

Marty slowly went into the ocean, splashing himself with a little
water as he did so. I laughed as I watched him. Maybe that's the
answer I thought. In a way he's funny. Maybe I shouldn't take him
so seriously. When he swam nearer to me, I soaked him with a huge
splash. He let out a big yelp.
  "Aw, come on," I said. "Stop acting like an old lady."
  "I'm not. You sure the water is clean." he repeated.
  "Stop being so clean and stop repeating yourself so much." I said as
I swam closer to him. Soon I was in his arms. I forgot everything as I
felt his softness and hardness.
  "Won't someone see us?" he asked.
  "Who will see us? A fish? There's nobody around. You know Marty,
you're funny. I should take your remarks and habits with a grain of
salt. If only you didn't spend so much time washing. The dripping of
the faucet is like torture."
  "I don't wash as much as I used to. I feel secure with you. Little by
little I'll get better," he said before he swam a few laps back and forth.
  I charged my master card every day for the room at the Versailles
Hotel. I seriously thought of buying the lovely room Marty and I
shared so that we would have a get-a-way. I had saved about $80,000
on my name over the almost 30 years I was married to Leo. The real
trouble was that I didn't know how I could live with Marty, especially
in one room, and not lose my mind because of his irritating habits.
He had improved a great deal but still spent almost two hours in the
bathroom taking a shower or washing his hands. Some of the people
had a carpenter convert the one room into two so I thought of doing
that. Still we would have to live in two small rooms and the thought of
that was very unpleasant after my living in a large house.
  When I put my arms around Marty in one of the double beds we
slept in, his body was so wet that I'd have to take a shower in the middle
of the night because I felt so uncomfortable. I couldn't understand

why he sweated so much, as the room was cool from the ocean breezes that gently wafted into the room from the large windows.

I wasn't sleeping well and sometimes, in the middle of the night I'd hold Fuffy tightly in my arms, as if doing this would clear my head and give me answers. No one in my family knew about Marty and me except that we were friends who sang together at different hotels.

Marty called his mother two or three times a day from the phone in the hotel lobby. He told her that he'd like to stay away a few more days because that lady friend of his, Evelyn, had taken a room in a hotel on the beach and that he'd like to visit her. His mother asked why he wasn't with Herbie anymore. He said that Herbie went to New York, which was a fib. It surprised me that he only turned a little purplish as he said this. He asked his mother if she had enough food in the house. She said, plenty, and asked Marty if she could come to see the room. I told him that it would be all right if she came.

I drove with Marty to his mother's apartment and picked her up. I was shocked at her appearance. Long earrings dangled from her earlobes and she wore a lace-trimmed dress with several rows of beads around her neck. She had heavy makeup on -- red lipstick and two circles of red rouge on her cheeks. Even her eyebrows were lined with some dark crayon, Perched on her head, was a white floppy hat that she always wore.

"Hello, Ma," Marty said when he saw her.

It didn't seem that he noticed anything different about her. She briefly nodded to me, not really saying hello. On the way to the Versailles, I asked her if she'd like to stop someplace for something to eat, but she said no. We took the elevator to my room, which was on the twelfth floor. She eagerly walked into it after I unlocked the door.

"This is a big room, very airy," she said.

She didn't pay any attention to Fuffy lying on the rug.

After a few minutes, she lay down on one of the double beds. She patted the bedspread and said,

"Martele, come, lay down besides me."

Staring at her, I forgot for a moment that the painted lady on the bed was Marty's mother and not some floozy who was definitely flirting with her own son.

"Betty" I said, "Marty isn't tired. He just likes to sit in a chair and look out at the nice view. Isn't the ocean beautiful?"

She didn't pay any attention to me and said again,

"Martele, come lie down besides me and take a rest!"

I looked at Marty who looked scared and very pale. His color was a sharp contrast to the magnificently colored sky. Betty continued lying on the bed, not the least bit interested in the view, which was breathtaking. I wanted her out of there, and fast.

"Betty" I said, "I have to take Fuffy for a walk. Come with me and you'll help."

"I can't walk," she said. "My feet are bad!"

"But you can dance." I said.

"Yes. I can always dance. Martele, you're coming to the dance Friday?"

"I'll try to Ma," he answered.

"Come, we better leave," I said to Marty and his mother. I don't want Fuffy to make in the room!"

"She'll make?" Marty said almost hysterically.

"Not usually, but I don't want to take a chance."

Betty slowly got up from the bed. I put a leach around Fuffy and went down the elevator with her, hoping no one would notice my small dog. After walking for half a block, we all got into my car and I drove Betty home. While I drove, she asked Marty when he was coming home.

"Soon Ma. I'm just taking a little vacation."

He acted like a small child when he said that, as if he had to obey his mother, or else. He was so relaxed earlier in the day when we were swimming in the ocean that the change in him now was shocking. He even walked differently when he was around her, sort of bent over. Again I knew I'd have to find a way to get him away from his mother and quickly. If I waited much longer, he'd never be able to leave her; he was so enmeshed with her. After the incident of his mother lying down on the bed in our room and flirting with Marty, I knew that she was not only sick, but sick in a very destructive way. She had said to me many times that she'd never remarry after Marty's father passed away, explaining that she had a husband --- Marty.

We stayed a few more days at the hotel and then I told Marty it was too expensive and that we had to leave. .

"D-Do you think I should go home?" Marty asked me while I was packing to leave the hotel.

"No. I don't think you should right now. You have some money that your brother sent you from your mother's estate so maybe we should go away someplace."

Marty's brother and sister were executors over his mother's trust.

"B-But my mother is very upset. You saw how upset she is."

"Marty, if you don't do something now, you'll never get away from her. Something is wrong with her, very wrong."

"I-It's me who has all these habits. She cooked for us and kept a nice house."

"That was years ago. She never let you grow up. She kept you a baby and I even noticed she gives you portions of food fit for a child. You never eat from a big plate."

"Well I have this condition. The doctor said it's hypoglycemia. My mother watches what she gives me."

"You never have a decent meal. She even boils hamburger meat. You don't eat any vegetables and hardly any fruit. No wonder you're so skinny. I can't stand it."

"You come over sometimes to my house and make meatballs and spaghetti. Once, you even made a turkey for Thanksgiving. You cook very well."

"Thank you for the compliment. Yes, she lets me cook once in a while now. I really don't want to change the subject but it's important that we talk and find some kind of solution for us."

"Did I tell you that Dr. Grossman said that I shouldn't live with anyone, that I have too many habits?"

"I'm not too worried about it, so why are you? I have to admit, though, that I was stupid not take more of an interest in money during my marriage but it's a little late to think about that now. Maybe a change of scenery will clear our heads."

"So, she'll be alright?" Marty repeated.

"Yes, she'll survive. O.K., now. How about going home and packing a small suitcase? You're very good with travel arrangements. Can you plan a nice trip for us?"

A new look of pride crept over Marty's face when I told him he's good at making travel plans. He traveled a lot with his father when he was alive and said that was one of the things he liked to do the most. He also told me he saw the White Mountains in New Hampshire with his father and never forgot it.

"How about me taking you to A.A.A. and you picking out a map and guide book for us?"

"Can I really do that?" Marty asked.

"Why not? I'm not good at those things at all. I'm a member of A.A.A. so you won't have any trouble getting anything you want."

"Did I tell you that I love maps?"

"And did I tell you that I hate looking at them. Well, I have to admit something. We don't have everything in common, do we?"

"No, but we have the important things!" Marty assured me. You really think we can go? I love to hike, especially along the Appalachian Trail."

"I like doing that too, although I haven't hiked in years. We'll have to take warm clothes along. You must have a warm jacket or coat because you've gone to New York in the winter. If you don't, we'll buy something."

"I have a lined coat."

"That will be fine. Also, if you have any long underwear, take it along. Before we leave, call your brother and tell him we're taking a little vacation for a week. Maybe he or your aunt can make arrangements for your mother to go to New York. We'll also do some shopping so your mother has food meanwhile. I'll even cook some meatballs and spaghetti so that she has some prepared food."

"You're very caring. So she'll be all right?"

"Yes. I'm sure your brother will help. You've never taken a vacation without her except for the few days at the Versailles. We need to get away and think things out."

Marty found reasonable airplane reservations and a small motel not far from the Pocono mountains. I packed at night when Leo was in his office. I didn't feel like going into details as to where I was going or where I had been. Leo was very upset with me but he probably thought I had finally flipped like my mother, something he told me many times would happen to me. I just told him that after so many years of taking care of our family, I needed to get away. I also told him that it would be best if we had an open marriage so that we could see other people. I added that we hadn't been happy together and that I was very lonely all the years I lived with him. Surprisingly, he agreed to this and a lawyer drew up the legal document. I guess he felt it was better than a divorce. At this point, so did I.

I had plenty of dog food for Fuffy and asked Leo if he would take care of her. He surprised me by agreeing, saying the little dog was good company.

I packed a heavy jacket, long-sleeved blouses, stockings and a flannel nightgown. At this time of the year, the temperature in Pennsylvania was about 30 degrees.

Marty ordered kosher food for our airplane trip because the regular food had gotten very skimpy. I cuddled up to him as the airplane took off. He insisted on sitting next to a window and pointed out every site as we took off. I read a junky Cosmopolitan magazine to keep me occupied. I felt happy sitting next to Marty. I thought that maybe we might work things out after all.

We landed in Newark Airport and took a bus to our motel. It was a beautiful ride. There were still smatters of red, yellow and gold leaves on the trees. I hadn't seen the fall in over 25 years and I felt as if I had landed in a different world. The air was cold and crisp and the aroma from the trees reminded me of years past when I spent time as a child in the Catskill Mountains. I had forgotten how lovely air could smell and inhaled deeply the perfume that the trees and leaves lying on the moist ground gave off. As I rode in the bus, I thought that perhaps Marty and I could live in Pennsylvania; it was better than Miami Beach.

Marty asked the motel owner for an upper floor and, as the place was very informal, we carried up our own suitcases. I loved the small room with its flowered cotton drapes and radiator that was already hissing as if to welcome us. The room even had a small glass decanter to make coffee. I filled the decanter with water, emptied the coffee packet into a paper cup, and put it on. Soon the room was filled with the aroma of fresh coffee. I added a packet of cream and prepared a cup for Marty and me. Sitting at a table by the radiator, I felt as if I had somehow been hurled into a different world instead of just reaching a different state than Miami. Do people really live like this,

I asked myself, a small charming town with old- fashioned general stores? I couldn't wait to shop at one of the stores. Christmas displays were already in the windows as it was almost November. I was hoping that the town of Stroudsberg would have a Christmas store where I could buy a small Santa Claus glass globe, perhaps one that would play music. I collected these globes and had a decent display of them on one of my bookcase shelves in Miami. I loved Christmas, even more than Chanukah, because as a child in Yonkers I lived mostly among Irish people who had magnificent Christmas trees. I would walk along the snow-covered sidewalks, look into their frosted windowpanes, and wish I had a tree like theirs.

It was a sort of "déjà vu" coming to Pennsylvania. In all the time I knew Marty, I didn't feel so sure that things would turn out all right as I now did.

We asked the owner of the motel where there was a decent restaurant and he said there was one only a few blocks away. We bundled up in our warm clothes and arm in arm, slowly walked to the Pocmont Restaurant, a family run business. Marty asked me if I wanted to share supper but I said no, that I was kind of hungry. I ordered fish and with much urging, got Marty to order a steak. With every bite he took, he asked if what he was eating was too expensive. No, I assured him, it was fine. How sad, I thought, that his mother never cooked a steak or any decent food for him.

It was getting dark by the time we finished our supper but I asked Marty if he would mind if I just browsed around a general store that was nearby. He said, sure. It was pretty cold by now so we put on our gloves that I had packed just in case. I didn't remember the last time I wore gloves. I bought a cinnamon loaf that was freshly baked and a pair of long, red wool stockings. I also bought a small musical doll with a purple dress, hat and white apron. When I wound up the tiny key on its back, it played "The Sun Will Come out Tomorrow" from "Annie." Maybe that's some kind of omen, I thought, when I listened to it.

The wind was blowing quite hard by the time we left the store but it only made us happily hold on to each other more tightly as we went back to our motel.

I couldn't wait to taste the fresh cinnamon loaf with some coffee for dessert. I turned on the faucet of the huge tub in the bathroom and quickly undressed to get into it. I loved taking baths, especially in oversized tubs. Marty busied himself unpacking. He took some tissues from the bathroom and wiped the bottoms of several drawers before he put in his clothes. It didn't bother me. It seemed as if nothing could bother me in the beautiful place I was in.

I threw on my flannel nightgown after my bath, cut a slice of cinnamon loaf for Marty and me, and poured the rest of the coffee.

"Marty" I said as I looked at the man I loved, whom, I thought, looked handsome, with a relaxed expression on his face, "how about living in Pennsylvania?"

"Are you serious?" he said, sort of bringing me back to reality.

"Why not? It's so lovely here, isn't it?"

"Yes, but we don't have anyone here. I can't be that far away from my mother and what about you? You have friends in Miami and a house. You can't just give everything up."

"Why can't I? I'll make new friends. As long as we're together, what else matters? Oh, look, it's just a thought. I hate going back and having to face a divorce, money problems and who knows what else. Life is just too short as the saying goes. I don't think it costs much to live here. We can buy a little house."

With that, Marty suddenly sang, "I'd like to live in a hut for two, two rooms and kitchen I'm sure will do!"

"You sing so nice. I'd rather listen to you than anyone else. What's that song from?"

"Thou Swell", from Rogers and Hart."

"Isn't that cinnamon loaf delicious? Maybe I can fatten you up here. Trouble is that I'll fatten myself up too."

"You're not fat. You're nice," Marty said, making me feel attractive and younger than my years.

I cuddled up to Marty in one of the double beds. The radiator stopped hissing but the room was not cold. In a few minutes, I heard Marty's quiet snoring. I was on my side with one arm around him. Soon, his body was drenched with sweat. I was determined to find out why he had these night sweats; that is if he knew why himself. I planned on speaking to him about this during breakfast at the Pocmont.

The restaurant had a lovely fireplace and at this time of the year, there weren't many people around.

I woke Marty to tell him to put on a "T" shirt because the room had gotten a little chilly. He mumbled that he wasn't cold but I got up anyway and got him a shirt. I looked at the windowpanes that were decorated with frost. I pulled the feather quilt over me that the motel provided and thought that I hadn't felt this content since I was a child, sleeping with my Baba in her apartment in Yonkers.

The next morning we went to the Pocmont Restaurant again for breakfast. In Miami, I tried to be kosher and avoided frying bacon in my kitchen. A customer at the table next to me was eating crisp bacon and eggs and when the delicious smell wafted over to me, I couldn't resist ordering a plate.

I sprinkled black pepper over my bacon and eggs and added some ketchup. I didn't say a word to Marty as I enjoyed the forbidden food. The coffee was delicious. It must have been the fresh cream I poured into the cup instead of the usual half and half that came in tiny cups or the powdered cream. I didn't care about gaining weight as I buttered two slices of whole-wheat toast and added some jam. I was so happy in the charming town of Stroudsburg that I seriously considered living in it permanently.

Marty sat next to me at the polished mahogany wood table and busied himself cutting up pieces of his cheese omelet. A fire glowed in the large fireplace along the brick wall of the restaurant.

"Really, Marty" I repeated, "why can't we have a little happiness and live here? After my divorce and with the money your mother leaves you after she's gone, I think we'll have enough to live on. We can buy a small house and fill it with simple furniture. Imagine what it would be like seeing the fall leaves every year and snow again. What do you think?"

"My mother is still alive and you're not divorced yet," he said rather abruptly.

I was surprised at his down to earth answer. He didn't even stutter as he spoke. I guess it was just me who was dreaming.

"Marty, I'm going to serve Leo with divorce papers as soon as I get back to Miami. Hopefully, we'll settle the matter quickly and I won't have to go to court or anything. You know, it's only the lawyers who make money when you do that. I think Leo will be pretty fair. At least, I hope so."

Marty looked into his plate as I spoke and hesitated to eat.

"Go ahead, eat. I'm upsetting you and I'm sorry."

"T-That's alright! You're not upsetting me."

"I'm sorry, Marty. I shouldn't have mentioned the money you'll get when your mother passes away. I have a big mouth."

"No you don't. My mother is old and sick but I want her to live a long life."

"Of course!" I halfheartedly said.

Marty suddenly changed the subject.

"You haven't really been married, not emotionally, have you?" he asked for the millionth time.

"You're right. I have never been emotionally involved with Leo. You know, I don't think I would ever consider a divorce if I hadn't met you. Now I don't want to be parted from you. I miss you when I don't see you."

"You're the center of my universe." Marty repeated.

"You're so sweet. Let's finish our breakfast and go up to our cozy room."

Marty finished eating and, hand in hand, we walked the one flight of steps to our room. I wanted to talk to Marty about his mother and the strange way she acted at the Versailles, but that would have to wait at least an hour. I had such an urge to be with him that in a few minutes we made wonderful, unbelievable love.

Marty never fell asleep after our love making, so I boiled some water on a hot plate I had found in the general store and made two cups of tea.

"Did you put a lot of lemon in the cup?" Marty asked.

"Yes. Lots. Heh, we don't have that in common. I don't like lemon in my tea."

"Is that important?" Marty asked.

"No. I'm only joking. You're too serious but I like that about you. We have the important things in common. We're emotionally compatible, sexually compatible and intellectually compatible. Have you ever heard of such a thing between two people? Excuse the schmaltz, but it's as if I've been cut from your rib. I don't know the Bible well but there was something in it about Eve coming from Adam's rib. You have some *shticks,* habits that are getting better and better. You know, I'm not too perfect either. You think I am but I'm not."

We drank our tea and stopped talking for a minute. But only for a minute.

"Marty, if you don't mind, I'd like to ask you about the night sweats you have. You were drenched last night and it really upset me!"

"I do sweat a lot at night but you shouldn't be upset about it."

"I am. Do you have any idea why you do?"

"No."

"You know, your mother acted very strange at the Versailles Hotel. When she asked you to lie down next to her, she acted more like your girl friend than your mother."

"I can't understand you're saying that," Marty said, suddenly looking very drawn.

"I can. Look, I know this isn't going to be easy but I think it's important. Something traumatic must have happened to you as a child. Forgive me if I seem to be acting the "shrink" but there is something about the night that still upsets you. It goes into the unconscious mind and we think we forget these things, but really, we never do. Perhaps if you really concentrate, you can remember what happened to you so many years ago."

"You're not a psychiatrist." Marty said rather firmly. "I have one."

"You don't see him much anymore. You know all those shrinks didn't do you too much good. I don't think they know how to cure obsessive-compulsive problems. Maybe with medicine they can help a little but it has severe side effects. Isn't it wonderful that you don't take any? I only take a valium here and there and see Dr. Harris once in a while. We've been good for each other, don't you think?"

"Yes. But is it necessary to go back so many years. I don't know if I remember all that. I don't like talking about it either."

I took Marty's hand in mine and looked into his dark, soulful eyes.

"Marty, I really think that the past is important for you to remember. I know it's hard and not pleasant but I think it's the key to your night sweats, hand washing and other habits. Your sister and brother are at least ten years older than you, so they couldn't have been around much. You must have been constantly with your mother."

"Not always. My father took me with him on trips. You know I love to travel."

"I know and I love to travel with you. Let's get back to what we were talking about. Try to remember. Did you sleep in your own bed as a child?"

Marty closed his eyes for at least twenty minutes before he answered. He had a troubled expression of intense concentration on his face, as if he actually remembered those years of so long ago. Finally, he answered,

"Y-Yes. I had my own room."

"You told me your father traveled a lot. That means, he wasn't home much and you were alone a lot with your mother. Did you ever sleep with her in her bed?"

"I-I think so. All children do that, don't they?"

"Marty, I remember my Pop lying down in my bed once in awhile and I didn't like it; It didn't happen much, mostly when my mother was sick and in a state hospital. I told him to go back to his own bed even though he said he was lonely. I didn't feel that was an excuse to lie down next to me. I don't know how much that affected me. It's crazy but I once asked Dr. Harris if he thought I had lesbian tendencies. Years ago, I felt attracted to one of my friends. Dr. Harris assured me that everyone at times feels like that and it was normal because I never acted out any of my feelings. Marty, you are 'all man' so sleeping in your mother's bed didn't affect you that way."

Marty looked a little relieved when I said that. I didn't let up with my questions.

"Did you sleep with your mother often?"

"M-Maybe it was often. I just don't remember. Haven't we had enough of this?"

"No. I'm sorry. It's important to remember. You've often told me that sex is dirty. You even ask me that now even though we have a great sex life together. Maybe the dirty feeling you have has something to do with your washing your hands so much. You're not doing that so much anymore but you still hang around the bathroom a lot and have other habits that are annoying to you and to me."

I knew that I should stop for now, but I couldn't. The picture of Marty's mother actually flirting with Marty was still vivid in my memory. It bothered me a lot when she told me she didn't need another husband, that Marty was her husband. She was the sick one and she was the one who made poor Marty sick. I think she deliberately or maybe unconsciously made him sick so that he would never leave her.

I looked at Marty across the table and, now, he not only looked upset, but very pale. I knew I was taking a chance probing so much but I also knew I had to if he'd ever get completely well. Maybe I also liked the pseudo role I was playing as a shrink. I think it made me feel important.

"Do you want to take a walk?" Marty asked after we finished our tea. "It looks like it's about to snow!"

"O.K. Soon. I don't want to get off the subject. I know this is kind of painful but think, please. What happened when you slept in your mother's bed?"

"W-What do you mean, what happened? I don't know what you're getting at?"

"Did your mother ever touch you there? You know what I mean?"

Marty looked terribly distraught but I didn't let up. I knew what I was doing was risky, but I also knew I had to do it.

"D-Don't all mothers touch their children, especially when they diaper them?"

Marty, there's no way you can remember those years when you were an infant. Try to remember when you were older."

Marty closed his eyes again for about ten minutes. I just waited.

"I- I think I liked being in my mother's bed. It was warm and felt nice!"

"How old were you when it felt so nice?"

Marty closed his eyes again.

"I think about three or four."

"It seems that you are remembering. That's amazing. When you were in her bed, did she fool around with you? I mean touch you there, I asked again?"

"I-I think so. I did feel a little funny, maybe even guilty, because it felt so nice."

"Did you ever touch her?"

"W-What do you mean?"

"I mean just what I asked?"

"I I don't remember touching her. My father wasn't home much so I went into my mother's bed a lot. I shouldn't have, but I did!"

"You know what I think, Marty? I think that's why you have such night sweats. I also think that's why you feel sex is dirty. Maybe she took your hand and you touched her, her breast, or even down there!"

"N-No! I couldn't have done that!"

"Remember, you were only a child and a very lonely one at that. You know your Dr. Grossman encouraged you to have sex with me. He was very smart in telling you to do that. He wanted you to get over your feeling that sex is dirty. Did he ever ask you what I just did about your mother?"

"N-No. Never. Could we take a walk now?"

"Sure. I think that's enough so called therapy for today. Look, I'm sorry to have gone so deep into such unpleasant things. No one really knows what causes excessive hand washing."

I had to admit I was impressed with myself as I said "excessive hand washing."

"Marty, thank you for putting up with me. We'll talk some more but it really is enough for today. Heh, we did real good. Made some inroads into things. You're so wonderful, Marty, to let me do what I'm doing."

"W-Well, you're only trying to help me. Come, let's go!"

We bundled up in our jackets and went down the staircase.

"How about going back to that general store. I love looking around there. I need a wooden bowl and a chopper. My mother had one but I don't know what happened to it. If anyone has it, that store does. They practically have antiques."

"I like looking around there also. I'd like to buy a few picture post cards. Maybe I'll write to my cousin in New York."

"Sure. You're the only person I know who still writes cards and letters. My mother loved to write. You know, Marty. You're kind of like my mother, father, best friend and brother. Years ago, Dr. Harris said I didn't have a clear cut identity as to who I was because I had such a sick mother as a child and weak father. Now, I feel like a woman, attractive and loved."

Marty managed a small smile as I said that.

"I'm not your brother, mother or father."

"I meant, sort of. Anyway, you know what? You're going to get completely well in time and then I'm afraid you won't want me."

"You're the center of my universe!" he said again. "I'll always want you!"

I curved my arm and put Marty's hand through it. He had bought a pair of wool gloves in the general store when we were there last and wore a hooded, lined jacket. The wind swirled around us but it only made us take deeper breaths of the refreshing cold air.

"After I buy a bowl and chopper at the store, that is if I can find them, let's go to that steak house across the street from the store. After all you've been through, you can use a good supper. I think I'll get one also. I haven't eaten steak in a long time."

"It's expensive. Do you want to share one?"

"No. Not today. I'm going to have my own. And you know what else? I'm going to order a Bloody Mary. I love that! And maybe you'll order a beer."

"I can't drink!" Marty said. "I get a little *shika,* drunk".

"That's good. It'll relax you. You're not driving so what does it matter?"

"I like a little beer."

"Good, but I'm afraid it'll make you even sexier. I won't be able to handle that." I laughed.

"You think I'm a 'matsiah'?"

"What does that mean?"

"Didn't your father or mother ever say that? It means a bargain."

"Yes, I think you're a bargain."

We went into the general store that also had a glowing fire. As Marty looked at the post cards, I searched for a wooden bowl and chopper. As I did this, I found another woolen decorated Christmas stocking that I planned on hanging up at Christmastime. I always celebrated both Chanukah and Christmas, loving both holidays equally.

Chapter 5
Early Childhood

I had mixed emotions whether it was a good idea helping Marty remember his early childhood. Actually, I was amazed that he was able to recall events when he was three or four. I knew I was taking risks, encouraging him to go back so many years and dig up unconscious memories of sexual encounters with his mother. After all, I wasn't a trained "shrink"; yet all the doctors he had seen over the years hadn't helped him.

The next night I asked Marty if he would go to sleep a little earlier than usual. He was a night person and usually didn't crawl into bed until 1:00 or 2:00 A.M. I was anxious to take him around as his body felt silky next to mine. I told him he had a soft, yet sexy body, but saying this bothered him.

"I'm a man. Don't you think I'm a man?" he asked.

"Yes, Marty. It's just that I don't like men who are too muscular. Some of them work out and have muscles bulging all over the place. You're just right."

I slept through the night, something I hadn't done in a long time. I realized that this was because Marty didn't get drenched in the middle of the night as he usually did. Could it be that his talking about his mother and his childhood helped his night sweats? It was really too soon to tell but I was delighted to get a decent night's sleep. Of course, I didn't have to hold on to him so tightly when I lay next to him but I really couldn't control this. I was so crazy about him that I practically had to lie on top of him when we slept together.

He slept without pajamas and even though I still slept in flannel nightgowns, out of habit, I would lift my gown up to feel him.

I could now bury myself in his body because he had some flesh on him.

When I woke up, I put ground coffee and water in an old-fashioned aluminum coffee pot I had bought in the general store. I then connected my hot plate and soon the delicious aroma of fresh coffee filled the small room. The manager of the motel had given me a small refrigerator. I filled it with some apples, corn muffins and a glass bottle of fresh milk. I had drunk most of the milk already and just had a little left over for the coffee. Everything tasted so good from the small general store that I felt as if I hadn't really tasted food in years.

As I drank my coffee, I watched Marty sleeping. I wanted to cuddle up to him again but was afraid I'd wake him. He slept very quietly, hardly making a sound. At other times, he snored rather loudly, which bothered me. Now he looked peaceful and calm. Again I wondered if this had to do with his bringing up hidden memories of when he was a child and dealing with them.

Even though it was only around 8:00 A.M., heat was coming up from the floorboards. I thought I'd ask the manager if he had a room with a fireplace. I was crazy about fireplaces although I never had one, even when I was a child in Yonkers. My grandmother had small coal stoves in some of her rooms and I loved to open the latch doors and watch the glittering coals. When they cooled and turned to ashes, I would pick some up and rub them between my fingers. I loved the velvety feel of them.

I felt so content with Marty that I actually thought I could live forever in the small motel room. I hated the thought of going back to Miami and facing a divorce and dealing with Marty's mother. Reality seemed very far away in the cozy room of Stroudsburg, Pennsylvania.

Marty finally stirred so I jumped into the bed, put my arms around him and, with my cheek against his chest said,

"Good morning! I have some fresh coffee and buns. I guess that'll hold you until we have a bigger breakfast at the Pocmont."

"I'm getting fat with all this good food."

"No you're not, Marty. You were much too skinny. I'm the one getting fat. You know? You didn't sweat last night."

185

"I didn't?" he said gently getting out of my clutch.

"No. I hope I didn't torture you or anything yesterday. We do have to talk some more but not today. It looks like it's about to snow. Am I in heaven or what?"

"I'm worried about my mother!" he suddenly said, breaking the reverie I was in. I better call her. I tried yesterday but there was no answer. Do you think something happened to her? There was no one to take care of her when I left. Do you think something happened to her?" he repeated.

"You act like you're her only child. If it'll make you feel better, call her again" I said, getting up to dress. "But first, have some of this delicious coffee I made and a bun."

"T-That's very nice of you." Marty said as he went to the bathroom.

I heard the water run for what seemed forever. Maybe he washed so much whenever he thought about his mother. Perhaps it brought back hidden, forgotten thoughts of her and made him feel dirty. Whatever it was, she was a kind of poison to him but I still didn't know how I'd help him leave her.

I drank a second cup of coffee when Marty left to make a call. He was gone a long time and when he finally came back, he looked very scared.

"There's no answer," he said. "Now I'm sure something happened to her. I better call my brother, Jules."

"O.K. but it's kind of expensive to keep calling in the morning. Could you somehow last the day and call at night?"

I knew I was not being nice but in a way I didn't care. I was really sick of his mother and the problems Marty had because of her.

"Oh, alright, I'll call Jules tonight."

We ate at the Pocmont, without hardly saying anything. I didn't enjoy eating my forbidden scrambled eggs and bacon, Marty picked on his cheese omelet, his mind far away.

"Do you want to go for a walk after we eat?" I asked him. "I love that general store. Maybe I'll buy another hot cinnamon bread there. I don't know what it is but the store reminds me of Yonkers when I was a kid. There was a store like it in Getty's Square and I used to go there with my brother. Of course we just had a few pennies on us but I still liked to look around!"

"A few pennies? You mean you were so poor. You poor thing."

"No. I'm not a poor thing. I have you now and I can buy things. Please, Marty, try to stop worrying about your mother at least until tonight. Let's try to have a nice day."

"Alright. I'll go for a walk with you but won't we catch a cold if we do? It's really cold out."

"No. It's invigorating. We're bundled up with jackets and gloves. We even put on long underwear this morning. I love to feel the cold wind against my face. It helps headaches. You know in Miami I usually have a headache but here I feel better. How about you?"

"I love the cold weather. I hate Miami with the heat and humidity."

"Me, too. You know, we have so much in common. It's really amazing!"

We walked a few blocks before it started to snow. There weren't many stores in the small town of Stroudsberg, just the general store that also served as a grocery and drugstore, a barber, a post office and bank. As far as I was concerned, the town had just about everything I needed.

Marty and I sang as we walked along. We did music from Broadway and the Big Bands, which I loved.

"You know, Marty? I'd rather listen to you than Frank Sinatra. I'm so lucky. I have my own, personal singer."

"You're prejudiced."

"No. I mean it. Sometimes I feel like crying when you sing, especially anything from Cole Porter or George Gershwin. It's so touching. I guess you have so much feeling when you sing because of all you've been through."

"I didn't go through so much."

"You didn't? Twenty years in and out of state hospitals isn't much? You never complain or anything."

"I have a good life. You didn't have such a picnic."

"No, I didn't. So far I've managed to stay out of a mental hospital, thanks to you and Dr. Harris. As long as I'm with you, I feel I'll be all right. None of what happened to you was your fault. Oh, I shouldn't talk about this now. I hope it snows enough so that I can throw a snowball at you or even make a snowman with a carrot for a nose. I haven't done that in years."

The snow, which began like light iridescent flakes, soon got heavier and the wind picked up. Even though I wore a lot of clothes, I shivered. I hated to leave the snow that had always been my friend and go back to the motel.

When we got to our room, I undressed quickly and crept into bed. I pulled the down comforter over me and asked Marty if he wanted to lie down. He said he didn't want to undress in the middle of the day so he sat down at the table to write cards. I watched the small television set that showed old movies in black and white. I admired Spencer Tracy and Katherine Hepburn and marveled at their acting. The windows of the small room were frosted so it was hard to look out. I did make out, though, that there was a fierce storm outside, something I hadn't seen in many years.

Marty looked up from his writing and startled me by saying, "I'm going to call my brother now. Is it alright?"

"Sure. Do you have enough money for the telephone?"

"No, no I don't. D-Do you have some change?"

"I think so. Look in my pocketbook. You can also get some change at the desk downstairs. We have travelers' checks so the manager will gladly change them."

Marty was again gone a long time. When he came back, he looked very pale.

"I got Jules. My mother is with him in New York. He went to Miami to get my mother. She's been very upset. I knew I shouldn't have run away with you the way I did. She's sick and upset. What did I do?" Marty asked himself as he walked to the bathroom. I followed.

"So what if she went to New York?"

"So what? You know what Jules said? He said that my mother set up a new trust for him, my sister and me, an irrevocable trust. My sister and brother are the trustees."

"What? What did you just say? An irrevocable trust? That's awful. You sure you heard right?"

"Y-Yes. I heard right. Now what am I going to do?"

"You had asked her a few months ago to separate your money into a separate trust. She said she'd do it to protect you. And she did this? Now you have no protection and I'm afraid there goes our future. When something happened to her, you were supposed to get one-third of the money. That would have added up to at least $150,000. I was sure that with what I'd get from Leo we'd have enough to get married. Now, I don't know. This is awful. I wonder why she did that."

"Jules said she was very upset that I went off with you, a married woman. She was afraid you were after my money."

"Your money? That's ridiculous. You don't have a lot of money. I wish you did. She just doesn't want to let you go. I think she gave birth to you to never let you go!"

"Don't say that. She cooked and baked over the years and took care of us!"

"Oh, yeah!" She took care of herself, not you. You would have never gone to hospitals at all if it wasn't for her. You have a brilliant mind and could have been or done anything you wanted. Oh, what's the use? I better be nice to her because it seems she holds our future in her hands. When is she coming back to Miami?"

"Jules said she wants to come home. We better make plans to leave."

Suddenly the cozy room felt chilly and seemed darker. Why, I asked myself, can't I have a little happiness? I've had a lousy life and it wasn't even my fault. I just had the bad luck of having a sick mother. I had to get married to escape the crazy bin of a house I lived in with her. Well, I thought, it was no use dwelling on that now.

I turned to Marty who sat on a chair, waiting for me to tell him the next thing to do.

"Alright, Marty. See what reservations you can get."

"Should we leave tomorrow, if I can get reservations?"

"Why not? It's no fun here anymore. Now I have a new worry on my mind."

"I- I'm sorry I cause you so much trouble."

"It's not your fault. Maybe your mother will still help you but I sure don't know how to go about it now. She has to see an attorney to try to break that trust and set you up a separate one. If she ever has to go to a nursing home or anything, your share could be used up and there will be nothing for you. No one ever looked out for you. How sad."

"My mother won't go to a nursing home. I don't want her to. I'll take care of her."

What about us? Our future?"

"We'll be together, you'll see. It'll work out," Marty tried to assure me but I didn't believe any of it. I decided right then and there that we'd live on whatever I got from Leo. We had a small income from our adult education jobs so we would just have to increase the hours and pay.

I threw some clothes into my suitcase while I looked around the small room. I had six days of complete happiness in that room. I didn't think that was much considering I was over 50. I felt very sorry for myself.

I took the frail, small musical doll off the television set, wrapped it in some tissue paper, and gently put it in one of my sweaters. Its head was loose. I had planned on getting some glue to strengthen it. Now I'd just have to hope it stayed on as the suitcase was thrown around in baggage.

I looked one more time at the doll with its dark, curly hair, tiny white apron tied on a maroon printed dress and black shoes. It had a beautiful face and I loved looking at it. I turned the silver key on its back and listened to its happy song. I wound it up several times and then put it to rest amongst my clothes.

The flight on Continental Airlines went very smoothly. Marty had ordered some kosher food ahead of time so we enjoyed corned beef sandwiches on onion rolls with a slice of sour pickle. I didn't want the flight to come to an end because of what I had to face in Miami.

When we were at the Pocmont Restaurant, I asked someone to take pictures of Marty and me. I had put them in a small linen carrying bag and now took them out to look at them. At least I had that and wonderful memories to look back on.

When the plane stopped at Miami International Airport, Marty and I took separate super shuttle vans to get home. I missed him the minute we were apart and felt bad that I wouldn't be sleeping with him that night, all warm and cuddly against him. His mother was due to get back from New York the next day. I told him I'd buy some ground beef and bring it over to his house and cook some spaghetti and meatballs for him and his mother. That is if she'd let me. I had to soften her up somehow so that she'd change her trust to protect Marty.

Leo wasn't home when I got to my house and I felt grateful for this. He was still living at home, not having any desire to leave. I certainly wasn't going to force him to do so. After all, it was his house also, one which he had put a great deal of effort into. He had already met a woman and planned on spending weekends at her place, even though he didn't want to marry her.

Leo asked me if I wanted to see a marriage counselor with him but I told him I didn't think that would make us more compatible. I added that we stayed together for over 30 years for the sake of the children. Now that both our children were away, there wasn't much point to it anymore.

Actually I was glad Leo had met someone so that he would not be alone when and if our divorce went through. As the father of my children, I hoped that in time we would be friends and not go through a bitter court battle as most couples did.

I shopped in Marty's neighborhood and bought lean ground chuck, Ragu spaghetti sauce and spinach spaghetti. I added a cinnamon loaf which Marty's mother loved. With the bag of groceries in my hands, I went up to Marty's apartment and lightly knocked on the door. No one answered so I just walked in. Marty's mother was taking a nap and Marty was in the bathroom, as usual. He didn't hear me come in, with the water running in the sink. I was sure he was washing his hands again and again, until they were raw. That's the effect his mother had on him. I called his name through the bathroom door.

"Hello there!" he said rather breezily when he saw me, and walked out of the bathroom with wet hands.

"Well, you seem to be in a good mood."

"I'm glad my mother is alright. She's resting! You know, she asked me if I'd take her to the dance downstairs Friday night. They have a dance in the large social hall every week and she loves to go. She says she has trouble walking but not dancing."

Marty looked quite pleased as he said this, which annoyed me.

"I guess you didn't have a chance to ask her about that trust, did you?"

"No. I don't want to upset her. She's been through a lot."

"She's been through a lot! What about us? You know, maybe I shouldn't go through with my divorce. You only care about your mother, not me. You act like nothing happened in Pennsylvania. Didn't we make some kind of breakthrough there?"

I didn't wait for him to answer.

"You know Marty. I'm finally losing hope. I thought you grew up and became a man. You acted so different in Pennsylvania when you were just with me. You even looked different. Now you need a shave and you're wearing baggy pants again. It's like you get brainwashed when you're around your mother."

I knew I was acting very mean but couldn't seem to control myself.

"You're not getting a divorce because of me, are you?" Marty sheepishly asked. "I mean I didn't break up your marriage, did I? You said you weren't emotionally involved with your husband. You would get a divorce even if you hadn't met me. Isn't that right?"

"Yes, I guess so," I said. "You know, I feel like I don't want to go through with it. What's the point? I already have a legal open marriage so I can go out with whomever I want. At least with Leo I have financial security. Maybe I can have the best of two worlds, as the saying goes -- have him and you. He's met someone but doesn't really care enough about her to want to marry her. In a way, I feel sorry for him, even after some terrible years we had together. You're not helping the situation by only thinking about your mother and her needs. What about mine?"

"You're the center of my universe, you know that!"

"I do? What good is it? I don't think you'll ever get away from your mother nor do you want to. I thought you'd be miserable away from me and yet I heard you singing in the bathroom. Oh, what's the use! I bought some food for supper and might as well cook it while your mother is sleeping. I don't feel like taking it back."

"That's very nice of you."

"Yes. I guess it is. You probably didn't have anything prepared for supper. I feel sorry for you and for myself. I can still try to persuade your mother to help you but you're going to have to help also. You have to tell her that you won't have any security if something happens to her, that she has to protect you. I think she cares for you in her own peculiar way and really wants you to be well. Maybe if you acted like a grownup man who has a girlfriend, she'd know her role as a mother. She mentions that she doesn't need a husband because she has you. You know, that's not normal. Maybe she didn't realize what she did to you over these many years, and still doesn't. I have to be nice to her so that she trusts me. I bought a cinnamon loaf for her. I even bought a bottle of coca-cola. She likes that too and so do you."

"I don't know how to thank you."

"That's alright," I said as I took a fry pan out of a cupboard in the kitchen and prepared meat and seasonings for meatballs. When I opened Marty's refrigerator to get some pepper, I noticed nothing in there except a few eggs and a quart of milk that was probably sour.

"How come you didn't shop yet? You have nothing to eat in there," I said as I cracked an egg.

"I had breakfast. I cooked some oatmeal for my mother and me. My mother was very tired so we didn't go to Washington Avenue yet. When she gets up, we'll go. I'll help her shop."

I finished cooking the meatballs and spaghetti and placed the cinnamon loaf and soda in the refrigerator. I couldn't wait to get out of the apartment. I didn't like how Marty acted or looked. His mind was completely on his mother and her problems -- as if all the time we spent together in Pennsylvania never happened.

As I went down the elevator I asked myself, even at this late date, what I was doing with my life. I had been unhappy with my marriage but there were all degrees of unhappiness. I didn't want to be poor again as I had been as a child. I wanted to try to live the way I was accustomed to. One thing I didn't do with Leo was worry about money. What would I have now? I asked myself. A guy who still washes his hands over and over, who has just about nothing in the way of finances and who is tied to his mother permanently. I felt very down as I walked to my car.

As Leo and I were legally allowed to see other people, I decided it was best for me to continue living in the house with him and just go out with Marty. As long as his mother was alive, I knew he'd never leave her so I didn't feel there was any benefit in me getting divorced and struggling with money. Leo agreed with the arrangement so

I continued cooking for him and looking after him. He sat at the kitchen table and worked most of the time so I hardly saw him anyway. Actually I liked the arrangement. All the bills were paid and I had the freedom to do more or less what I wanted. So did Leo.

In time, I did convince Marty's mother to see an attorney to try to break her trust to protect Marty. After many costly trips to the lawyer, he said that it was near impossible to break an irrevocable trust. (I still have her voice on a cassette tape as I asked her if she realized what she had done in New York. She said she didn't and that she loved Marty and wanted him to have enough money after she was gone.)

I found this very touching and said to her, "Betty, thank you for trying so hard. I'm sure you didn't mean to hurt Marty in any way."

She looked very old and tired as she said,

"No. He's a very good and honest person. No. I want him to have enough to have a nice life."

The lump in her thyroid was getting larger and at times she could hardly breathe. I did most of the shopping and cooking for her and Marty. I cut up kosher frankfurters for her and practically fed them to her. She had cinnamon bread and ice cream for dessert and was able to keep her weight up this way. At 90, she was still an attractive lady, with her silver hair cut in bangs. She always wore a clean cotton dress and even though she complained of swollen legs, she wore neat stockings and shoes. One day, sort of out of nowhere, she said to me that it was a miracle that Marty met me and got away from "that terrible place with the sick people -- Friendship Haven." I was very touched by this and began to like "the old lady" as I called her when I spoke of her to Marty.

One Friday, as I was preparing chicken and soup for the Sabbath weekend, Marty and I noticed a hissing sound. It came from Betty who was bent over while sitting in her favorite yellow armchair. I asked her, "What is it Betty, what's wrong?"

She managed to say, in a hoarse voice, that she couldn't breathe. We rushed her to the emergency clinic at Jackson Memorial Hospital. After many tests, a head and neck specialist there said that she had thyroid cancer. The doctor asked Marty why he hadn't taken care of his mother sooner, when she was younger and the lump wasn't so large.

The doctor added that he'd try to operate but didn't hold out much hope for it. Marty was devastated.

"I let her down!" he moaned. "I ran away with you and didn't look after her. She was all alone."

"Stop blaming yourself, Marty. She only wanted to go to her own doctor at the clinic. Dr. Porter never suggested operating on her. He said it would be too risky and to leave her alone to live out her years. She had a lot of faith in that doctor, don't you remember?"

"D-Do you really think I did everything I could?" Marty pathetically asked me.

"Yes. You did, and more. You took care of her your whole life and she was never alone because of you."

I didn't want to say anything at the moment about the kind of life he had.

"Look, Marty. She still might make it."

"Y-You think so? You really think so?"

"Who knows? She's a tough old bird."

I knew that if she came through the surgery and still lived on, Marty's share of his money would be used up for her care. I couldn't tell Marty how I really felt as he was filled with guilt. Also, I felt sorry for the old lady.

I told Marty that it would be a good idea if he stayed with me while his mother was in the hospital. I added that it would be too depressing for him to be alone in his apartment. He agreed, and slept in one of my small bedrooms. Leo didn't mind as he was seldom home now.

Marty's mother lived through the surgery. When we went to visit her, she had an oxygen mask on which she kept trying to pull off. It was terrible to see her like that. Marty asked her if he should call his sister, Inez, so that she could visit. His mother whispered that she didn't want to see her because she didn't really care about Marty. I asked her why she felt that way and she explained that it was because his sister, one of the trustees, didn't want to give Marty his share of money ahead of time. She added, again, in a raspy voice we could hardly hear, that she wanted Marty to have a good life and to have enough money.

I sat down next to her bed, took her cold hand in mine, and told her that I'd always take care of Marty; that she shouldn't worry about him.

"Do you like me Betty?" I added from out of nowhere.

"Like you. I love you!"

"I love you too." I said.

I turned away from her so that she wouldn't see the sadness in my face. I didn't want to cry as that wouldn't do Marty any good.

I faced her again.

"You know, Betty. You're a good lady. And you sing very well also. You helped us with our shows by playing the tambourine. I liked dancing with you too. I want to tell you something. I'm going to marry Marty and he's going to have a very happy life."

"How could such a thing happen?" she barely whispered.

"It's from God. You know, a destiny. Try to rest a little now. You'll be all right. You'll go dancing again."

She closed her eyes and as she did, Marty and I left the white room.

Two days later, she died.

Leo answered the phone, when it rang. The physician who had treated her told him the news. Leo knocked on Marty's bedroom door to tell him what happened but I stopped him, saying that it is "better for me to speak to Marty".

That day is very vivid in my memory as most of the others I shared with Marty. I expected him to be devastated but he wasn't. He just said to Leo and me that his mother didn't die, that she just went dancing.

"Yes!' I said. "She's dancing and having a good time!"

Leo, Marty and I lived in the same house for close to four years and got along very well. Leo told me that his girlfriend threatened to break off with him if he didn't marry her. He wasn't eager to do this but knew there wasn't any chance of us getting together. He even said that he thought Marty and I were very compatible. He seemed more like my father than a husband when he said this. Perhaps in a way he had been sort of a father figure as I never felt I really had parents. Over the many years we were married, I often felt grateful to him for marrying me and getting me away from my poor, sick mother and weak father.

We were divorced in 1989 in a very amicable way. We never went to court to fight about money. I got the house, the furniture and enough stocks and bonds to live on. Marty's money remained intact and his brother, who was very honest, gave him his full share over the next year.

It is very strange but when I think about it now, at least fifteen years later, I realize that Marty was sort of a chameleon. It was as if he had been brainwashed and jumped to his mother's commands, not always consciously. After Marty's mother passed away, he became much more mature. Living with me in my house made him happier than he had ever been. He busied himself washing dishes and vacuuming rugs, which he loved to do. He was terrific with stocks and bonds and now watched not only his money but mine also. He earned a driver's license and surprised me by telling the clerk at the bureau his real age, which was now 58. I was happy that he was only four years younger than me.

I noticed that he washed his hands less and less. I asked him if he could explain this and all he said was that he felt secure with me. I was now able to go out with him and other couples, without being embarrassed. When I introduced him to my friends, he shook hands with a man if he was along. I encouraged him to dress better and went shopping with him to buy new pants and shirts. He looked very handsome in his new clothes and took meticulous care of them. With Marty, and my affectionate Fuffy in the house, I felt secure as a family.

We still couldn't get married because if we did, Marty would lose his disability income that he received from his father's work record. Instead, we had a very religious engagement ceremony called "Tonoyim", which was done in College Station, Texas. My daughter arranged to have a Rabbi there and Marty and I both wrote on a sheet of paper that we intended to get married in a year or so. How this would happen, I still didn't know, but with God's help, and with my prayers, I knew that some day it would. I didn't like living with someone without the benefit of marriage. I probably felt that way because of my religious upbringing with my Baba. I wanted the respect of my children as a married woman. It didn't matter if we had a civil ceremony first but I also thought about having a big wedding also, with Marty and us both singing songs and exchanging vows as we stood before a Rabbi. Even though I painted a picture of this in my mind, which seemed a bit corny, I still wanted it. That way, I could show off Marty to my family and friends; he handsome in a dark suit or tuxedo, and me, in a pretty light-colored dress.

Chapter 6
Civil Ceremony

The miracle did happen. A few years after our religious engagement ceremony, we got married. Marty's disability income would not get affected by this and I would get half of Leo's social security. Adding up what we'd have, we decided we could manage. On March 3rd, 1994, we took the metro train downtown to civil court for a ceremony. I wore a light pink two-piece dress, beige stockings, and black shoes with small heels. My outfit was nothing like the low cut dresses and high heel shoes I wore to attract Marty years ago. Marty wore his best pair of gray pants with a dark blue jacket. As usual, I told him to comb his hair and perhaps pick up a small flower for me to wear on my dress.

"It's only a civil ceremony," Marty said a little grumpy.

"Yes, but we're still getting married. I don't know if we'll have anything else. I didn't tell my children anything about our getting married. Leo has been very sick with asthma so I didn't think it was the right thing to do at this time. I guess that's silly. I did get a Jewish *Get*, divorce, from Leo so we could get married in a religious ceremony, but so much time has gone by, that now I don't feel like bothering."

"You don't feel like bothering?" Marty said as he fumbled around on the worn cushion of the metro train going downtown.

"You think what I'm sitting on is clean? You think someone made on it or something?" he whispered to me as I sat on one of the seats next to him.

"Gee, Marty!" I said with impatience. "Must you always think about dirt and everything? No one made on it. Why don't you move if you're uncomfortable?"

"You think I should?"

"Here we are getting married and you still can't make a small decision. Yes, move. Aren't you a little excited? I mean I've known you for over 14 years. That's a long time. I never expected this day to really happen. Did you?"

Marty didn't answer right away as he had gotten up to inspect other seats on the train. Finally he sat down a few seats away from me and said,

"I hope this seat is alright. Yes, we've been with each other for a long time. Isn't that almost the same as being married? I mean you told me you were never emotionally involved with Leo. I didn't break up your marriage, did I?" he repeated.

"Of course not. You know. I feel bad about Leo. I think I told you he wanted to go for counseling but that Dr. Harris said we were incompatible and that there was no point to it. Leo has mellowed some over the years. It's funny how we've all become close friends. I've even spoken to Leo's girlfriend and I get along with her also. To get back to what we were talking about, I still think having a ceremony or a piece of paper, whatever, is very nice. I wouldn't like my children to think I'm just living with a man, even the man I love. You know, I'm also kind of religious so having a ceremony does mean something to me! Are you still fidgeting around? Don't you think we should sit together today?" I asked him.

I didn't want anyone on the train to hear our conversation but it was impossible not to raise my voice to speak to Marty who wasn't sitting next to me.

"I can't find a clean seat. This train used to be so nice but look at it now!"

"We should have driven downtown, don't you think?"

"Well it's a long drive. It's easier this way."

"Oh well," I said to myself. "This is it now, day after day!" Even at this late stage, I wondered if my love for Marty could withstand his driving me nuts.

My divorce papers and our driver's licenses in hand, we arrived at Government Center and walked half a block to a civil court building. Admiring young women dressed in white, holding colorful corsages, and young men bedecked in their best suits with white carnations in their lapels, we filled out marriage applications. Afterwards we waited in a small room for our names to be called. Forty-five minutes later, a clerk called us. We walked into a flowered wallpapered room and were directed to stand underneath an artificially flowered canopy. A justice of the peace asked us "Do you take this man to be your lawful wedded husband?" After I answered, "I do," he repeated the same vow to Marty, "Do you take this woman to be your lawful wedded wife?" Without stuttering, Marty answered, "I do". Marty placed a wedding band that I had bought in Penny's on my finger and little more was said after that. We kissed lightly and someone took our picture.

Afterwards, I felt empty, thinking that a Jewish ceremony would be so much more meaningful.

Riding back to South Miami on the train again, I told Marty that it would be nice to also have a Rabbi marry us.

"Where would we do that?" Marty asked. "Why did we have a civil ceremony? We don't have so much money to have a big affair in a hall or someplace," he wisely said.

"Maybe we can have a few people in Sonny's house."

Sonny was a drummer I had met while playing the piano at the South Dade Jewish Community Center and over the years he had become my best friend.

"You don't want to have it in your house?" Marty asked.

"No, because my son might come by and see it."

"So what if he does?"

"Like I said before, it's silly, but the timing seems wrong with Leo being so sick with asthma."

"But he got married and didn't ask our permission."

Was that some new maturity I sensed about Marty since we became husband and wife? Could he really have grown up so fast?

"I know Leo didn't ask our permission but I still feel funny about letting my kids know about our marriage just now!"

"Whatever you want," Marty said, always trying to please me.

Marty was very uncomfortable on the train again, sitting on the edge of his seat and wiping off the cushion with a napkin from his pocket. I watched the ritual, saying nothing.

We picked up my car at the South Miami station and drove to Steak and Ale on Kendall drive for our wedding supper. It was chilly outside so Steak and Ale had a fire going in their fireplace. We asked to sit at a table next to it.

I ordered baked salmon, the salad bar and a bloody Mary.

"Isn't that drink expensive?" Marty asked.

"No, it's not. It's the early bird dinner and they give two drinks for the price of one. That way, you can have one too."

"Sometimes I get an upset stomach when I drink. You think I should?"

"Well, it is a special day. Marty, you're too worried about money. We have enough. You'll get your trust money intact from your mother and I think I got enough from my marriage settlement. Let's just enjoy ourselves. O.K.? We've gone through a lot to get to this point, don't you think?"

"You're right. You poor thing."

"Why do you always tell me I'm a poor thing?"

"Because you put up with me!"

I looked into Marty's dark brown serious eyes as I sipped my drink and munched on a celery stick. Poor thing? I felt that I was the luckiest lady in the world to have survived both an awful childhood and a crummy marriage. Here I was, cozy and warm, sitting next to my new husband, enjoying a wonderful supper of salmon, baked potato with sour cream, chives and assorted salad and fruit from the salad bar.

The young waiter placed a small home-baked bread on our table. Marty loved bread and immediately cut off half of it. As he buttered it he asked,

"Should I order the steak? It's not too expensive?"

"Why not? Order what you want."

"It's O.K. to order the steak?"

"Didn't you just ask me that? Please, Marty, don't repeat yourself, O.K.?"

"I'm sorry" Marty said, as he tried to get the attention of the waiter. Soon he was meticulously cutting up his steak, removing any grizzle from it and tearing up his napkin in little pieces.

I knew I was being a nag but, as usual, couldn't control myself.

"You still tear up the napkin? Maybe you can get over that. I have friends I'd like us to both go out with and it doesn't look right the way you tear up your napkin."

"Alright. I won't do that," he said as he pressed his glass of water against his teeth. He had some strange idea this would push in his front teeth that he felt stuck out and embarrassed him.

As much as I enjoyed it, I couldn't wait for the meal to end so that we could go home and make love, free from fear of being caught or anything. Our own home, private, with just a dog to keep us company. What could be better? I asked myself.

Before we had our drink, Marty and I toasted our glasses and lightly kissed each other.

"To our long, happy life!" I said as we did this.

"You're the center of my universe." Marty said looking straight at me. I thought I felt a chill run up and down me as he said this. I had such a strong chemistry for him that I felt then and there that we could overcome anything from now on that life threw us. I loved him and recalled Dr. Harris' words, "*If you love someone you can put up with anything. If you don't, you don't want to put up with any little thing.*"

"After our kiss, Marty asked me, "Did anyone see us?"

"For Pete's sake, Marty. We're married!"

"But nobody knows!"

"They will soon!"

I watched Marty tear up another napkin and wipe his mouth with each little piece of it. This time I laughed. It was better than bursting from irritation. He picked up his water glass and again pushed his teeth against the rim.

"Do you think that's going to actually push in your teeth? That's silly, Marty. And you're not a silly person. You're intelligent! And also very sweet."

"How can I be sweet and annoy you so much?"

"You can be sweet and annoying too."

"You poor thing!"

"Marty went back to the salad bar. I sat at my table, drinking my Bloody Mary. It was very refreshing. I felt relaxed. A small candle was lit at our table. It was my favorite restaurant and here I was, a married woman, again.

Marty came back in about twenty minutes with a full plate of beets, melon, egg salad, lettuce, tomatoes, macaroni, jello, sliced cucumbers and cottage cheese. Blue cheese salad dressing was heaped on his plate. He sat down, tore up another napkin, and dug into his plate.

"Do you want any of this?" he asked me.

"No. I've had enough but, thank you," I said, as I watched him tear his napkin again into tiny pieces.

"Where did you get another napkin from?" I asked as I watched him slowly eat and dab his mouth with his paper napkin. "You know, Marty, they have nice cloth napkins here."

"I don't want to use those fancy napkins. I always carry paper napkins with me! They come in handy."

"I guess they do."

I finished my drink and Marty finally finished his salad and steak. By this time, I really looked forward to going home and again thought of the privacy of our own room and comfortable bed.

It was dark by the time we left the restaurant and went home. As I turned my key in the lock, I heard Fuffy barking at the door when I opened it.

"Heh, Fuffy, you sweet little dog. You do a good job of protecting the house." She turned over for me to rub her belly.

Marty startled me as he suddenly blurted out,

"Did you get bit? I think something bit me!"

He rolled up his pants and carefully examined his leg as he stood in the hallway inside the house.

"No. I didn't get bit."

"What could it be?" Marty asked with a terribly worried expression on his face.

"Maybe a mosquito or a small stray flea."

"Does Fuffy have fleas? OH MY GOD!"

"What do you mean, 'Oh my God?' Is that the worst thing in the world? I've had fleas before and took care of them."

"You did? How?"

"I had the house fogged and Fuffy treated. Don't worry," I said as if that was possible for Marty to do.

"Fleas!" he said again. Oh my God!"

"Marty!" I said in a very patronizing voice. "It'll be alright. Actually, I looked over Fuffy the other day. I didn't really see anything. Even if she has a flea for two, it's no big deal. I'll take care of it. You know, this is our wedding night."

It didn't matter. Wedding night or not. Any spell that we might have had was dampened. What was surprising, though, was that it didn't bother me too much. Actually, I had gotten used to Marty's ways. Also, I knew that in time his habits would get better and better.

Marty was my husband. I wasn't alone or lonely anymore. I looked forward to wonderful years with him. I even looked forward to his using a whole napkin like other people did. Right now, it wasn't too important.

Marty, rubbing his leg, sat down at his desk and looked over some stock market reports. He was very experienced at this, having helped his mother over the years with her finances. In a few minutes, I heard him snoring slightly. He suddenly woke up and said,

"I can't understand it. I must have dozed off. I'm sorry. It must have been that drink."

"Oh, that's alright. We have plenty of chances to be together now. Do you feel like putting your arms around me?"

"Of course but I don't know if I can do anything. I don't know why I'm so tired!"

"Well, it has been a long day. That's O.K. You don't have to do anything. Just holding each other is enough."

Marty slowly undressed and neatly folded his pants and underwear over a chair. He washed. This did take some time but I patiently waited. We lay in bed and put our arms around each other. After all this time, I still marveled at the feel of his body.

He didn't have to worry. He was very virile and we made wonderful love. He didn't fall asleep afterwards because, somehow, our love making always gave him renewed energy. He got up, dressed and went back to his desk to look over some more papers. I lay in bed, relishing how relaxed I felt. I thought about the day and went over it again and again in my mind. Somehow, something was missing and I knew what it was. I wanted to have a religious ceremony with a Rabbi. I thought about it some more and finally fell asleep.

The next morning, I told Marty that I'd like to have a religious ceremony, nothing fancy, just simple and meaningful.

"I'll call Rabbi Shapiro and maybe he'll do us the honor. How do you feel about that?"

"If that's what you want" Marty said. "I've felt married to you for a long time. Don't you feel the same?"

"Yes, I do. You know we became intimate with each other during the time you were in the Greater Miami Opera chorus. Wasn't that something? You remember what Dr. Harris said? He told me it was important to find out if you were a man before I became even more serious with you. No problem there. You were wonderful and even the good doctor was surprised. I think I told you that I went to Temple Zion, Rabbi's Shapiro's synagogue, and prayed that it was the right thing to do. I was already separated from Leo but still felt the need to do this. I was concerned about being with you at such a stressful time as your being in the opera. I mean 'Simon Boccanegra' and "The Merry Widow' were difficult operas to memorize and perform but you did great. You looked so handsome in 'The Merry Widow'. I remember you waltzed with beautiful ladies dressed in pastel colored, long dresses of that period. You wore knickers with long black stockings, a white ruffled shirt and dark jacket. The makeup people also pasted a fake, black goatee on your upper lip and from that time on, you wear a tiny mustache."

"You were also in the opera," Marty said. Why are you making such a big deal about my being in it?"

"It is a big deal. They took you right away as a first tenor. I was a standby and they took me later. We even shared that together. Don't you think we're made for each other, that our getting together was a destiny? You know I couldn't have met you anyplace. Something pulled me to Friendship Haven, like a magnet. It's very strange."

"Did I tell you that you're the center of my universe?"

"Well, you didn't tell it to me today yet but the day isn't over. Now, how about us talking about our Jewish wedding? I don't want it to be in our house because, as I told you, my son can come by and see us. Maybe Sonny will let the Rabbi perform the ceremony in his apartment. I'll call and ask him."

I called Sonny and he was very happy to have the ceremony in his place. He said,

"Sure. Sure 'nough. It's an honor. Ya want music? I have some great tapes of Jewish music. I can play my drum to them. I can have wine and cake. Oh boy! That's great!"

"Sonny. Did I tell you lately that you're my best friend? You're so kind hearted. You know, Marty and I got married yesterday at county court. I plan on having the Jewish ceremony in a week, maybe on a Sunday."

"Kin you get married again?" my sweet friend asked.

"Sure but this time it will be very special; you know a Rabbi, a Chupah and everything else!"

"Sure 'nough. How many people you gonna have?"

"Well, I'll call my cousin Milty, as a best man, and also my friend, Milton Spitz. I guess I can have two best men. Milty has a video camera so he can take pictures. I'll invite Genia, you know my Russian friend who sings so nicely, to be my best girl and let's see, who else?"

"That's how many people?"

"Well, Sonny, with the Rabbi and his wife, my cousin Milty and his wife, my friend Milt Spitz, me, you, Genia and Marty, of course, let's see, that makes nine, I think. How's that? You have room for that many people?"

"Sure. Wow, it's great. Ya want me to play my temple blocks also?"

"Why not? It's going to be a great wedding. I'll call Rabbi Shapiro and arrange it. You know it's good I had a 'Get'. You know what that is, a Jewish divorce, or else Rabbi Shaprio, who's almost Orthodox, wouldn't marry us. O.K. Talk to you tomorrow. I love you Sonny."

Rabbi Shapiro said he'd be delighted to do the ceremony.

CHAPTER 7
Religious Ceremony

We all met at Sonny's house around 5:00 P.M. Sonny had set a lovely table with a white tablecloth. He had a bottle of Manishevitz wine on the table, gold trimmed small glasses assorted cakes and a challah. About six black yarmulkes rested near the glasses. Already, Jewish wedding music was playing on his cassette tape recorder and he was sitting at his temple blocks playing along to it.

"Heh, Sonny, I asked. How come you're not wearing your cowboy hat?"

Sonny always wore a cowboy hat when I saw him.

"I didn't think that would be right. You mean I should wear a hat instead of a yarmulke? Is it alright to wear the yarmulke underneath?"

"That would be fine. You look good in your hat, very handsome!" Sonny had to be the plainest looking man I had ever seen but his heart of gold shown through to actually make him look handsome at times.

Everyone came promptly at 5:00 P.M. to Sonny's apartment and we all introduced ourselves to each other. The men were dressed in jackets and ties and the women in pretty dresses. I wore my pink dress again but this time, Marty bought and pinned a lovely white orchid to the collar of my dress. Marty also had a white carnation on the lapel of his jacket.

As the music played in the background, two women and two men held up the long sticks of the blue silk clothed Chupah which we stood under. It was fragile and hard to hold up, but somehow, everyone managed. The Rabbi first spoke in Hebrew and then translated the words into a special blessing for Marty and me, a blessing for our good health and happiness. After that he asked, "Do you, Martin David, take this woman to be your lawfully wedded wife, to love, honor and cherish her throughout your life?"

Marty answered, "I do"

"Do you, Evelyn, take this man to be your lawfully wedded husband, to love, honor and cherish him throughout your life?"

Looking at Marty who kept wiping his brow with his hand, I said, "I do."

"Havah Nagilah" was playing in the background and Sonny was softly playing along with it on his drums.

Marty placed my wedding band, which I had removed earlier, on the index finger of my right hand. The Rabbi continued the ceremony.

"I've known this couple for a long time. They came to my synagogue every Friday night and it was a pleasure to see them. I don't think I know any two people who are more *barsheit (destined)* for one another. They've gone through a lot. Today I'm solemnizing their marriage in answer to the Lord."

We made a blessing over the wine and broke the glass, actually a light bulb that was wrapped in a towel.

"Mazel tov, mazel tov, everyone said to us. We all burst out into song, "Chussen, Kalle, Mazel Tov", meaning a blessing to the bride and groom. Genia sang "Katushia" a Russian love song, in a high soprano voice and afterwards, danced to it. At 75, she was still very agile. I helped my friend, Milty, sing "Oif'n Pripetshik", an old Yiddish song about a brick oven in Russia that people baked in and which also warmed the house. Marty sang to me "All the Things You Are" by Cole Porter and I also sang a few verses to him. Rabbi Shapiro gave us a beautiful gold printed Ketubah in Hebrew, a certificate of our marriage.

It was such a warm, lovely wedding, that today, when I look at the video, I get choked up.

Marty and I treated our guests to a lovely dinner at Steak and Ale afterwards. The Rabbi didn't join us because the food wasn't strictly kosher.

It is now over fifteen years later. Marty and I have made improvements in our house and take great pride in fixing it up. We share almost everything together -- music, movies, plays, traveling, friends and most of all, a love that gets stronger and stronger. Did all of his habits disappear? No, but over the years, they are hardly noticeable. Besides, as I once told him, "If you were so perfect, you wouldn't want me." When he goes out with friends, they are happy to be with him. He's so intelligent and well read that people say he has a photographic memory. As time goes on, I become more and more proud of him.

No one knows about his past except my children. I didn't want others to treat him differently, looking for mental quirks. He has fit into the so-called normal world beautifully. I might add, here, that he never took any medication for his obsessive-compulsive problems, something my son, who is a doctor, said hasn't been done. He suggested that I get in touch with the New England Journal of Medicine and give them this information.

As I promised myself to do a long time ago, I did help one person who was diagnosed as mentally ill, although erroneously. Actually, I was helped just as much and never spent time in a mental hospital as I feared I would. Perhaps, in a way, writing this book also helped me to finally understand my mother's illness and how she suffered.

Was all of this an important reason to write this story? The reader will have to answer that.

I can only end this book, which took me years to live and write, by saying,

"Marty, I'm very proud of you and love you. I always will."